China as the Workshop of the World

Is China becoming the "workshop of the world," in the same way that Britain and the United States once were? Or is China—as some multinational companies believe—simply a processing segment in global production networks? This book examines China's role in the international division of labor: it analyzes the scale and scope of China's manufacturing; the type and relative sophistication of its exports in the world market; and its position in the global value chain. It shows that China monopolizes industrial production by being the processing center of the world.

Based on extensive original research, this book examines the structure of production in global manufacturing industries, applying both qualitative and quantitative methods. It analyzes each segment of the value chain, exploring in depth several specific industrial sectors. It concludes that China has become deeply integrated into the global manufacturing industry; and that China's position in the value chain is still quite low, with relatively low R&D and other similar high-value activities; but that, in some sectors, China is catching up rapidly, especially in newly emerging sectors.

Yuning Gao is Post-Doctoral Research Associate at the Winton Centre for Financial History, University of Cambridge, UK.

Routledge Studies on the Chinese Economy
Series Editor: Sinyi Professor, *Judge Business School, Chair, Development Studies, University of Cambridge*
Founding Series Editors: Peter Nolan, *University of Cambridge* and Dong Fureng, *Beijing University*

The aim of this series is to publish original, high-quality, research-level work by both new and established scholars in the West and the East, on all aspects of the Chinese economy, including studies of business and economic history.

The Growth of Market Relations in Post-reform Rural China
A micro-analysis of peasants, migrants and peasant entrepreneurs
Hiroshi Sato

The Chinese Coal Industry
An Economic History
Elspeth Thomson

Sustaining China's Economic Growth in the Twenty-First Century
Edited by Shujie Yao and Xiaming Liu

China's Poor Regions
Rural–urban migration, poverty, economic reform and urbanisation
Mei Zhang

China's Large Enterprises and the Challenge of Late Industrialization
Dylan Sutherland

China's Economic Growth
Yanrui Wu

The Employment Impact of China's World Trade Organisation Accession
A.S. Bhalla and S. Qiu

Catch-Up and Competitiveness in China
The case of large firms in the oil industry
Jin Zhang

Corporate Governance in China
Jian Chen

The Theory of the Firm and Chinese Enterprise Reform
The case of China International Trust and Investment Corporation
Qin Xiao

Globalisation, Transition and Development in China
The case of the coal industry
Huaichuan Rui

China Along the Yellow River
Reflections on rural society
Cao Jinqing, translated by Nicky Harman and Huang Ruhua

Economic Growth, Income Distribution and Poverty Reduction in Contemporary China
Shujie Yao

China's Economic Relations with the West and Japan, 1949–79
Grain, trade and diplomacy
Chad J. Mitcham

China's Industrial Policy and the Global Business Revolution
The case of the domestic appliance industry
Ling Liu

Managers and Mandarins in Contemporary China
The building of an international business alliance
Jie Tang

The Chinese Model of Modern Development
Edited by Tian Yu Cao

Chinese Citizenship
Views from the margins
Edited by Vanessa L. Fong and Rachel Murphy

Unemployment, Inequality and Poverty in Urban China
Edited by Shi Li and Hiroshi Sato

Globalisation, Competition and Growth in China
Edited by Jian Chen and Shujie Yao

The Chinese Communist Party in Reform
Edited by Kjeld Erik Brodsgaard and Zheng Yongnian

Poverty and Inequality among Chinese Minorities
A.S. Bhalla and Shufang Qiu

Economic and Social Transformation in China
Challenges and opportunities
Angang Hu

Global Big Business and the Chinese Brewing Industry
Yuantao Guo

Peasants and Revolution in Rural China
Rural political change in the North China plain and the Yangzi Delta, 1850–1949
Chang Liu

The Chinese Banking Industry
Lessons from history for today's challenges
Yuanyuan Peng

Informal Institutions and Rural Development in China
Biliang Hu

The Political Future of Hong Kong
Democracy within communist China
Kit Poon

China's Post-Reform Economy—Achieving Harmony, Sustaining Growth
Edited by Richard Sanders and Chen Yang

Eliminating Poverty Through Development in China
China Development Research Foundation

Good Governance in China—A Way Towards Social Harmony
Case studies by China's rising leaders
Edited by Wang Mengkui

China in the Wake of Asia's Financial Crisis
Edited by Wang Mengkui

Multinationals, Globalisation and Indigenous Firms in China
Chunhang Liu

Economic Convergence in Greater China
Mainland China, Hong Kong, Macau and Taiwan
Chun Kwok Lei and Shujie Yao

Financial Sector Reform and the International Integration of China
Zhongmin Wu

China in the World Economy
Zhongmin Wu

China's Three Decades of Economic Reforms
Edited by Xiaohui Liu and Wei Zhang

China's Development Challenges
Economic vulnerability and public sector reform
Richard Schiere

China's Rural Financial System
Households' demand for credit and recent reforms
Yuepeng Zhao

Sustainable Reform and Development in Post-Olympic China
Edited by Shujie Yao, Bin Wu, Stephen Morgan and Dylan Sutherland

Constructing a Developmental Social Welfare System for All
China Development Research Foundation

China's Road to Peaceful Rise
Observations on its cause, basis, connotation and prospect
Zheng Bijian

China as the Workshop of the World
An analysis at the national and industry level of China in the international division of labor
Yuning Gao

Routledge Studies on the Chinese Economy—Chinese Economists on Economic Reform

Chinese Economists on Economic Reform—Collected Works of Xue Muqiao
Xue Muqiao, edited by China Development Research Foundation

Chinese Economists on Economic Reform—Collected Works of Guo Shuqing
Guo Shuqing, edited by China Development Research Foundation

China as the Workshop of the World

An analysis at the national and industry level of China in the international division of labor

Yuning Gao

LONDON AND NEW YORK

This edition published 2012
by Routledge
2 Park Square, Milton Park, Abingdon, Oxfordshire OX14 4RN

Simultaneously published in the USA and Canada
by Routledge
711 Third Avenue, New York, NY 10017

First issued in paperback 2014

Routledge is an imprint of the Taylor & Francis Group, an informa business

© 2012 Yuning Gao

The right of the Author to be identified as author of this work has been asserted by him in accordance with sections 77 and 78 of the Copyright, Designs and Patents Act 1988.

All rights reserved. No part of this book may be reprinted or reproduced or utilised in any form or by any electronic, mechanical, or other means, now known or hereafter invented, including photocopying and recording, or in any information storage or retrieval system, without permission in writing from the publishers.

Trademark notice: Product or corporate names may be trademarks or registered trademarks, and are used only for identification and explanation without intent to infringe.

British Library Cataloguing in Publication Data
A catalogue record for this book is available from the British Library

Library of Congress Cataloging-in-Publication Data
Gao, Yuning.
  China as the workshop of the world: an analysis at the national and industry level of China in the international division of labor/ Yuning Gao.
  p. cm.—(Routledge studies on the Chinese economy; 43)
  Includes bibliographical references and index.
  1. Industries—China. 2. Industrialization—China. 3. Industrial productivity—China. 4. China—Commerce. I. Title.
  HC427.95.G366 2011
  338.0951—dc22   2011003027

ISBN 13: 978-0-415-60405-5 (hbk)
ISBN 13: 978-1-138-81685-5 (pbk)

Typeset in Times New Roman by
Florence Production Ltd, Stoodleigh, Devon

To my son, Hongyi, born together with the book

Contents

List of figures		xi
List of tables		xv
Acknowledgments		xxi
List of abbreviations		xxiii
1	Background, theoretical framework, and literature review	1
2	Scale and scope of the "world workshop": China's place in world production	21
3	Pattern and sophistication of the "world workshop": China in the world market	59
4	The competitiveness of the "world workshop": China's place on the service part of global value chain	96
5	Comparative study of three of China's industries in the international manufacturing division	133
6	Conclusions	197
	Appendix 1: The broad economic categories	202
	Appendix 2: The International Standard Industrial Classification, Revision 3	203
	Appendix 3: The Standard International Trade Classification, Revision 3	206
	References	209
	Index	221

Figures

1.1	Share of FIEs in export	2
1.2	Industrial output of United Kingdom, United States, and China, 1750–2000	4
1.3	Merchandise exports of United Kingdom, United States, and China, 1820–2006	5
1.4	Pattern of the United Kingdom as a "world workshop"	13
1.5	Pattern of the United States as a "world factory"	14
1.6	China's share of merchandise exports, 1985–2006	15
2.1	Gross manufacturing output (current US$)	22
2.2	Manufacturing value added (current US$)	22
2.3	Share of manufacturing value added in the world (exchange rate method, %)	23
2.4	Share of industrial value added and GDP in the world (PPP method, %)	24
2.5	Share of manufacturing value added in the world (PPP method, %)	25
2.6	Share of high- and medium-technology products	26
2.7	China's manufacturing value added according to OECD classification	28
2.8	FIEs in China's industrial value added	29
2.9	China's share in world's output of raw materials	34
2.10	China's share in world's output of household appliances	35
2.11	Share of world CO_2 emissions	36
2.12	Amount and share of manufacturing CO_2 emissions	36
2.13	Share of world's gross capital formation (PPP method)	38
2.14	Share of capital stock in 101 sample countries	40
2.15	Share of manufacturing energy use	43
2.16	Share of manufacturing in final energy consumption	43
2.17	Industrial labor force as share of the world's	46
2.18	Undergraduate admissions in ISIC Review 3 classification	48
2.19	China's industrial capital–output ratio, 1960–2006	50
2.20	Manufacturing energy-consumption intensity (exchange rate)	51

xii *Figures*

2.21	Manufacturing energy-consumption intensity (PPP method)	51
2.22	Manufacturing labor productivity (US = 100, in 1997 constant international dollars)	52
2.23	China's relative unit cost (US = 100%)	53
2.24	Growth of China's TFP	55
3.1	Share in world merchandise exports (%)	59
3.2	Share of world merchandise imports (%)	60
3.3	Share of merchandise trade in GDP (exchange rate)	61
3.4	Proportions of China's different exports, 1981–2007	62
3.5	China's adjusted share of world merchandise exports, 1981–2005	63
3.6	China's balance of general merchandise trade with the world, by firm type	64
3.7	RCA in descending order (SITC Revision 3, 3-digit, 2005)	67
3.8	Share of the world's labor-intensive manufacturing exports	68
3.9	Processing share in China's exports by technological level, 1992–2005	72
3.10	Share of high-tech exports in total manufacturing exports	74
3.11	Share of high-tech exports in world market	75
3.12	Export of ICT goods (US$ billion)	76
3.13	Export of high-tech products by trade type	76
3.14	Export of high-tech products by ownership	77
3.15	Composition of China's trade surplus	81
3.16	China's parts and components trade, 1992–2003	85
3.17	Descending GL index in 2005 (SITC Revision 3, 3-digit)	87
3.18	China's descending GL index (SITC Revision 3, 3-digit)	88
3.19	GL index of China's merchandise trade groups	89
3.20	VS share of manufacturing	93
4.1	Share of BERD in total business value added	99
4.2	Number of business R&D researchers per 1,000 employees	100
4.3	Structure of manufacturing business R&D by technological intensity, 2004	101
4.4	China's share of world's resident invention patents	105
4.5	China's service trade, 1982–2007	111
4.6	Surplus of royalties and license trade	113
4.7	Foreign corporate R&D centers in China	114
4.8	China's ODM revenue from electronic systems, 2003–2008	115
4.9	China's EMS revenue from electronic systems, 2003–2008	115
4.10	Share of FIEs in wholesale and retail enterprises	117
4.11	Revenue of Fortune Global 500 firms to GDP	122
4.12	Country distribution of DTI top business R&D firms (by individuals)	124
4.13	Expenditure of R&D scoreboard firms to BERD	125
4.14	Share of manufacturing sector in outward FDI	130
4.15	Share of leasing and business services sector in outward FDI	131

Figures xiii

5.1	GIO of main non-structural-pottery producers (US$ billion)	136
5.2	GIO of main structural-pottery producers (US$ billion)	137
5.3	Export structure of China's ceramics products	141
5.4	Export of non-structural ceramics (666) (US$ million)	142
5.5	Export of structural ceramics (66244-5) (US$ million)	142
5.6	History and ownership transition of Sanhuan Group	145
5.7	Pattern of value added of Sanhuan Group and New Zhongyuan	153
5.8	Shares of major steel producers from a historical perspective	154
5.9	Shares of main steel producers in the world's physical output	155
5.10	Industrial value added of iron and steel industry (3710/2710 + 2731; US$ billion)	156
5.11	Exports of main steel producers (US$ billion)	156
5.12	Shares of main steel producers in the world's physical export	157
5.13	Export share of physical output	157
5.14	Share of flat and tube products in physical output	159
5.15	Share of flat and tube products in physical export	160
5.16	Descending export unit value of 5-digit iron and steel products, 2007	161
5.17	Physical labor productivity (ton/person/year)	163
5.18	Concentration ratio (CR5) of main steel producers	165
5.19	Labor productivity of Baosteel Group and Baoshan Iron & Steel Co. Ltd.	168
5.20	Output share of high-value-added products of Baoshan Iron & Steel Co. Ltd.	169
5.21	Labor/capital productivity of Fortune 500 steel producers	178
5.22	Pattern of value added of Baosteel Group and Heibei Iron and Steel Group	179
5.23	World energy production by fuel type, 1850–2007 (mtoe)	180
5.24	World new renewable-energy production, 1970–2007 (mtoe)	181
5.25	Pattern of value added of Suntech and LDK Solar	195

Tables

1.1	Regional shares of world manufacturing output	1
1.2	Products of which China has the largest physical output in the world, 2002	6
1.3	The generations of rival concepts of control	7
1.4	Successive waves of technical change	8
1.5	Stages of marketing and technology assimilations	10
1.6	Projected development stages in managing globalization	10
1.7	Share of merchandise trade in East Asia and Pacific area (%)	16
2.1	Medium- and high-technology manufacturing ISIC	26
2.2	Manufacturing industries classified according to their global technological intensity	27
2.3	Structure of industrial value added (%)	29
2.4	Share of high-tech industry in manufacturing value added	30
2.5	China's high-tech manufacturing industries' value-added revenue	30
2.6	Value added of high-tech industries from FIEs	31
2.7	Manufacturing divisions where China was ranked first (ISIC Revision 3)	32
2.8	China's main manufacturing products (ISIC Review 2)	33
2.9	China's share of transport equipment manufacture	34
2.10	Share of world computer production	35
2.11	Share of world gross capital formation (exchange rate method)	38
2.12	GFCF for manufacturing	39
2.13	Manufacturing share of FDI inflow	39
2.14	Market capitalization of listed companies	40
2.15	Manufacturing corporation assets	41
2.16	Manufacturing in FDI stock	42
2.17	Share of primary energy consumption	42
2.18	China's metal ore production	44
2.19	China's industrial raw materials futures contracts, 2009	44
2.20	Share of total labor force	45
2.21	Manufacturing employment of China and OECD	46
2.22	Share of world's human resources	47

2.23	Stock of skilled labor in China and United States (millions of people)	47
2.24	Inflow of skilled labor in China and US (1,000 people)	48
2.25	Manufacturing capital–output ratio	50
2.26	Manufacturing unit costs of China and United States	54
2.27	China's relative unit cost by industry (US = 100)	56
2.28	Relative TFP of China's manufacturing	58
3.1	Top ten economies with goods ranking first in world export market	60
3.2	Share of merchandise trade in GDP (PPP)	62
3.3	China's trade structure	65
3.4	Share in world market and RCA of China's exports	66
3.5	Technological classification of exports	69
3.6	China's competitiveness in world trade	70
3.7	Exports of China's industries according to OECD classification	70
3.8	Share of exports of FIEs in manufacturing sectors	71
3.9	Share of FIEs in high-tech export by industry	72
3.10	Current definition of high-tech trade in China	73
3.11	High-tech trade as a percentage of merchandise trade and manufacturing trade	74
3.12	Structure of high-tech exports (HNTP classification)	75
3.13	Export structure similarity and relative unit values	78
3.14	Relative unit value in SITC (Revision 3, 3-digit) sectors in 2005 (China = 1)	78
3.15	Unit value: China's color video monitor exports to the world (US$)	79
3.16	Relative unit value of ICT exports in 2005 (China = 1)	79
3.17	Classification of intermediate goods by BEC	80
3.18	Structure of China's trade under BEC classification	81
3.19	Share of intermediate trade in the world market	82
3.20	Structure of China's intermediate goods trade	82
3.21	Parts and components trade	84
3.22	Parts and components trade in world market	85
3.23	Share of parts and components of China	86
3.24	GL index of China, Japan, Korea, US in 2005 (SITC Revision 3, 3-digit)	88
3.25	GL index of China, 1992–2007 (SITC Revision 3, 3-digit)	89
3.26	China's share of different trade patterns (SITC Revision 3, 3-digit)	91
3.27	Share of different trade patterns in 2005 (SITC Revision 3, 3-digit)	92
3.28	VS share of manufacturing sectors	94
4.1	Evolution of the classification of business services sectors	97
4.2	Structure of China's service sector	98

Tables xvii

4.3	Total business enterprise R&D (billions of international dollars)	98
4.4	Total business personnel and researchers (1,000 FTE)	100
4.5	Doctoral degree graduates (persons)	101
4.6	R&D intensity across sectors, 2004	103
4.7	R&D intensity in high-tech industries, 2003	104
4.8	Share of non-domestic and foreign-funded enterprise, 2004	104
4.9	R&D expenditure structure	104
4.10	Share of total invention patents	105
4.11	Share of enterprises in resident patents	106
4.12	Total manufacturing patents by technological intensity, 2004	106
4.13	High-tech-related patent applications by field of technology (2001–2005 average)	107
4.14	PCT international applications by country of origin	108
4.15	ISO member bodies' contribution	109
4.16	Pattern of standards in force	109
4.17	China's current ICT standards	110
4.18	Service trade in total goods and service trade	112
4.19	China's commercial services trade, 2006 (US$100 million)	112
4.20	Share of wholesale and retail FIEs across sectors, 2004	118
4.21	Country distribution of *Business Week*'s 100 Top Brands	119
4.22	Incomplete statistics for China's acquired national brands	120
4.23	Net share of manufacturing output of the top 100 firms, 1909–1963 (%)	121
4.24	Country distribution of Fortune Global 500	121
4.25	Country distribution of *Financial Times* Global 500	122
4.26	Market value of *Financial Times* Global 500	123
4.27	Country distribution of Top 50 non-financial TNCs in developing countries	124
4.28	Number of top business R&D firms (individuals)	125
4.29	Patterns of national champions	126
4.30	Main indicators of national champions	126
4.31	National champions in China's capital market (year end 2007)	127
4.32	Industrial distribution of national champions	128
4.33	Share of outward FDI of the world	129
4.34	China's FDI outward stock structure of sourced enterprises	131
5.1	Scope of the classification of the ceramics industry	135
5.2	Physical output of China's ceramics industry	137
5.3	Physical indicators of different ceramics products of upper-scale enterprises	138
5.4	China's kaolin clay trade	139
5.5	Employment and productivity of main ceramics producers	140
5.6	Export unit value of structural ceramics	143
5.7	Export unit value of non-structural ceramics (US$/kg)	143

5.8	R&D intensity through sectors, 2004	144
5.9	Main economic indicators of Sanhuan Group (10,000 yuan)	146
5.10	Distribution of different production modes of Sanhuan Group (10,000 yuan)	147
5.11	Main OEM brand of Sanhuan Group	147
5.12	Total input of technical activity	148
5.13	Main indicators of daily-used-ceramics producers	151
5.14	Operating indicators of main daily-used-ceramics producers	152
5.15	Length of time taken by major steel producers to expand production from 1 to 100 million tons	154
5.16	Steel product classification	158
5.17	Steel consumption by end-use sector, 2008 (%)	159
5.18	Export unit value of main steel producers (US$/kg)	161
5.19	Labor input and labor productivity of main steel producers	162
5.20	Physical energy and CO_2 intensity of iron and steel industry	163
5.21	R&D intensity of iron and steel industry (2710)	164
5.22	Scale distribution of China's iron and steel enterprises	164
5.23	Main indicators for Baosteel Group	166
5.24	Main indicators for Baoshan Iron & Steel Co. Ltd.	167
5.25	Physical output of Baosteel Group and Baoshan Iron & Steel Co. Ltd., 2006	168
5.26	Domestic sales share of major flat and tube products (%)	170
5.27	Share of exports in total sales (%)	170
5.28	Global market share of top five automotive and automotive-steel producers in 2006	172
5.29	R&D expenditure and personnel	172
5.30	Physical output and structure of Heibei Iron and Steel Group	174
5.31	Physical output of Fortune 500 steel companies	175
5.32	Labor productivity of Fortune 500 steel companies	176
5.33	Main indicators for Fortune 500 steel companies	177
5.34	Existing capacity of renewable energy generation (GW)	182
5.35	Existing capacity of solar energy generation (GW)	182
5.36	Physical output of global solar cells (MW)	184
5.37	Conversion efficiency and market breakdown of different cell types (%)	185
5.38	Global pattern of crystalline-silicon solar-module production, 2006	186
5.39	Demand and supply of silicon materials and their price (tons)	186
5.40	Employment in China's solar PV industry (people)	187
5.41	Main indicators of Suntech (US$ million)	188
5.42	Regional market breakdown for Suntech (US$ million)	188
5.43	Product price and margins for Suntech	189
5.44	R&D intensity for Suntech	190
5.45	Main technology standards issued	190
5.46	Main indicators of LDK Solar	191

5.47	Margins of LDK Solar and its products	192
5.48	Top ten solar-cell producers (MW)	193
5.49	Indicators of main solar-cell producers	194
6.1	Adjustment of the definition of world factory	197

Acknowledgments

I would like to express my greatest gratitude to my supervisor, Professor Peter Nolan, for the guidance, support, and help demonstrated through all the discussions on my work. His penetrating advice gave me clear direction for my research, from the drafting of this book to its revision. His extensive academic insight also has become the model for my own study. Furthermore, I would like to thank my advisor, Dr. Jin Zhang, for the suggestions made during group seminars.

I would also like to acknowledge the Sun Hung Kai—KWOK's Foundation Cambridge bursary, awarded to me by the funding body, the Cambridge Overseas Trust. I am also grateful to Dr. Jinghai Zheng, who employs me as a part-time research assistant, both for the professional economics techniques I learn from him and the financial support it provides.

I would also like to acknowledge the part played by Professor Angang Hu, who led me through the gate of academic research and especially into the field of Chinese studies. Without his kind help, the successful fieldwork in China for this book would have been unimaginable. In addition, discussions with my colleagues in the China Big Business Programme, at the University of Cambridge, and in the Center for China Studies, at Tsinghua University, have given me the opportunity to examine my research from many different perspectives.

During my time in Cambridge, my parents have always given my career their unreserved help. I am also deeply grateful to my wife, Zhenzhen, for her patience, tolerance, and warmest support in sharing all the ups and downs of these years with me.

Finally, the author would like to thank Taylor & Francis Journals for kind permission to reprint material from Yuning Gao and Angang Hu (2009) "A comparative study of the development mode of China's iron and steel industry," *Journal of Chinese Economic and Business Studies*, Vol. 7, No. 3: 283–297.

Abbreviations

AS	aircraft and spacecraft
ASEAN	Association of Southeast Asian Nations
ATP	advanced technology product
BEC	broad economic categories
BERD	business enterprise research and development
BERR	Department for Business, Enterprise & Regulatory Reform (UK)
BOD	biological oxygen demand
BOP	balance of payment
BPO	business process outsourcing
BRIC	Brazil, Russia, India, China
BSI	British Standards Institution
CCC	China compulsory certification
CCCI	China Certification Center, Inc.
CDMA	code division multiple access
c.i.f.	cost, insurance, and freight
COE	computers and office equipments
CSRC	China Securities and Regulatory Commission
DIUS	Department for Innovation, Universities & Skills (UK)
EBOPS	expanded balance of payment service classification
ECM	electronic contract manufacturing
EMS	electronic manufacturing services
EPZ	export processing zone
ETE	electronic and telecommunication equipments
EU	European Union
FATS	foreign affiliates trade in services
FDI	foreign direct investment
FIE	foreign investment enterprises
f.o.b.	free on board
FTE	full-time equivalent
GB	Guo Biao (National Standard)
GFCF	gross fixed capital formation
GIO	gross industrial output

GL	Grubel–Lloyd (index)
HNTP	high and new technology products
HRST	human resources for science and technology
HS	harmonized system
ICT	information and communications technologies
IEA	International Energy Agency
IEC	International Electro-technical Commission
IEEE	Institute of Electrical and Electronics Engineers
IFS	International Financial Statistics
IISI	International Iron and Steel Institute
IIT	intra-industry trade
ILO	International Labor Organization
IMF	International Monetary Fund
IPO	initial public offering
ISIC	International Standard Industrial Classification
ISO	International Standard Organization
ITU	International Telecommunication Union
LME	large and medium enterprises
JSA	Japanese Standards Association
M&A	merger and acquisition
MEM	medical equipments and meters manufacturing
MLSS	Ministry of Labor and Social Security (China)
MNC	multinational company
MOC	Ministry of Commerce (China)
MOF	Ministry of Finance (China)
MOST	Ministry of Science and Technology (China)
NBS	National Bureau of Statistics (China)
NDRC	National Development and Reform Commission (China)
n.e.c.	not elsewhere classified
NIE	newly industrialized economies
NYSE	New York Stock Exchange
OBM	original brand manufacturing
ODM	original design manufacturing
OEM	original equipment manufacturing
OECD	Organization for Economic Development and Cooperation
PCT	Patent Cooperation Treaty
PIM	perpetual inventory method
PPP	purchasing power parity
PV	photovoltaic
R&D	research and development
RCA	revealed comparative advantage
SAC	Standardization Administration of China
SAFE	State Administration of Foreign Exchange (China)
SASAC	State-owned Assets Supervision and Administration Commission

SITC	Standard International Trade Classification
SOE	state-owned enterprises
TFP	total factor productivity
TNC	transnational company
UNCTAD	United Nations Conference on Trade and Development
UNDP	United Nations Development Program
UNEP	United Nations Environment Program
UNIDO	United Nations Industrial Development Organization
UNSTA	United Nations Statistics Division
VS	vertical specialization
WIPO	World Intellectual Property Organization
WLAN	wireless local area network
WTO	World Trade Organization

1 Background, theoretical framework, and literature review

Historical background

China: "world workshop," "world factory," or nothing?

It was in 2001, the year that China became the 143rd member country of the World Trade Organization (WTO), that, for the first time, China was described as a "world factory," in a report by some Japanese scholars from the Research Institute of Economy, Trade, and Industry (Zhang, 2006). In 2000, China's manufacturing value added had just passed US$200 billion, which made China the fourth-largest manufacturer of the world. However, according to the forecasts of Global Insight (2007), China would overtake the United States before 2015, to become number one, in its high-growth-rate scenario (see Table 1.1). If so, China would be more like a "world factory" than at any other time in its history as a modern country.

The skyrocketing of the merchandise trade during the transition period of China's entry to the WTO was another aspect of the process. China's merchandise exports surpassed Japan's in 2004 and reached 6.5 percent of the world's total. UN trade statistics show that China had the most products ranking first in 2005, 958 of which are among the 5,113 items in the six-digit

Table 1.1 Regional shares of world manufacturing output

	Manufacturing value added (US$ billion)		Change	Annual growth rate on 1997 price (percent)
	2006	2015		
US	1,879 (22.3)	2,577 (16.6)	(−5.7)	2.8
China	910 (10.8)	3,090 (19.9)	(9.1)	9.1
World	8,424 (100.0)	15,527 (100.0)		3.8

Note: Numbers in brackets are the share of world's total.
Source: Global Insight (2007).

2 Background and theoretical framework

harmonized system (HS) catalogue (Korea International Trade Association, 2007). The statistics from the WTO show that China's exports in the second half of 2006 exceeded those of the United States to become the second largest after Germany's, and it also forecast that China might take first place after 2008, the year of the Olympics (WTO, 2007). This seems to provide very strong proof that China would take the title of "world workshop."

Nevertheless, arguments from many other scholars offer opposing evidence. The debate over the measurement of China's total industrial output, between exchange rate and purchasing power parity (PPP), leads to the first questions as to *how big China's manufacturing industry is, and whether it is big enough to make China a "world factory."* However, a more common viewpoint focuses on the industrial structure. A real "world factory" should provide advanced products of its time, which means it should stand at the top of the "quality ladder" (Grossman and Helpman, 1991). Further questions relate to *what the pattern of China's products is*, and *what its position on the "ladder" is*.

The ensuing debate noted that foreign investment enterprises (FIEs)[1] have become more and more important in China's exports. In 2003, their share in China's total exports reached 54.8 percent, and that was because they accounted for a large proportion of China's processing exports (78.7 percent) and machinery/electronics exports (68.9 percent). Although some researchers think that they have been overestimated, because of the use of domestic intermediaries (Ping et al., 2005), the role of FIEs still raises another question, as to *whether China has its own competitiveness in the world market*.

The third main problem concerns the role of FIEs in China's high-tech sectors. Although they form only 10.4 percent of the total number of industrial enterprises above a designated scale,[2] they share about 20.9 percent of the gross

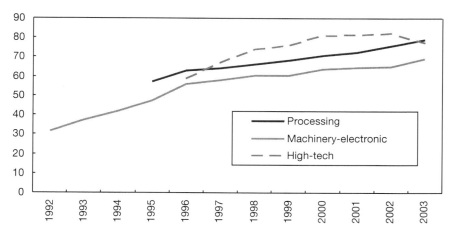

Figure 1.1 Share of FIEs in export
Source: Author's calculation, based on Zhang (2006).

industrial output (GIO), 19.1 percent of research and development (R&D) expenditure, and 25.4 percent of the total number of invention patents (National Bureau of Statistics (NBS), 2006). Besides, FIEs also represent a very large proportion of China's high-tech exports—over 80 percent during the peak time from 2000 to 2002. These facts raise the associated questions of *what the role of FIEs is in China*, or *whether a foreign-funded China can be thought of as a "world factory."*

The arguments sometimes omitted, which no one will consider in respect to China when talking about the highest end of the global value chain, involve the technology standard of world industries and the world-famous brands. I believe that they are indeed the real "soft power" (Nye, 2004) of a "world factory" today. That is why many people think China should be called a "world workshop" instead of a "world factory"(Xinhua News Agency, 2004).

What is a workshop, factory, firm, or company?[3]

A *workshop* is a room or building that provides both the area and tools (or machinery) that may be required for the manufacture or repair of manufactured goods. Apart from the larger factories, workshops were the only places of production in the days before industrialization.

A *factory* (previously manufactory) or manufacturing plant is a large industrial building where workers manufacture goods or supervise machines processing one product into another. Most modern factories have large warehouses or warehouse-like facilities that contain heavy equipment used for assembly-line production. Archetypally, factories gather and concentrate resources—workers, capital, and plant.

A *firm* (sometimes *enterprise*) is an economic term used to describe a collection of individuals grouped together for economic gain, according to Coase (1937). It also refers to the basic unit for the organization of production, which Penrose (1959) considers, not as a "legal person," but, by analogy, as an "economic person."

A *company* (sometimes *corporation*) refers to a legal entity (technically, a juristic person) formed to have a separate legal identity from its members and ordinarily incorporated to undertake commercial business. Although some jurisdictions refer to unincorporated entities as companies, in most jurisdictions, the term refers only to incorporated entities.

"World workshop"/"world factory" in history

The appellation "world workshop" was commonly used to describe the United Kingdom after its Industrial Revolution. Hudson (2001) points out that the Industrial Revolution promoted the world's first industrial and consumer-oriented society in Britain and made Britain the workshop of the world. Chambers (1961) thinks, "Britain can be described as the workshop of the world . . . in a variety of definitions," in his book, *The workshop of the world*.

4 Background and theoretical framework

These definitions include monopoly of the supply of manufactured goods, vital components of her export trade, shipping and credit agencies, and mutually advantageous relationships and funds for the lubrication of the wheels of the world's commerce.

The historical data show us the "world workshop" according to the first two definitions.[4] In the 1870s, the United Kingdom's manufacturing output constituted 22.9 percent of the world's, and its export 21.8 percent. In 1860, the United Kingdom produced 53 percent of the world's total output of pig iron, 50 percent of coal and brown coal, and 50 percent of the total cotton wool consumed; its total modern-industry production capacity reached 40–45 percent of the world's. Trade from the United Kingdom accounted for one-fifth of the world's merchandise trade and two-fifths of manufacturing; the United Kingdom's merchant fleet also formed one-third of the world's total (Kennedy, 1987). Before the First World War, London was undoubtedly the world financial center, and, in 1914, the United Kingdom's share of accumulated foreign direct investment (FDI) from all round the world was 45.3 percent (Dunning and Lundan, 2008).

The United States reached an even higher peak share of world manufacturing output—44.7 percent—in the early 1950s, but its export peak was only half that of the United Kingdom. This difference shows that the industrialization of the United States relied on its domestic markets much more than on the foreign markets. Besides, the United States also had a preponderant shipping power and contributed 48.3 percent of the global FDI till 1960 (Dunning and Lundan, 2008). The world financial center after the Second World War, New York, helped the United States to become a new "world workshop" at that time.

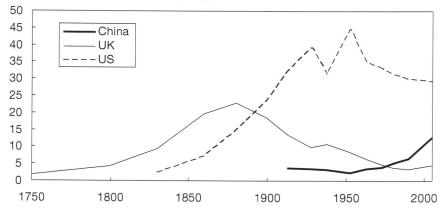

Figure 1.2 Industrial output of United Kingdom, United States, and China, 1750–2000

Source: Author's calculation, based on Bairoch (1982) and World Bank (2007b).

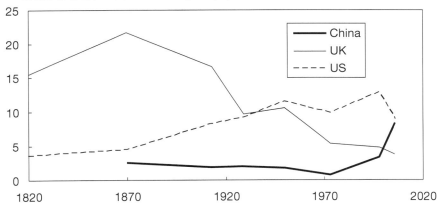

Figure 1.3 Merchandise exports of United Kingdom, United States, and China, 1820–2006
Source: Author's calculation, based on Maddison (2003) and WTO (2007).

In fact, the United States has several advantages that the United Kingdom never had. First of all, although its share in the Fortune Global 500 has decreased from half of all to one-third over the past thirty years, and it was almost caught up by Japan in 1995 (Fortune, 2009), the United States still has the largest group of the most powerful companies around the world. Second, it shares more than 40 percent of the world's business R&D expenditure (Department for Innovation, Universities & Skills (DIUS) and Department for Business, Enterprise & Regulatory Reform (BEPR), various years), which has become the source of the United States' national innovation system. Third, the United States also owns half of the world's most famous brands (Interbrand, various years), and this is believed to be a sign of the soft power of the "world factory" today.

When we talk about China today, the most impressive thing is that China has become the largest producer of numerous products, but most of them are still raw materials or low-value-added ones. These facts usually lead to the result that China's share of the manufacturing output in the world is close to the estimation of PPP, which was 18 percent in 2007. With this kind of measurement, China has reached the level of the United Kingdom in the 1850s, which leads people to think that China has emerged as a "world workshop."

China's merchandise export also rose sharply, especially after its entry into the WTO in 2001. China's share in the world reached 8.8 percent in 2007, which is 0.4 percent higher than that of the United States. However, it is still at only half of the United States' peak and a quarter of the United Kingdom's peak. From historical comparison, it seems China can only be treated partly as a "world workshop," but is still far from being a "world factory." This is still a very rough assessment of the problem. If we would like to make this view clearer and more accurate, we need to investigant the determinants further.

Table 1.2 Products of which China has the largest physical output in the world, 2002

Sectors (ISIS Rev 2)	Products
31 Food & beverages	Edible vegetable oil, monosodium glutamate (50%), citric acid (30%), xylitol (80%), cigarettes (33%)
32 Textiles & wearing	Cotton yarn, cotton cloth, silk (70%), clothing, light pig leather, light sheep leather (21%), heavy bovine leather (22%), goat skin, leather shoes (34%)
33 & 34 Wood & paper products	Wooden pencils (55%)
35 Chemicals	Sulfuric acid, soda, chemical fertilizer (20%), terramycin (65%)[a], cephalosporin, hydrochloric acid doxycycline, vitamin C (50%), penicillin (60%), chemical fiber, rubber overshoes (50%)[a], plastic film, plastic sacks, plastic shoes
36 Non-metallic mineral products	Cement (37%), glass (31%), glass attemperatord (33%), everyday pottery (70%), artificial diamonds (60%)[a]
37 Metal & metallic products	Pig iron (23%), steel (15%), lanthanon material (70%)[a], Containers (83%), nail clippers (40%), zippers, metal lighters (80%)[a], clocks and watches (75%)
38 Equipment	Tractors (83%), sewing machines (50%), motorcycles (44%), bicycles (40%), micro motors (60%) disposable batteries (40%), washing machines (24%), vacuum cleaners, refrigerators (16%), electric fans (50%)[a], air conditioners (30%), kitchen ventilators, microwave ovens (30%), electric cookers, color TVs (29%), radio-tape recorders (70%), VCD players (70%), digital program-controlled switchboards, telephones (50%)[a], displays (42%), cameras (50%)[a]
39 Other manufacturing industries	Toys (33%)

Note: The number in brackets refers to China's share in the world.
a At least the share.
Source: Great Wall Enterprise Strategy Institute (2004).

Long waves: stages of industrial evolution

The United Kingdom is recognized as the cradle of the Industrial Revolution, and one of the most important characteristics of this revolution was the specialization of craft production that came from the ideas of Adam Smith, the division of labor. The United Kingdom became the first integrated market in the world, and the British also tried to integrate their colonies into the market. The booming manufacturing became the most powerful "weapon" of this new "world workshop," and even Napoleon could not prevent his enemy's products from pouring onto the French market.

The United Kingdom faced a different competitor in the international restructuring race (Ruigrok and Tulder, 1995) over the following 100 years' peace and was finally defeated by the United States. As Marx (1996 [1859], p. 132) pointed out,

In general understanding [of the subject] the answer [which is given to that inquiry] amounts to the generality that an industrial nation enjoys the height of its production at the moment at which it occupies its general historical height. In fact, a nation is at its industrial height so long as gain is not yet the main thing, but [the process of] gaining. So that Yankees are ahead of English.

Industrialization in the United States brought a brand new concept of production control, and scientific management (Taylor, 1911) and Fordism became the characteristics of the so-called Second Industrial Revolution. The success of the United States came from horizontal specialization, which meant the scope of specialization went down to the whole manufacturing procedures of the products. As productivity skyrocketed, the manufacturing output of the United States increased eightfold between 1870 and 1913, whereas the United Kingdom's doubled, and Germany's quadrupled (Bairoch, 1982).

Another century after overtaking the United Kingdom, the United States had to face its own challenge: a new generation of the concept of control from Japan—network specialization. People usually use vertical specialization to describe this new mode, but here I would like to use "network," because it is in fact an expansion of working procedures and forms a specialization network of the product parts. This change from the 1980s was thought to be the beginning of the Third Industrial Revolution. Network production later led to the concept of module production (Baldwin, 2000), which has become the internal organization mode of the East Asian economies.

Japan had 147 companies in the Fortune Global 500 in 1995, compared with the 150 from the United States, and its gross domestic product (GDP) also reached its peak, 72 percent of the GDP of the United States. The disadvantage was that Japan held few technology standards and world-famous brands as its "soft power," compared with the United States. China today is integrating itself into the world's specialization network, but it still has a long way to go, even if it seems to be the most powerful potential challenger in the new generation of industrial revolution.

The generation of industrial revolution is more a historical concept than an economic one and is usually treated as the national life cycle in a macro-history

Table 1.3 The generations of rival concepts of control

	First	*Second*	*Third (forthcoming)*
Concept	Craft production	(Neo-)Fordism	Toyotism
Supply	Flexible specialization	Horizontal specialization	Network specialization
Technology	Invention	Predominance	Standardization
Lead Country	UK	US	Japan? China?

Source: Author's design based on Ruigrok and Tulder (1995, p. 61).

context (Braudel, 2002), or even the internal movement of the modern world system (Wallerstein, 1974). Therefore, our next question will concern what the economically driven forces of the industrial revolution are. The most obvious economic explanation of the cycle of industrialization may be the long wave theory in economic history.

The most well-known long waves in economic history are Kondratieff (1935) waves. These long waves became famous especially after Schumpeter (1939) explained them in relation to innovation. He pointed out that the long cycle of factor price that Kondratieff had observed was because of the movement of key technological innovations. Freeman and Soete (1997) specified the characteristics of the Kondratieff waves from the 1780s. They thought the United Kingdom's age comprised the first and second long waves, and the United States' age comprised the following two long waves.

Freeman and Soete (1997) specified the characteristics of the Kondratieff waves from the 1780s (see Table 1.4). The United Kingdom's age comprised the first and second long waves, when it led the breakthrough in specialized production of textiles and the use of steam power and railways. These key innovations came from its system of inventor as entrepreneur in the first long wave and the emergence of institutions of different forms of engineering in the second long wave. The production of textiles led to the formation of numerous small firms, and the production of iron produced many bigger ones. However, their modes are all of the flexible specialization, which belongs to the first industrial revolution.

The United States' age comprised the following two long waves. The United States led the world into the age of electricity and steel and also had

Table 1.4 Successive waves of technical change

Kondratieff waves	Key features	Energy system	Innovation system	Organization form
First 1780s–1840s	Factory production of textiles	Water power	Inventor–entrepreneur	Small firms
Second 1840s–1890s	Steam power and railway	Steam power	Institutions of engineering	Big firms
Third 1890s–1940s	Electricity and steel	Electricity	"In-house" R&D department	Giant firms
Fourth 1940s–1990s	Automobiles and synthetic materials	Oil	Specialized R&D department	MNCs
Fifth 1990s–	Micro-electronics and computer networks	Gas/oil	Integrated national system	Firm network

Source: Freeman and Soete, *The economics of industrial innovation*, London: Pinter, 1997, pp. 19, 65–70.

a monopoly of manufacturing products. After the Second World War, the specialized R&D of automobiles and synthetic materials finally helped the United States to become the true "world factory" during the golden age of the Western world, which was also the ascendant side of the fourth long wave. In addition, the emergence of multinational companies (MNCs), based on the giant firms that appeared at the turn of the nineteenth and twentieth centuries, is in fact the source of the United States' key power.

Although scholars still do not agree about the starting time of the fifth long wave, there is no doubt that we are now on the ascendant side of it. Today, the mode of specialization has expanded from pipelining to a network, and innovation activity has also become an integrated national innovation system (NDRC, MOC, and Nelson, 1993). The possible new form of organization, the firm network, provides new chances for a latecomer such as China, but there are certainly many more ladders (Chang, 2002) for China to climb than there were for the United States a century ago.

A review of the analysis framework

Levels versus stages: an alternative perspective

Based on the generation of industrial revolution and the long waves in economic history, scholars developed some more general models of the stages of economic development, which were thought of as parts of a large-scale "life cycle" (Duijn, 1983). The Rostovian take-off model (Rostow, 1960) divided the process into five stages: traditional society, the preconditions for take-off, take-off, the drive to maturity, and the age of high mass consumption. Michael Porter (1998) provides a division into the four stages of economic development: the factor-driven stage, the investment-driven stage, the innovation-driven stage, and the wealth-driven stage.

The stages of industrial evolution are closely related to those stages. The change of leading sectors and organization forms through the Kondratieff waves provides us with a clear division of the stages. Hobday (1995) provides some more characteristics of the market and technology through different stages.

Akamatsu (1962) brought out his theory of the "flying geese paradigm" to describe the dynamic process of industrial upgrading among antecedent countries and catching-up countries, especially in the east Asian area. According to his theory, Japan, newly industrialized economies (NIEs), the Association of Southeast Asian Nations (ASEAN), latecomers (such as China), and latest comers (such as Vietnam) are in the order of their different stages of growth, from information and communications technologies (ICT) to garments. When they globalize their own economy, they will also experience different development stages.

If we assume that all the countries will proceed through the same stages of industrial evolution in order, or at least some of the stages, different countries

Table 1.5 Stages of marketing and technology assimilations

Market stages	Technology stages
1 Passive importer-pull; cheap labor assembly;	Assembly skills, basic production capabilities; mature products dependent on buyers for distribution
2 Active sales of capacity; quality and cost-based; foreign-buyer dependent	Incremental process changes for quality and speed; reverse engineering of products
3 Advanced production sales; marketing dept. established; starts overseas marketing; markets own designs	Full production skills; process innovation; product-design capability
4 Product marketing push; sells direct to retailers and distributors overseas; builds up product range; starts own-brand sales	Begins R&D for products and process; product-innovation capabilities
5 Own-brand push; markets directly to customers; independent distribution channels, direct advertising; in-house market research	Competitive R&D capabilities; R&D linked to market needs; advanced product/process innovation

Source: Hobday (1995, p. 40).

Table 1.6 Projected development stages in managing globalization

Globalization within	Stage 1:	Localization overseas of marketing capacities. Expend exports to stimulate the market.
	Stage 2:	Localization overseas of production capacities. Set up a production system integral with the matter.
	Stage 3:	Localization overseas of R&D capacities. Strengthen technological support for oversea production, product development integral with the market, technological development, the research system, etc.
Globalization outside	Stage 4:	Reconstruction of management style based on local standards. Establish corporate roots locally, with locals included in management.
	Stage 5:	Management innovation to make the company suitable for Globalization. Practice true internationalization.

Source: Japan Commission on Industrial Performance (1997, p. 246).

at various levels of evolution can be considered to be at different stages of the process. This hypothesis is the most important alteration from stage to level. It means all the characteristics of the stages in the economic history of industrial evolution are also those of the corresponding levels of the countries today. Therefore, the countries that are at the low end of the global value chain are commonly thought to be still in the early stage of industrial evolution.

Levels of industrial evolution

Industrial production becomes more and more complex through its evolution. During the four stages of marketing and technology assimilations in Hobday (1995), the form of its organization has been upgraded, from simple processing workshop at the beginning of the Industrial Revolution, to production factory, to operating firm, and to global business today. This is also the process of its extending at both ends of the global value chain.

Processing

Processing is the basic level of the generalized value chain. It includes the processing from raw materials to semi-finished products, or parts of final products, and their related inbound logistics. This level usually finishes with workshops, which are similar to the small firms at the first stage of industrial evolution.

Production (including trading)

Production includes the process of output of final products and their outbound logistics–trading. This level lies within the factory, and the production scale is more likely that of the big firm in the stage of the second long wave.

Operation (including R&D, sales)

Operation has a similar meaning to production in the standard value chain. I would like to treat it as a wider concept that includes R&D and sales.[5] This level corresponds to the stage of the giant firms whose key competitiveness comprises technology and sales channels. The operations of these firms should not only involve production, and the roles of R&D and sales have become very important.

Global business (including standards, brands)

The standard value chain does not include the parts that can bring more and more value added today: standards and brands. The brand of Coca-Cola was estimated to be worth US$67 billion in 2006, and it is much more valuable than any patent or fixed capital of the company. At this highest level, this kind of "soft power" is in fact the real source of the MNC's and places them at the top of the value chain.

Steps in a generalized value chain

The standard value chain has two parts (Porter, 1985): the "primary activities" include inbound logistics, operations (production), outbound logistics, marketing and sales, and services (maintenance); the "support activities" include administrative infrastructure management, human resource management, R&D, and procurement. Compared with the stages of industrial evolution, the "support activities" of the standard value chain can be reintegrated into the "primary activities" to form a generalized value chain along the direction of the addition of value.

Standards and R&D

From a wider perspective, the function of processing and the standards beyond that usually come before the raw material, and so they are in fact the beginning of the "value." The more intensive the technology in the product, the more R&D activities play an important role in processing progress. Although its function may be similar from one product to another, and the standard beyond may be the same through the whole life cycle of the products, we still cannot deny that standards are "quoted" each time products are "supplied" to the consumer.

Processing and trade

These are actually the key parts of a value chain in any kind of concept. Here, I only would like to expand the range of trade to a broad concept of input and output. The input part is composed of procurement (logistics relating to raw materials should also be included here) and import, and the output part concerns the logistics of the products and their export.

Sales and brand

The traditional concept of the value chain treats sales as its end, but I would like to argue that consumers today are usually hit first by the brands of the products, from advertisements or other channels. Although brands are not a method of physical access by which the final products reach consumers, even compared with service, I still believe they are the real end of a generalized value chain.

Framework of the chain and levels

Pattern of the "world workshop"

A "world workshop" is concerned with a limited part of the framework. The United Kingdom, a typical "world workshop," started its revolution from the bottom of the evolution level and also the middle of the value chain, that is, the processing of manufacturing products. The production boom greatly enhanced its production capacity, which appeared as the sharp increase in the merchandising trade, and especially the export of the main manufactured products.

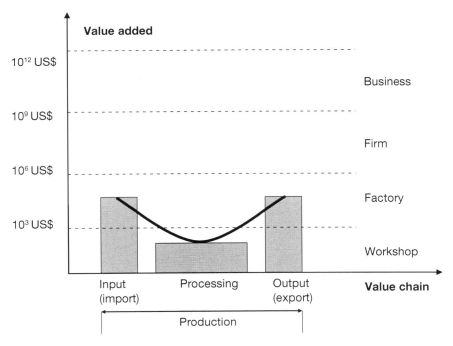

Figure 1.4 Pattern of the United Kingdom as a "world workshop"
Source: Author's design.

The scope of the "world workshop" only extends to processing and trade, and its scale of organization usually ranges from workshop at the beginning to bigger factories later. The source of technology is individual invention. This, on one hand, can be easily supported by them and, on the other hand, fits the mode of product specialization well.

Pattern of the "world factory"

A "world factory" has much wider scope in terms of industrial evolution levels and expanded to include the total generalized value chain. In history, the United States led the new industrial revolution. The horizontal specialization therefore required more specialized R&D, but not just individual inventions. This trend later led to the appearance of the group of standards, from processing level to design level, which became the key soft power of the "world factory."

Furthermore, the end of the generalized value chain also extended to include sales. The giant firms went beyond output or export and began to provide sales and service to customers. Today, most consumers are usually reached first by

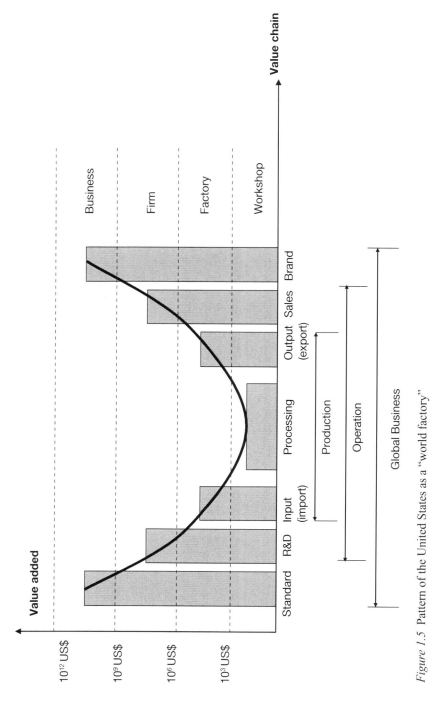

Figure 1.5 Pattern of the United States as a "world factory"
Source: Author's design.

businesses' brands, and these are also another kind of soft power, the identities of the "world factory."

Hence, the value chain's level rose to operation at the beginning and later to the level of global business. More than a hundred years ago, the businessmen of the "world workshop" talked about the value added of processing in pounds and of trade in thousands of pounds. Today, the businessmen of the "world factory" talk about their R&D expenditure in terms of millions of US dollars and their brand in terms of billions of US dollars. This is how the world has changed, and it may be the only way for those countries that want to become a "world workshop," or even a "world factory," in the future.

The inside and outside impetus

The "pull" from inside: China's development in the East Asia mode

China's economic development after entering the WTO

There are many different evaluations of the impact of China's entry of the WTO. *The China Quarterly* (Fewsmith, 2001) and *The China Economic Review* (Chun et al., 2001) launched special issues, and a large number of books associated with the subject were also published (such as Panitchpakdi and Clifford, 2002; Lardy, 2002). Other scholars carried out quantitative research on the impact of China's trade liberalization (McKibbin and Tang, 2000; Gilbert and Wahl, 2002). Yet other researchers (Martin and Ianchovichina, 2001; Shafaeddin, 2004) focused on the impact of China's WTO accession on other countries and the WTO itself.

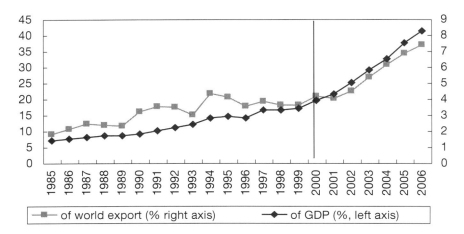

Figure 1.6 China's share of merchandise exports, 1985–2006

Source: Author's calculation, based on NBS, various years; WTO, various years.

16 *Background and theoretical framework*

The most optimistic prediction thought that China's share of world exports would rise from 4.4 percent in 2001 to 7.8 percent by 2007 (Martin and Ianchovichina, 2001), but China's exports rose even higher than that, to 8.2 percent in 2006. Although its GDP annual growth rate exceeded 10 percent by 2002, the annual growth rate of its exports tripled at the same time. This meant that the share of exports in China's GDP increased sharply, from 20.1 percent in 2001 to 36.9 percent in 2006.

Dynamics of flying geese

When Akamatsu (1962) brought out his "flying geese paradigm" theory in the 1930s, he could hardly have imagined that Japan's leading position might be taken by China one day. In fact, the term of the "flying geese" is a dynamic one, not a static one, and the rise of China totally changed its order. Data from Global Insight shows that China caught up with Japan in the share of manufacturing value added in 2006. From 2001, when China entered the WTO, to 2006, Japan declined from its peak of about 18 percent to about 11 percent, and, at the same time, China rose from 7 percent to the same share.

Related to the booming output, China's merchandise trade became dominant in East Asia and the Pacific over a period of 5 years. In 2000, China's share was a quarter of the total merchandise trade of the area, which was 20 percent less than that of Japan, but only 5 years later, their positions had been totally reversed through China's sharp growth and Japan's stagnation. China's share of the merchandise trade reached 42 percent, closing to the share of Japan in 2000, but at the same time Japan's share decreased to about 33 percent. This means the engine of the regional trade had moved to China from Japan.

China's position is described as that of a "hub" of regional trade by the International Monetary Fund (IMF). China shared one-third of the intraregional trade in 2004. The IMF (2005, p. 36) believes that,

> this acceleration in regional trade with China has reflected to a large extent a supply-side driven reorganization of production processes, with China emerging as a regional assembly hub, countries in the region export inputs to China for final assembly and shipment to the EU, Japan, and the United States.

Table 1.7 Share of merchandise trade in East Asia and Pacific area (%)

	1980	*1985*	*1990*	*1995*	*2000*	*2005*
China	9.36	14.80	13.78	18.68	25.17	42.11
Japan	66.83	65.40	62.45	51.78	45.57	32.87

Source: Author's calculation, based on World Bank (2007b).

The "push" from outside: the vertical specialization network in globalization

Disintegration of production and integration of trade

Helleiner (1973) notes that the rise in manufacturing exports from developing countries is closely related to the vertical specialization of international manufacturing. Finger (1975) studied the offshore assembly operation in the United States in the 1960s. The Dixit and Grossman (1982) model analyzed the spread of multistage working procedures among different countries and its influence on international division. Jones and Krueger (1990) called this fragmented production and pointed out its two driving forces, the comparative advantage and the increase in returns to scale. Arndt (1997) thought that this international division included global sourcing, offshore sourcing, subcontracting and intraproduct specialization etc. Feenstra (1998) called this the "*disintegration of production* in the global economy."

From the 1990s, research in the field of international economics began to pay attention to the phenomenon that saw more and more different countries participating in different sections of supply or the production of specific products. Scholars gave various names to this multinational chain or network. For example, Krugman (1996) called it slicing the value chain; Leamer (1996) concluded that it was delocalization; Antweiler and Trefler (2002) introduced the concept of intramediate trade, Hummels et al. (2001) called it vertical specialization; and Feentra (1998) used the phrase "*integration of trade*" in the global economy."

In addition, there was also much research into the disintegration of production from the perspective of the value chain (Porter, 1985), firm networks (Jarillo, 1988), industrial clusters (Schmitz, 1995), and modular production networks (Sturgeon, 2002). The key concept of this new production mode was the network. Network production is based on vertical specialization, or disintegration of continuous-flow parts, which was horizontal specialization of craft production. This new mode brought great opportunities when developed countries transferred part of their networks to developing countries, because of pressures of cost or the attraction of the market. China, which has a nearly infinite labor force and huge potential market, seemed to be the best choice when it decided to open up to the world.

Specialization of R&D and sales

China's production within vertical specialization is in fact a kind of across-the-board original equipment manufacturing (OEM). With the demand for R&D booming and the upgrading of enterprises in host countries, some OEM has come to incorporate more design of the products being manufactured and become original design manufacturing (ODM), which involves another kind of "outsourcing." This brings developing countries opportunities, not only

18 *Background and theoretical framework*

in the production process, but also in the total operation of the generalized value chain.

The ODMs later expand into the sales and service part of the value chain and created a new form of outsourcing, electronic manufacturing services (EMSs).[6] EMSs provided design, logistics, processing and assembly, distribution, and even customer service. EMSs appeared in the late 1990s and became a popular form in the world's information and communications industries. An EMS has much higher value added than an ODM, which is only one of its parts, and EMSs have just begun to transfer to some of the most competitive developing countries.

From OBM to what?

After the OEM and ODM stages, enterprises in developing countries began to build up their own brands. Although their brands are only familiar to the stockist, this new mode, called original brand manufacturing (OBM), still expanded rapidly through the leading firms. OBM brought them much greater profit than the traditional modes and also brought them the opportunity to build up their own brands that could be familiar to customers, which are the truly valuable "brands." Most of China's enterprises are still in the early stages, and so, in the context of "brands," China still has a long way to go.

China's generality and specialty: a further discussion

Gross and average output

When talking about China's place in the world economy today, people are used to beginning with its GDP, which makes it the third (after the United States and Japan) or even the second-largest (under the PPP method) economy in the world. However, even under the PPP estimation, the GDP per capita of China was still only two-thirds of the world average in 2006. Throughout history, the "world workshops" all started from a much higher level of GDP per capita and rose from being above the world average to the leading position. The rise of China in global manufacturing is the first time a "world workshop" has appeared with poor "workers."[7]

This basic condition means that the way China has become a "world workshop" is completely different from the original mode of the "modern economic growth" of today's leading industrialized countries. For them, the income level of labor naturally reached a high level as they became a "world workshop." For China, however, even if its share of GDP or industrial output reaches a very high proportion in the world, the per capita level is still quite low. China may create a brand-new mode for developing countries to emerge in the world economy, where a lower–middle-income country can have great influence because of its total economic scale.

The power of scale mainly comes from the large physical number of products with low average value added, just as the GDP per capita. In total, they form the massive output of the second-largest manufacturing producer of the world today. Together with the large range of products dominated by China, the volume of products creates a very broad but thin basis of this world workshop.

Whether this basis can support a so-called "world workshop" may be one of the most important debates, and a further analysis of the scale and scope of "made in China," from both the output and input side, is particularly needed.

Amount and structure of exports

China's position in the world market has rapidly risen because of its booming exports in recent decades. As the second-largest exporter, with a share of nearly 9 percent of the world market, China reached the proportion that the United Kingdom and the United States had in 1920, just before the Great Depression. However, the main argument of whether China's large share of the world market can make it a "world workshop" is similar to the argument whether its manufacturing output can do so. The question is whether China can be competitive in the world market.

The problem also concerns the value added. More than half of China's exports are in the processing trade, and so the value added of these exports is quite low compared with the original export products. When the United Kingdom and the United States became "world workshops" in their time, most of their exports were inter-industry exports, which means most of the value added of the export products was retained within their borders. China's exports, however, are so-called intra-industry exports, and so China is only a processing center for the international manufacturing division.

Supporters believe that this kind of processing center is just the "world workshop" within today's disintegration of production, based on the mass cross-border inflow of intermediate products, which transfers the main value added out of the traditional value chain of global production. Opponents think the definition of "world workshop" should concentrate on the main part of the value added, which they believe is the source of real competitiveness.

A comprehensive analysis of the pattern of China's export products is therefore very necessary to establish whether China has its own competitiveness in the world market.

Source of competitiveness: foreign or domestic

Some researchers believe there was an earlier wave of globalization when the United States became the "world workshop" dating from the First World War, because of the high ratio of trade in GDP, but globalization today is more about factor flow than products. A large amount of capital came into China with the search for a low-cost labor force and formed half of China's total manufacturing exports. Even considering the domestic factors involved, this ratio is still higher than 20 percent.

A further problem with China's competitiveness therefore stems from the role of FIEs. On the one hand, the Organization for Economic Development and Cooperation (OECD) (2005a) reported that China became the biggest exporter of information technology goods in 2004, surpassing the United States and the European Union (EU). On the other hand, about 80 percent of China's high-tech exports (ICT included) comes from the FIEs. A "world workshop" had never before met this kind of problem, which could only appear in the light of today's deep globalization.

Critics think that FDI gained huge profits but brought little in the way of a technology upgrade to China's industries (Huang, 2003). No one can deny, however, that China has shown rapid progress through "learning by doing." The key problem is that the MNCs in China hold a large amount of "soft power," from standard to brand, that only belongs to those "made in China" but not "made by China."

The source of China's competitiveness as a "world workshop" in fact needs a deep analysis of the role of FDI in China's economy. Through that, we can then understand the specialty of China much more clearly.

Notes

1. FIEs refer to all industrial enterprises registered as joint ventures, cooperatives, sole (exclusive) investment industrial enterprises, and limited liability corporations, with foreign funds.
2. Revenue higher than 5 million RMB yuan.
3. Based on the definitions from Wikipedia.
4. They were thought to be the result of the Victorian boom and were clearly shown at the Great Exhibition (Hudson, 2001).
5. Management is indirectly related to the addition of value and so is not include in the generalized value chain.
6. This is sometimes called electronic contract manufacturing (ECM).
7. Chinese workers were selected as "People of the year" by *Time* magazine at the end of 2009.

2 Scale and scope of the "world workshop"

China's place in world production

Output side: statistical and physical

The output of total industry, especially manufacturing, is certainly the most direct measurement of a "world workshop." Chambers (1965) used the "monopoly in world manufacture" as the first condition. The main methods of measurement can be divided into two main kinds, the value-based method and the physical-output method.

The value-based method is most commonly used in almost all statistical research, but the problem is that we face several ways of estimating a country's manufacturing output. Different methods of measurement may have different results, and so a comparison of these methods is necessary when our conclusion relies heavily on them.

Manufacturing output

Gross industrial output

GIO is "a general measurement of the total output value of the industry/manufacture/sector (or even plant) during a certain period of time, which is usually one year" (NBS, various years). Since 2000, China's gross manufacturing output has experienced quite high growth, which exceeded Germany's in 2003 and caught up with Japan's in 2005, reaching more than US$2.6 trillion. The GIO of Japan has fluctuated over the past 15 years, but the United States' rose from US$2.82 trillion in 1991 to more than US$4.6 trillion in 2005, although there was a small decline following the "dot.com" bubble. The United States' manufacturing output was still 1.8 times larger than China's overall in 2005, and it still dominates world manufacturing.

Industrial value added

Industrial value added (IVA) refers to the "final results of industrial production of industrial enterprises in money terms during the reference period" (NBS, various years). China's average growth rate of manufacturing value added is 9.3 percent from 1995 to 2000, 6.1 percent higher than that of industrialized countries and 4.0 percent higher than that of developing countries. Between

22 Scale and scope of the "world workshop"

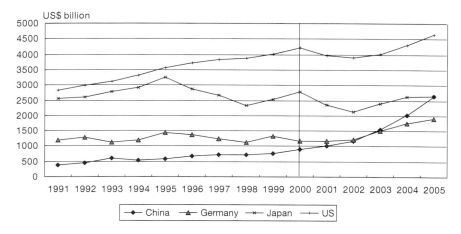

Figure 2.1 Gross manufacturing output (current US$) (Data for 2005 were estimated by the author)

Source: Author's calculation, based on UNIDO (2008) and US Census Bureau (various years).

2000 and 2006, China's growth rate speeded up to 11.2 percent, 9.4 percent higher than industrialized countries and 4.2 percent higher than developing countries. In 2000 and 2004, China overtook the United Kingdom and Germany to become, respectively, the fourth and the third-largest manufacturer in the world. China's manufacture value added in 2005 was still one-third of that of the United States, which was nearly US$700 billion.

According to the constant price data of the United Nations Industrial Development Organization (UNIDO), China's share in the industrial value

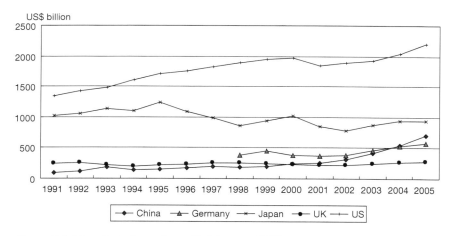

Figure 2.2 Manufacturing value added (current US$)

Source: Author's calculation, based on UNIDO (2008) and US Department of Commerce (2006).

Scale and scope of the "world workshop" 23

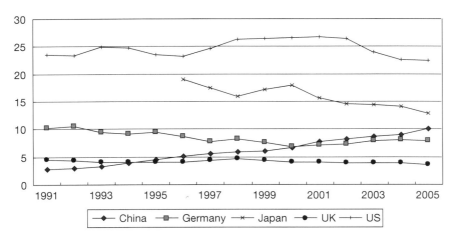

Figure 2.3 Share of manufacturing value added in the world (exchange rate method, %)
Source: Author's calculation, based on World Bank (2008).

added of the world increased from 5.1 percent in 1995 to 11.4 percent in 2007 (Cui, 2008). The statistics from UNIDO (2010) show that China was in second place in 2009 and shared 15.6 percent of the world's value added, following the United States with 19 percent.

Current price data from the World Bank show that, in 1995 and 2001, China shared 5.1 and 7.7 percent, respectively, of the world's total value added and became the fourth and the third-largest manufacturer. Furthermore, until 2005, there was still a 2.7 percent gap between China and Japan in terms of proportion of the world's total value added. These data show that the United States shares 22.3 percent under current US dollar estimates, which is a decline from its peak in 2001 of 26.7 percent.

Interestingly, the ratio of value added to gross output appears quite stable in some of the main economies, such as the United States, Japan and China. The United States has the highest share, which kept steady at between 46 and 49 percent over the last 15 years, Japan stayed at between 36 and 40 percent, and China remained at 25–27 percent. As the value added is a measure of gross output, similar to the gross profit from sales, the value added ratios of these three economies reflect a basic feature of their manufacturing outputs, each of which has a quite different capacity to generate "value added," while having the same output. This is why there's a wider gap between China and the other main economies in terms of its manufacturing value added than in terms of gross output.

Purchasing power parity

PPP is a widely used method to adjust exchange rates between economies. According to the "one price law," the exchange rate of a country will converge to its aggregate price level in the long run. Although debates about its effectiveness have been continuous over recent decades (Rogoff, 1996; Lothian and Taylor, 2000; Taylor and Taylor, 2004), the PPP method provides us with a platform to compare the relative scales of economies using a much more stable converter.

The original version of China's price level was based on a census of a basket of commodities, in 1986, by the World Bank and China's National Statistics Bureau. The PPP converter was estimated to be 1.8 in 1986 and did not change much over the following 20 years. This converter is widely used by international organizations such as the World Bank and the IMF and academic databases such as the Pennsylvania World Table. However, China's price level changed a lot with such a high growth rate after 20 years, and this converter has already overestimated China's economic scale. For example, under the original version of the PPP converter, China has the same energy efficiency (energy consumption per unit GDP) as Nordic countries. The new International Comparison Program of the World Bank set up a series of new converters based on a basket of commodities in 2005, and China's converter was changed to 3.45 in 2005 (World Bank, 2007a). This means the economic scale of China is 40 percent smaller than the original estimation.

We can compare the two versions of PPP estimation. Under the original version, China's GDP had reached 14.4 percent of the world's total in 2005, and its share of industrial value added even reached 24.5 percent, which was 7.9 percent higher than the United States. The new version of the converter adjusted China's share of GDP to 10.1 percent, and its share of industrial value added to 17.3 percent in 2006. Although some researchers think the new version is an underestimate, because the adjusted prices are weighted averages of data from eleven cities, and rural China always has lower price levels

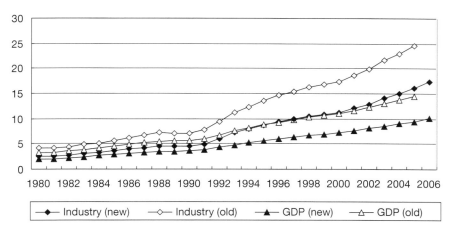

Figure 2.4 Share of industrial value added and GDP in the world (PPP method, %)
Source: Author's calculation, based on World Bank (2008).

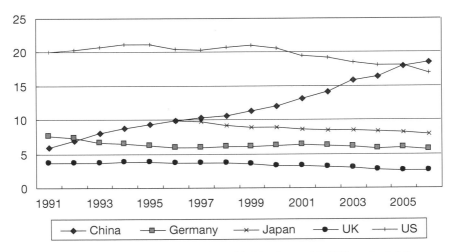

Figure 2.5 Share of manufacturing value added in the world (PPP method, %)
Source: Author's calculation, based on World Bank (2008).

(Brandt and Holz, 2004; Chen and Ravallion 2008), Deaton and Heston (2008) believe the proportion is less than 10 percent for GDP. I think it is even smaller for the industrial sector, which is mainly located in urban areas.

With this new estimate, China's manufacturing value added has already surpassed the United States' from 2006 and Japan's of 10 years ago. China's proportion reached 18.5 percent in that year, which is 1.6 percent higher than that of the United States. This may be an overestimate of China's figure when the PPP/exchange rate converter is directly used, because the PPP method includes, not only commodity prices, but also the price of services, and the difference in the prices of industrial products between China and developed countries is much smaller than that of the service sector. Nevertheless, it at least shows us the upper bound of the relative scale of China's manufacturing.

Industrial structure and high-tech industries

Of the four indicators used to measure "industrial competitiveness," UNIDO (2004) uses the proportion of medium- and high-tech industries to reflect the technical structure of a country's manufacturing. According to their definition, medium and high technology includes printing and publishing (division 342 in International Standard Industrial Classification (ISIC) Revision 2), industrial chemicals (351), other chemicals (352), plastic products (356), and the groups of basic metal industries (37) and all machinery and equipment (38, excluding 381).

According to this classification, China's share was quite low in the early 1980s, even 10 percent lower than India's. From 1985 to 1998, China kept a

26 *Scale and scope of the "world workshop"*

Table 2.1 Medium- and high-technology manufacturing ISIC

ISIC	Division or groups
Revision 2	342, 351, 352, 356, 37, 38 (excl. 381)
Revision 3	22, 24, 252, 27, 29, 30, 31, 32, 33, 34, 35

Source: UNIDO (2004).

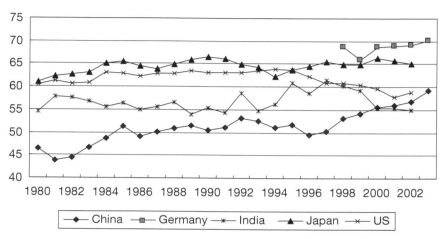

Figure 2.6 Share of high- and medium-technology products
Source: Author's calculation, based on UNIDO (2008).

quite stable level of about 50 percent, which is 10–15 percent lower than the United States and Japan. From 2000, China overtook India and caught up with the United States within the next three years, but was still 5 percent lower than Japan and 10 percent lower than the highest country, Germany. This method can be used for international comparison, but cannot reflect the whole manufacturing structure of a country.

The classification of manufacturing industries according to technology intensity is defined by OECD (2003) and comprises four groups: high-tech industries, medium–high-tech industries, medium–low-tech industries and low-tech industries. This division was established after long-term (1973–1992) observation of the R&D intensity of OECD countries and was based on three indicators, two direct intensity indicators (share of R&D expenditure in value added and gross output) and one overall intensity indicator (includes indirect R&D).

We use this classification to divide China's manufacturing value added from 1995 to 2005. The proportions are not very volatile. First, the share of low-tech industries seems to be replaced by high-tech industries and fell from 33 percent in the mid 1990s to 27 percent in 2005. The share of medium-high and medium–low-tech industries kept the same levels, of about 38 percent and 25 percent, respectively, although they fluctuated, but the share of high-tech industries almost doubled, from 6.2 percent in 1995 to 11.5 percent in 2005. This kind of transition is sometimes called China's "leapfrogging," as the proportion of manufacturing value added directly shifted from low-tech sectors to the high-tech sectors. However, as we find out later, the leading businesses here are FIEs.

The structure of FIEs is quite different from that of domestic enterprises. The share of high-tech sectors in the value added of FIEs increased from 17.2 percent in 1996 to 24.3 percent in 2007, and, during the same period of time, the share in domestic enterprises even dropped from 7.14 percent to 6.89 percent. This meant that the ratio expanded from more than double to about quadruple. However, the share of medium–low-tech industries in FIEs is just less than half that of domestic enterprises, and that of the low-tech sector also dropped from 6 percent higher to 3 percent lower than domestic enterprises.

Table 2.2 Manufacturing industries classified according to their global technological intensity

Industry name	ISIC Revision 3 codes
High-tech	
Pharmaceuticals	2423
Aircraft & spacecraft	353
Medical, precision, & optimal instruments	33
Radio, television, & communication equipment	32
Office, accounting, & computing machinery	30
Medium–high-tech	
Electrical machinery & apparatus	31
Motor vehicles, trailers, & semi-trailers	34
Railroad & transport equipment	352 + 359
Chemical & chemical products	24–2423
Machinery & equipment	29
Medium–low-tech	
Building and repairing of ships and boats	351
Rubber and plastics products	25
Coke, refined petroleum products, and nuclear	23
Other non-metallic mineral products	26
Basic metals and fabricated metal products	27 + 28
Low-tech	
Manufacturing n.e.c.; recycling	36 + 37
Wood, paper, printing, publishing	20 + 21 + 22
Food products, beverages, and tobacco	15 + 16
Textiles, textile products, leather, and footwear	17 + 18 + 19

Source: OECD (2003).

28 *Scale and scope of the "world workshop"*

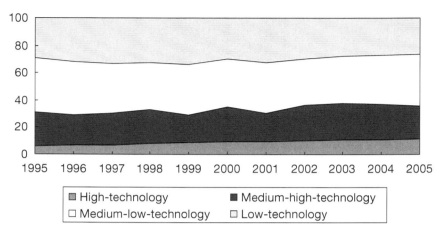

Figure 2.7 China's manufacturing value added according to OECD classification
Note: This estimation is based on the ISIC Revision 2 classification (Hatzichronoglou, 1997).
Source: Author's calculation, based on UNIDO (2008).

Because of the different structures of FIEs, their shares of the four manufacturing-sector groups are also quite varied. Although they only share one-third of China's total industrial value added (similar to their share in medium–high-tech and low-tech industries), their share in the high-tech sectors reached more than 60 percent of China's total in 2004. In contrast, their share in medium–low-tech sectors, which are mainly capital-intensive ones, was only 17.5 percent in 2007. This means high-tech manufacturing in China is overwhelmingly reliant on FIEs but not on its domestic firms.

Compared with other main manufacturers in the world, the share of high-tech industry in China's manufacturing value added had almost caught up with Germany in 2004, but was still 5 percent lower than that of Japan and the United States. Germany's lower proportion was because its advantage came from many intermediate goods, such as machinery and electronic equipment used as capital input, which are classified as belonging to the medium–high-tech sector. In contrast, Korea has such a high ratio mainly because of its concentration in ICT production and because of the "small economy effect," like Finland. This result also reflects the limitation of the OECD classification, in that only using a two- or three-digit level of division can omit the big technology differences among the subdivisions within, especially for a country such as Germany.

The NBS released the *Catalog for high-technology industrial statistics classification*, in July 2002, which placed aircraft and spacecraft (AS), electronic and telecommunications equipment (ETE), computers and office equipment (COE), pharmaceuticals (Ps), and medical equipment and meter manufacturing (MEM) in the statistics for China's high-technology industries.

Scale and scope of the "world workshop" 29

Table 2.3 Structure of industrial value added (%)

	1996	2000	2005	2007
Total enterprises	100.00	100.00	100.00	100.00
Low-tech	33.95	31.02	27.61	26.52
Medium–low-tech	24.15	22.74	25.38	26.40
Medium–high-tech	32.95	32.02	32.65	34.57
High-tech	8.95	14.22	14.36	12.51
FIEs	100.00	100.00	100.00	100.00
Low-tech	38.76	29.57	25.23	24.10
Medium–low-tech	12.89	11.80	12.76	14.33
Medium–high-tech	31.14	32.22	33.70	37.26
High-tech	17.21	26.41	28.31	24.31
Domestic enterprises	100.00	100.00	100.00	100.00
Low-tech	32.90	31.58	28.80	27.67
Medium–low-tech	26.61	27.00	31.66	32.15
Medium–high-tech	33.35	31.95	32.13	33.29
High-tech	7.14	9.47	7.42	6.89

Notes: Data are agglomerated from 2-digit codes of China's National Economic Industrial Classification (GB/T4754—1994 and 2002) and are not comparable.
Source: Author's calculation, based on NBS (various years), NBS, NDRC, and MOST (various years).

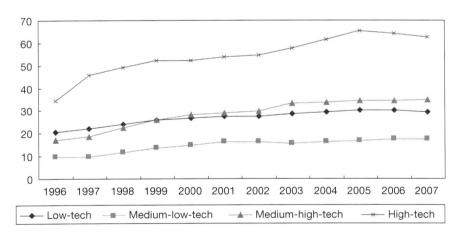

Figure 2.8 FIEs in China's industrial value added

Note: Data are agglomerated from 2-digit codes of China's National Economic Industrial Classification (GB/T4754—1994 and 2002) and are not comparable with data in Chapter 2.
Source: Author's calculation, based on NBS (various years); NBS, NDRC, and MOST (various years).

Table 2.4 Share of high-tech industry in manufacturing value added

	1999	2000	2001	2002	2003	2004	2005
China[a]	8.7	9.3	9.5	9.9	10.5	11.5	11.5
Japan	17.8	18.7	16.8	15.9	16.8		
Korea	22.6	24.4	22.2	22.9	23.5	25.3	24.6
Germany	10.4	11.2	10.5	10.8	11.4	11.8	12.4
USA	17.9	18.8	17.6	16.8	16.7	16.5	16.7
Finland	21.4	23.5	20.2	23.3	23.7	21.6	21.9

a Calculated from data from all industry enterprises.
Source: Author's calculation, based on NBS, NDRC, and MOST (various years).

The definition is comparable with OECD's classification of high-technology industries. China's data are published in the *China statistics yearbook on high technology industry*, 2007.

According to statistics from the National Science Board (2008), we can easily establish that ETE shared half of China's high-tech industrial value added revenue before the mid 1990s, and COE replaced Ps and MEM after the late 1990s and reached 39 percent in 2005, which is just 3 percent lower than ETE.

However, in the world market, China's COE industry share, which reached nearly half of the world's output in 2005, represents a much higher proportion than the ETE industry, a much broader and larger sector. The proportion is close to four times that of 2000, and China's ETE industry also tripled during

Table 2.5 China's high-tech manufacturing industries' value-added revenue

	1985	1990	1995	2000	2005
Structure of value-added revenue					
Aerospace	4.76	4.61	6.23	8.62	3.05
Ps	13.85	15.70	16.40	16.64	9.86
COE	2.67	3.86	7.35	27.30	38.98
ETE	65.64	65.18	59.85	41.25	43.01
Medical, precision, and optical instruments	13.08	10.65	10.18	6.19	5.10
Total	100.00	100.00	100.00	100.00	100.00
Share in world total					
Aerospace	0.32	0.43	1.53	4.51	6.41
Ps	1.07	1.42	2.28	4.58	8.14
COE	0.46	0.69	2.11	12.11	46.00
ETE	3.47	3.82	5.16	4.84	15.26
Medical, precision, and optical instruments	1.03	1.10	1.90	2.32	5.85

Source: Author's calculation, based on National Science Board (2008).

Table 2.6 Value added of high-tech industries from FIEs

	1995	2000	2005	2006	2007
Structure of value added					
Aerospace	1.76	0.60	0.55	0.59	0.74
Ps	14.15	10.83	7.40	7.32	8.57
COE	12.97	19.56	31.25	28.09	28.28
ETE	65.35	64.90	56.36	58.63	56.80
Medical, precision, and optical instruments	5.77	4.10	4.44	5.38	5.61
Total	100.00	100.00	100.00	100.00	100.00
Share in value added of total enterprises					
Aerospace	10.51	8.20	14.05	15.69	18.45
Ps	25.59	24.56	25.75	26.17	27.30
COE	66.98	75.11	91.20	86.02	90.64
ETE	57.59	63.40	74.72	74.06	71.25
Medical, precision, and optical instruments	27.66	33.92	43.06	44.79	42.58

Source: Author's calculation, based on NBS, NDRC, and MOST (various years).

that period of time. This is the result of outsourcing from the United States and EU and the transition from the original production basis, like the NIEs.

In 2007, FIEs shared 90.64 percent of the COE value added and 71.25 of the ECE. They also shared 42.58 percent in MEM. Although some dropped from 1995 to 2000, the shares in all five industries increased between 2000 and 2007. With the exception of aerospace and pharmaceuticals, the other three are all dominated by FIEs. This is a typical feature of China's being the "processing center" for the world's high-tech industry, with offshore outsourcing by multinational companies, especially those from the ICT sector.

Production capacity of major industrial products

According to the *Industrial statistics databases* (UNIDO, 2008), China has taken first place in seven of the twenty-two manufacturing divisions of the ISIC (Revision 3), where China contributes nearly half of the world's tobacco products, a quarter of textiles and clothing, and one-third of electrical machines and other transport equipment measured in value added. Furthermore, in seventeen of the other eighteen divisions (excluding manufacturing of motor vehicles, trailers, and semi-trailers), China was ranked above sixth place.

Based on more than 80 top products in 2002 (see Table 1.1), China had 172 top products in 2006 (Cui, 2008), of the 616 products covered by UNIDO industrial-product statistics. Here, we pick up several products dominated by China since 2005. Apart from medium-tech chemicals and basic metals, this new list still includes several products with higher levels of

Table 2.7 Manufacturing divisions where China was ranked first (ISIC Revision 3)

ISIC manufacturing division	Share
16: Manufacture of tobacco products	49.8
17: Manufacture of textiles	29.2
18: Manufacture of clothes, dressing and dyeing of fur	24.7
19: Tanning and dressing of leather; manufacture of luggage, handbags, saddlery, harness and footwear	33.4
27: Manufacture of basic metals	23.8
31: Manufacture of electrical machinery and apparatus n.e.c.	28.2
35: Manufacture of other transport equipment	34.1

Source: Singtao Net (2008).

sophistication compared with those of 2002, such as computers. Its surprisingly high share of 84 percent is, on the one hand, related to China's share of 46 percent in the world's total computer and office equipment industry, and, on the other hand, a result of the global outsourcing that results in computer production in China being dominated by FIEs.

We also followed the trends of some of China's important products. Its share of world cement production tripled from 15.4 percent in 1985 to half of the total; that of steel production doubled within 5 years from 15 percent in 2000 to 30 percent in 2005; and China's fertilizer production is one-quarter of the world's total, which is one of the most important bases of its large agriculture sector. The proportions of Chinese steel and fertilizer in the world even rose to 46.6 and 35 percent, respectively, in 2009 (Ccthere Net, 2010).

Besides that, China also had a high ranking in transport equipment, being the second-largest shipbuilder and motor vehicle manufacturer and the largest motorcycle and bicycle producer. For the three main indicators of shipbuilding, completions, new orders, and orders booked, China ranked second after South Korea in 2007. In 2009, for the last two indicators, China overtook Korea to become the largest, especially with its share of 61.6 percent of all new orders (Ccthere Net, 2010). China's share of world passenger-car production doubled from 5.57 percent in 2004 to 12.80 percent in 2007, which raised its ranking from sixth to second, just after Japan (18.8 percent). In 2002, China had become the second-largest commercial vehicle producer, but its production was still one-third of the United States' (27.6 percent in 2008). In 2009, however, China's total car production increased 48 percent to 13.79 million, about a quarter of the world's total, and it became the largest producer for the first time (China Association of Automobile Manufactures, 2010).

In 1993, China became the largest motorcycle manufacturer, surpassing Japan, and it produced 3.35 million units that year. The total broke 10 million in 1997 and 20 million in 2006. China shared 40 percent of the world's output in 2003, and its share reached nearly half the total in 2006 (Zhang, 2008). China also produced more than one-third of the world's bicycles, which was

Table 2.8 China's main manufacturing products (ISIC Review 2)

	Year	Share of world's total (%)	World ranking
31: Food & beverages			
Beer	2005	19.1	1
Wine	2005	19.1	1
33 & 34: Wood & paper products			
Paper	2005	15.3	2
35: Chemicals			
Sulfuric acid	2005	23.6	1
Urea	2002/03	26.8	1
Phosphate fertilizer	2002/03	23.3	1
Granulated sugar	2005	7.7	3
Synthetic rubber	2005	13.5	2
Chemical fibers	2005	44.7	1
36: Non-metallic mineral products (except products of petroleum and coal)			
Ammonia[a]	2005	43.0	1
Cement[a]	2005	46.6	1
37: Metal & metallic products			
Iron	2005	35.5	1
Crude steel	2005	30.9	1
Copper (refined)	2004	13.7	2
Aluminum	2004	22.1	1
Lead (refined)	2004	26.1	1
Zinc	2004	25.2	1
382 & 384: Machinery and transportation			
Metalwork lathes	2006	11.8	3
Shipbuilding contracts	2006	27.2	2
Ship completed	2006	15.0	3
Motor vehicles	2006	10.5	3
Motorcycles[b]	2006	> 50.0	1
Bicycles[b]	2006	> 33.0	1
383 & 385: Electricity and ICT			
Color TVs	2005	40.5	1
DVDs	2005	79.1	1
Digital cameras	2005	52.9	1
Mobile phones	2005	39.7	1
Computers	2005	84.0	1

a From IEA (2007).
b From Zhang (2008) and Wang (2008).
Source: Tsuneta Yano Memorial Society (2007, p. 65).

34 Scale and scope of the "world workshop"

87 million in 2007, and China also exported 56 million in that year, which represented a share of more than 60 percent of the world market (Wang, 2008).

Manufacturing of household appliances became China's strength in the late 1990s. In 2000, China's share of the world's television production was about 30 percent, that of washing machines was 25 percent, and that of refrigerator production was 18 percent. These shares were about 10–20 percent in 1990, and, in 2006, they all reached more than one-third of the world's total.

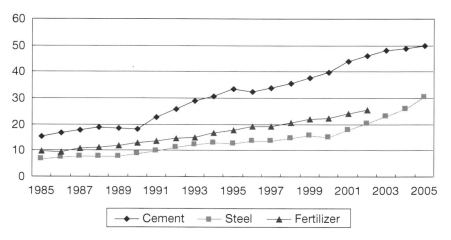

Figure 2.9 China's share in world's output of raw materials
Source: Author's calculation, based on UNSTA (2003) and NBS (2008a).

Table 2.9 China's share of transport equipment manufacture

	2000	2001	2002	2003	2004	2005	2006	2007	2008
3841 Shipbuilding and repairing									
Completions					14	17	19	23	29.5
					(3)	(3)	(3)	(2)	(2)
New orders					16	23	30	42	37.7
					(3)	(3)	(2)	(2)	(2)
Orders booked					15	18	24	33	35.5
					(3)	(3)	(3)	(2)	(2)
3843 Motor vehicle manufacturing									
Passenger cars	1.47	1.77	2.66	4.81	5.57	8.38	10.49	12.03	12.80
	(14)	(14)	(11)	(7)	(6)	(6)	(3)	(2)	(2)
Commercial vehicles	8.53	9.90	12.39	12.97	13.81	13.40	10.13	12.44	14.57
	(3)	(3)	(2)	(2)	(2)	(2)	(2)	(2)	(2)

Note: Numbers in brackets are China's world ranking.
Sources: China Association of the National Shipbuilding Industry (various years); International Organization of Motor Vehicle Manufacturers (various years).

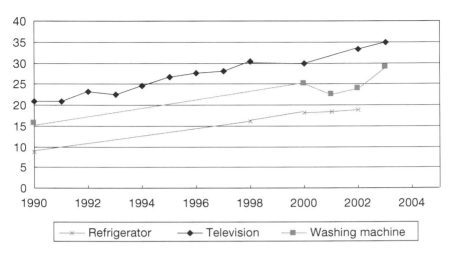

Figure 2.10 China's share in world's output of household appliances
Source: Author's calculation, based on UNSTA (2003); NBS (2008a).

Table 2.10 Share of world computer production

	2000	2001	2002	2003	2004	2005
China	19.2	24.6	44.7	68.3	80.0	83.5
Japan	7.7	5.1	4.4	3.0	2.8	2.6
Korea	5.7	5.8	6.8	4.4	2.7	3.0
Asia total	62.1	76.0	90.4	93.2	95.0	96.8

Source: Tsuneta Yano Memorial Society (2007, p. 233).

China's share of the world's production of these three products reached about 60 percent, 48 percent and 40 percent, respectively, in 2009 (Ccthere Net, 2010).

More surprisingly, China's share of computer manufacture also skyrocketed, from 19.2 percent in 2000 to 83.5 percent in 2005. This means almost all computer assembly activities have been moved to China. However, we should remember that most of this "processing" is carried out by FIEs. It is the same for China's manufacture of telephones, which had a 70 percent share in 2003, and mobile phones, whose share rose from 40 percent in 2005 to 50 percent in 2009. What we need to remember is that all the core components of computers, such as CPUs etc., are still controlled by multinational companies such as Intel.

Undesirable outputs: China's emissions

In addition to all the products supplied by China, there is also a big challenge for this "world workshop"—the emission of carbon dioxide (CO_2) and other

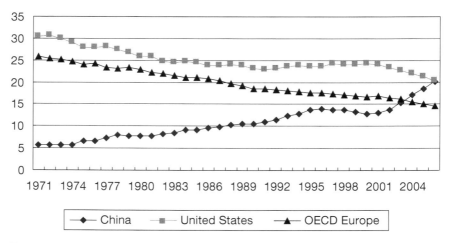

Figure 2.11 Share of world CO_2 emissions
Source: Author's calculation, based on IEA (2008).

waste products. International Energy Agency (IEA) data show that, in 2006, China had nearly caught up with the United States to become the second-largest CO_2 emitter, responsible for 5.6 billion tons in 2006. China's share of total world emissions reached 20 percent that year, only 0.3 percent lower than that of the United States. This proportion remained almost constant from 1996 to 2002, but later rose sharply and surpassed the total for OECD Europe in 2004.

However, if we only consider the manufacturing sector, China's share becomes much higher. The statistics from IEA show that China's emissions

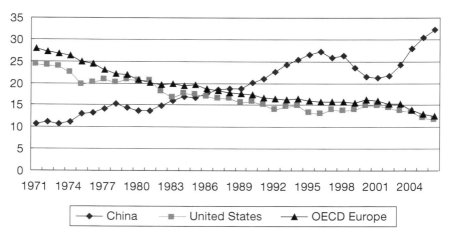

Figure 2.12 Amount and share of manufacturing CO_2 emissions
Source: Author's calculation, based on IEA (2008).

even exceeded those of the United States and OECD Europe in the late 1980s. Its first peak appeared in 1996, when it reached the level of the United States in 1971—about 27 percent of the world's emissions. China's emissions followed a "U" curve over the following 8 years and then reached 32.3 percent in 2006. Even under PPP measurement, China's manufacturing value added represented 18.5 percent in 2006, not to mention its figure of just 10 percent under the exchange method. This shows that China is still a very emission-intensive "world workshop."[1]

The issue concerns total emissions on a long-term basis, from the start of industrialization. The estimate from the United Nations Development Program (UNDP, 2008) shows that the United States has dominated accumulated CO_2 emissions since 1840, responsible for nearly 30 percent of the total. China's share is about 8 percent of the total, following Russia as the third largest. However, considering that China is merely a latecomer that only speeded up its industrialization over the past 30 years, this proportion is still quite an impressive one.

The more interesting analysis comes from Weber et al. (2008). They use environmental input–output analysis to separate the sources of China's CO_2 emissions into four parts: capital investment, household consumption, government expenditure, and export. Their research shows that,

> In 2005, around one-third of Chinese emissions (1700 million tons CO_2) were due to production of exports, and this proportion has risen from 12 percent (230 million tons) in 1987 and only 21 percent (760 million tons) as recently as 2002.

Within the export sectors, electronics contribute 22 percent of the total CO_2 emmisions, followed by metal products, which have a 13 percent share. China is therefore treated as the "pollution heaven" of the multinational companies, as well as their processing center.

Input Side: Capital, Labor, etc.

Capital: artificial capital and natural capital

Capital formation of China's manufacturing industry

The expenditure approach of national accounting divides GDP into three parts: final consumption expenditure, gross capital formation, and net export of goods and service. Gross capital formation (formerly gross domestic investment) consists of outlay on additions to the fixed assets of the economy plus net changes in the level of inventories. This part is the capital flow as the newly added part of the total production capital of an economy.

We can establish that China's share fluctuated between 1980 and 2000 and then almost doubled, from 5.9 percent to 11.1 percent in 2006, and, for the first time, surpassed Japan. The United States and European countries still

38 *Scale and scope of the "world workshop"*

Table 2.11 Share of world gross capital formation (exchange rate method)

	1980	1985	1990	1995	2000	2006
China	2.48	4.19	2.51	4.53	5.90	11.07
Euro area	26.60	17.90	25.76	22.43	19.27	21.48
India	1.27	1.92	1.49	1.41	1.60	2.90
Japan	12.87	13.77	19.47	22.14	16.64	9.42
Russia			3.03	1.49	0.68	1.87
United States	20.85	30.24	19.79	19.78	28.04	23.46

Source: Author's calculation, based on World Bank (2008).

dominated the capital formation of the world, their share being close to half the world's total, although the United States is 10 percent below its peak.

Like output measurement, the exchange rate method also underestimates the capital formation of lower-income countries such as China. We then use the ratio of gross capital formation in GDP and the GDP in international dollars to re-estimate the proportions. Under the PPP method, China exceeded Japan's share in 1998, the Euro zone's in 2003, and the United States' in 2006, and it reached 20.4 percent of the world's total at that year.

However, with regard to manufacturing, we think the role of fixed capital is more important. According to the World Bank's definition (2007b), gross fixed capital formation (GFCF; formerly gross domestic fixed investment) includes: land improvements; plant, machinery, and equipment purchases; and the construction of roads, railways, and the like, including schools, offices, hospitals, private residential dwellings, and commercial and industrial buildings.

In the 2004 census of the Chinese economy, there appear the structure data of GFCF by industries. Under this estimation, China overtook the United States

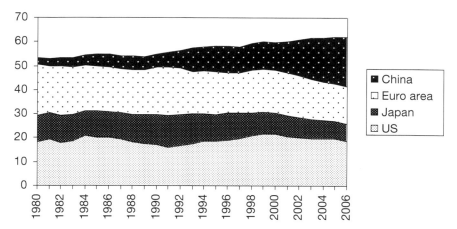

Figure 2.13 Share of world's gross capital formation (PPP method)
Source: Author's calculation, based on World Bank (2008).

in the GFCF of manufacturing in 2003, and it was 1.9 times that of the United States in 2006. This is not so surprising when we consider the big difference between the proportions of manufacturing in total GFCF. In China, the manufacturing share was 31 percent in 2006, four times that of the United States in the same year. This is certainly one of the most important bases for China to be considered a "world workshop."

FDI is another capital inflow to China's manufacturing. The role of FIEs in China's manufacturing has already reflected the importance of FDI. There is still a big gap between the total amount of FDI inflow to China and that to the United States, even in the last recession, when the FDI inflow to the United States dropped two-thirds between 2001 and 2002. However, there is a big difference between their structures, where manufacturing represents two-thirds of China's FDI but only one-third of the United States'. The result is that the FDI inflow to China's manufacturing rose steadily from 30.9 billion in 2001 to 40.9 billion in 2007, and it overtook that of the United States during 2002–2005.

Table 2.12 GFCF for manufacturing

	2000	2001	2002	2003	2004	2005	2006
Total amount (current US$ million)							
China				178,739	232,236	294,631	365,742
US	206,586	194,714	171,875	159,612	167,317	173,405	193,191
Proportion in GFCF (%)							
China				26.44	27.79	29.94	30.99
US	10.63	10.09	9.19	8.16	7.79	7.29	7.64

Note: China's share of manufacturing in total GFCF is assumed to be equal to its share of total investment in fixed assets before 2004.
Source: Author's calculation, based on NBS (various years); OECD (2005b); US Census Bureau (various years).

Table 2.13 Manufacturing share of FDI inflow

	2000	2001	2002	2003	2004	2005	2006	2007
China (US$ billion)								
Total FDI	40.7	46.9	52.7	53.5	60.6	60.3	63.0	74.8
Manufacturing	25.8	30.9	36.8	36.9	43.0	42.5	40.1	40.9
Ratio (%)	63.48	65.93	69.77	69.03	70.95	70.37	63.59	54.66
United States (US$ billion)								
Total FDI	335.6	147.1	54.5	63.6	86.2	91.4	165.6	276.8
Manufacturing	143.3	37.6	16.4	10.8	18.3	34.0	56.3	135.2
Ratio (%)	42.69	25.55	30.17	16.90	21.17	37.24	34.02	48.84

Source: Author's calculation, based on UNCTAD (various years).

Capital stock of china's industry

Capital stock is actually the overall capital input into the production of an economy during the observation period. The method generally used to estimate capital stock is the perpetual inventory method (PIM), in which the GFCF is treated as the newly added-in part. We use K06 here, which means the depreciation in PIM is 6 percent for all countries in the World Productivity Database from UNIDO.[2]

In 2000, China shared about 13.2 percent of the total capital stock of all 101 sample countries, which is about one-third of the United States' value, 36.1 percent. The EU-11 countries (EU-15, minus Austria, Belgium, Germany, and the Netherlands, because of absence of data) had a 26.7 percent share in 2000. This database is still waiting for the Penn World Table 7.0 to update itself, but there is no doubt that China's proportion will rise very quickly over the period from 2000 until now.

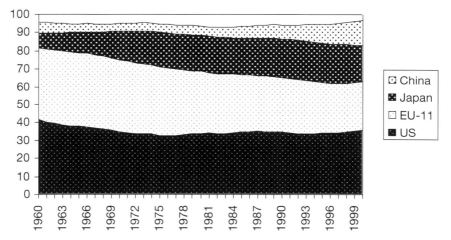

Figure 2.14 Share of capital stock in 101 sample countries
Source: Author's calculation, based on Isaksson (2007).

Table 2.14 Market capitalization of listed companies

	1991	1995	2000	2005	2007
China	0.02	0.24	1.81	1.80	9.64
India	0.42	0.72	0.46	1.28	2.82
Japan	27.58	20.62	9.81	10.93	6.90
Russia	0.00	0.09	0.12	1.27	2.33
United States	36.04	38.55	46.92	39.18	30.90
OECD Europe	23.28	24.04	28.96	25.86	26.25

Source: Author's calculation, based on World Bank (2008).

Another important measure of the business capital input of a country is its market capitalization. That of China did not have a significant share in the world before 2000, and it rose five times, from 1.80 percent to 9.64 percent of the world's total. In 2007, China overtook Japan for the first time to become the third-largest stock market, after the United States and OECD Europe. This boom provides more capital for China's manufacturing to expand its capital input.

In manufacturing, more widely used indicators are the total assets in a corporation account. The total assets of China's manufacturing firms, in current prices, almost quadrupled over the past 10 years, rising from one-quarter of those of the United States to half those of the United States. China's manufacturing firms' net assets also followed a similar trend. These figures show that China's manufacturing has at least accumulated sufficient assets for it to be considered a real "world workshop" over the past decade. Furthermore, because the inflow of assets, the GFCF, of China's manufacturing is twice as much as that of the United States, it can be predicted that the assets will catch up in the near future.

As for the FDI inflow, its stock also plays quite an important role in China's manufacturing capital stock. The total stock of China's FDI rose from 30 percent in 2000 to nearly 40 percent of that of the United States in 2007. Furthermore, the proportion of the manufacturing sector in China's total FDI stock rose from 53.4 percent in 2001 to 66.6 percent in 2007, but that of the United States dropped from 39.5 percent to 33.9 percent during that same period of time. The result of this structural change is that China's manufacturing FDI stock almost doubled from US$348.3 billion to US$805.7 billion, which was 40 percent of that of the United States in 2000, rising to 75.7 percent in 2007.

Table 2.15 Manufacturing corporation assets

	1995	1997	1999	2001	2003	2005	2007
Total assets (current US$ billion)							
China		979	1,069	1,221	1,546	2,234	3,490
United States		3,747	4,383	4,748	5,163	5,829	6,805
Net assets (current US$ billion)							
China	229	335	388	430	504	696	1,028
United States	1,457	1,584	1,714	1,800	1,809	1,957	2,110

Note: Net assets for China refer to the net value of fixed capital assets; for the US, they refer to net stock of private fixed assets.
Source: Author's calculation, based on NBS (various years) and US Census Bureau (various years).

42 *Scale and scope of the "world workshop"*

Table 2.16 Manufacturing in FDI stock

	2000	2001	2002	2003	2004	2005	2006	2007
China (US$ billion)								
Total stock	348.3	401.1	454.6	515.2	575.6	638.6	713.3	805.7
Manufacturing[a]		214.9	248.3	289.4	352.3	403.1	468.1	536.8
Ratio (%)		53.59	54.62	56.18	61.21	63.13	65.62	66.62
US (US$ billion)								
Total stock	1,256.9	1,344.0	1,340.0	1,378.0	1,520.3	1,634.1	1,843.9	2,093.0
Manufacturing	496.6		470.9	475.5	519.4	538.1	593.8	709.5
Ratio (%)	39.51		35.14	34.50	34.16	32.93	32.20	33.90

a Here we use foreign investor registered capital in manufacturing.
Source: Author's calculation, based on NBS (various years); UNCTAD (various years); US Census Bureau (various years).

Natural-resource input: energy and raw materials

Energy is so important for manufacturing that we would like to discuss it first of all the natural resources. According to BP's statistics, in 2007, China exceeded the Europe Union in primary energy consumption for the first time. This proportion had doubled from 1990 and might have been even faster without the slowdown caused by the Asian financial crisis. Although still 4.5 percent lower than United States, China has shared nearly half of the world's energy-consumption growth from 2001.

Talking about the manufacturing energy consumption, China has much higher share because of its high ratio of manufacture in total final energy consumption. The data from IEA is just the direct part of manufacturing in the final energy consumption where power generation sector (mainly electricity plants) is not included. Under this estimation, China's share even reached the level of OECD Europe in 1993, and then fluctuated during the following 10 years and 18.1 percent in 2003. After that China's share rose 6 percent within 4 years, which is close to 25 percent in 2006 (526 million tons of oil equivalents).

Table 2.17 Share of primary energy consumption

	1980	1985	1990	1995	2000	2005	2007
China	6.27	7.43	8.44	10.70	10.41	14.78	16.79
		(22.30)	(11.87)	(29.98)	(13.55)	(49.05)	(52.12)
US	27.33	24.58	24.18	24.71	24.85	22.19	21.27
		(−3.31)	(5.69)	(21.52)	(21.62)	(0.31)	(15.24)
Europe Union	23.55	22.29	20.27	19.11	18.40	16.86	15.72
		(36.72)	(−30.08)	(16.77)	(8.07)	(0.74)	(−15.14)

Note: The numbers in brackets are the share of the growth of the world's energy consumption.
Source: Author's calculation, based on BP (2008).

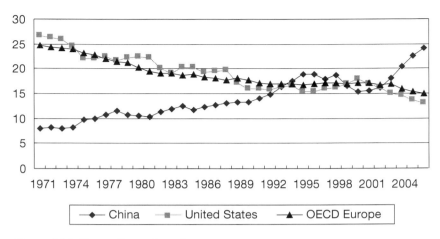

Figure 2.15 Share of manufacturing energy use
Source: Author's calculation, based on IEA (2008).

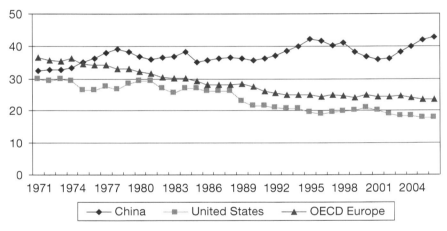

Figure 2.16 Share of manufacturing in final energy consumption
Source: Author's calculation, based on IEA (2008).

The most important reason for China's high manufacturing energy use is its high proportion of final energy consumption. Over the past 30 years, the shares of Japan, OECD Europe and the United States all dropped by about 13–16 percent, but China's share rose from 32 percent in 1971 to 43 percent in 2006.

Other natural resources important for manufacturing are mineral ores. In 2005, China was the top ore producer of aluminum, lead, zinc, tin, and tungsten. Most of these ores are used by China's own manufacturing industry.

Table 2.18 China's metal ore production

	Year	In world's total (%)	World ranking
Mine			
Iron ore	2005	16.6	3
Gold ore	2005	9.1	4
Silver ore	2005	12.4	3
Lead ore	2005	32.7	1
Zinc ore	2005	22.2	1
Tin ore	2005	41.3	1
Tungsten ore	2005	87.0	1
Molybdenum ore	2005	19.0	3
Vanadium ore	2005	29.2	2
Manganese ore	2005	10.5	4

Source: Tsuneta Yano Memorial Society (2007, p. 65).

Table 2.19 China's industrial raw materials futures contracts, 2009

	Trading turnover (million lots)	Trading volume (million tons)	Rank in world's exchanges
Copper	162.43	812.15	1
Aluminum	41.06	205.30	2
Zinc	64.51	322.55	1
Natural rubber	178.07	890.35	1
Fuel oil	91.51	915.05	5
Steel (reinforced bar)	323.14	3231.49	1

Source: CSRC (2010), Acworth and Burghardt (2010).

In addition, with regard to the basic metals, China consumed 32 percent of the world's steel, 30 percent of zinc, 25 percent of aluminum, 23 percent of copper, and 18 percent of nickel, in 2006 (Wolf, 2007).

With the boom in natural-resource consumption, the futures market for China's industrial raw materials also developed quite fast. Up until 2009, the trading volume of copper and zinc contracts on the Shanghai Futures Exchange (SHFE) has overtaken the London Metal Exchange to become the largest, and the SHFE steel contract, which began trading in 2009, has become, not only the largest of all exchanges, but also the largest contract of all traded metal around the world.

Labor force and human resources

Another important factor of production is certainly the labor. As the country with the largest population around the world, China also has a more abundant labor force than any other country. As its basis, China's labor force has accounted for more than a quarter of the world's labor force over the past 25 years, and its peak of 27.3 percent appeared in 1990. However, the gap between OECD countries and China has continuously increased, from 7.2 percent in 1980 to 10.1 percent in 2005, and the total for Brazil, Russia, India, and China (BRIC) reached 45 percent of the world's total in 2005. The main difference between them is that China has the highest participation ratio (labor force to working-age population) among the main economies, rising from 51 percent to 59 percent, but India has the lowest, which was still lower than 40 percent in 2005.

The more important indicator for a "world workshop" is the industrial labor force. China overtook the OECD countries in 1986 and reached about 30 percent of the world's total, and it has remained at that level, although the figure has fluctuated by around 4 percent. During the same period of time, the share of OCED countries dropped from 31.7 percent in 1980 to 17.9 percent in 2005, and, although India has two-thirds of the working-age population of China, its share of the industrial sector is much smaller than China's, at only a quarter of China's, and it only shared 8.2 percent of the world's total in 2000.

The decline of the OECD countries is because of their structure change: the share of the manufacturing sector in total employment dropped from 21.3 percent in 1980 to 14.2 percent in 2005. In contrast, China experienced structure change in a quite different way. A large number of manufacturing employees were laid off during the reform of state-owned enterprises (SOEs) in China from 1998, and the total amount dropped to 80 million in 2000. After China entered the WTO, strong demand for China's products made manufacturing employment increase quite fast, to 95 million in 2005, but this was mainly in private manufacturing enterprises.

Table 2.20 Share of total labor force

	1980	1985	1990	1995	2000	2005
Labor force						
Brazil	2.4	2.5	2.6	2.9	3.0	3.0
China	26.3	27.0	27.3	27.1	26.4	25.5
India	13.6	13.6	13.6	13.8	14.0	14.2
Russia	4.0	3.6	3.2	2.8	2.6	2.4
OECD24	19.1	18.0	17.2	16.6	16.1	15.4
Participation ratio						
Brazil	38.14	39.83	41.80	46.62	47.99	48.99
China	51.28	54.99	57.31	58.10	58.47	59.34
India	37.82	38.09	38.32	38.39	38.55	39.34
Russia	54.69	53.74	52.15	48.32	48.80	51.28
OECD24	46.15	47.24	48.91	49.15	50.02	50.40

Source: Author's calculation, based on World Bank (2007b).

46 *Scale and scope of the "world workshop"*

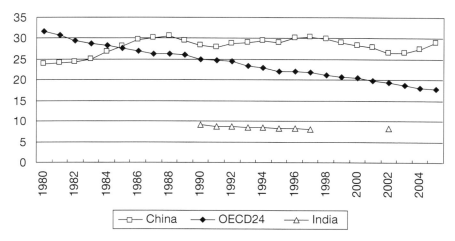

Figure 2.17 Industrial labor force as share of the world's
Note: OECD24 does not include the new members of OECD (those joining after 1994).
Source: Author's calculation, based on World Bank (2007b).

Table 2.21 Manufacturing employment of China and OECD

	1980	1985	1990	1995	2000	2005
Manufacturing employment (million people)						
China	59.0	74.1	86.2	98.0	80.4	95.2[a]
OECD24	77.6	73.2	76.0	71.9	70.5	66.3
Share in total employment (%)						
China	13.9	14.9	13.5	14.4	11.2	13.3
OECD24	21.3	19.0	18.5	16.8	15.7	14.2

a Not available and is estimated based on the growth rate of whole industrial labor force.
Source: Author's calculation, based on ILO (2008).

Human resources are recognized by the new growth theory as being another important factor, and a raw method to estimate the overall human resources of a country uses the product of average years of education and the population (above 15 years old). China's average years of education exceeded the world's average in 2000, which meant that China had a quarter of the world's human resources, which is double India's share. This huge base provides China with large numbers of skilled laborers and professionals.

Compared with the large numbers of the total labor force, China's skilled labor force is much smaller, forming less than 20 percent of the total. In contrast, skilled labor represents nearly 90 percent of the United States' labor force. China's low-skilled labor force—laborers with only secondary education—is still three times that of the United States, although it dropped from 103 million in 2003 to 93 million in 2006. China's highly skilled labor force—workers with tertiary education—is only about two-thirds the size of that of the United States, because its share of the total labor force is only one-tenth that of the United States.

Concerning the supply of low-skilled labor, the number of high-school graduates in China who did not go on to college was 2.5 times that of the

Table 2.22 Share of world's human resources

	1980	1985	1990	1995	2000	2005
Average years of education (years)						
Brazil	3.11	3.48	4.02	4.45	4.88	5.35
China	4.61	4.94	5.51	6.08	7.11	7.78
India	3.27	3.64	4.10	4.52	5.06	5.52
Russia	9.23	9.77	10.5	9.77	10.00	10.23
United States	11.90	11.60	11.70	11.90	12.11	12.32
World	5.92	6.17	6.43	6.44	6.66	6.87
Share of world's human resources (%)						
Brazil	1.38	1.51	1.70	1.94	2.11	2.25
China	17.60	18.70	20.20	21.90	24.00	25.24
India	8.40	9.06	9.98	11.10	12.30	13.27
Russia	5.69	5.30	5.05	4.26	4.06	3.64
United States	11.60	10.20	9.30	9.01	8.60	8.56

Notes: The education years for 2005 were estimated by linear extrapolation.
China's figures are according to its official census data.
Source: Author's calculation, based on Barro and Lee (1996) and World Bank (2007b).

Table 2.23 Stock of skilled labor in China and United States (millions of people)

	2002	2003	2004	2005	2006
Low-skilled (secondary education)					
China	98.47	103.03	102.65	93.66	92.89
	(13.1)	(13.6)	(13.4)	(12.1)	(11.9)
United States	37.76	37.93	37.83	38.20	
	(30.8)	(30.5)	(30.2)	(30.1)	
High-skilled (tertiary education)					
China	45.10	51.52	55.39	52.48	51.75
	(6.0)	(6.8)	(7.2)	(6.8)	(6.6)
United States	72.14	73.84	74.83	76.15	
	(58.9)	(59.4)	(59.8)	(59.9)	

Note: Numbers in brackets are the share of total labor force (%).
Source: Author's calculation, based on ILO (2008); NBS & MLSS (various years).

United States in 1990, but more than 4 times it in 2006. Furthermore, the boom in China's high-skilled labor force is quite impressive: the total number of Bachelor and associate graduates in China was only half that of the United States in 2000, but almost doubled in 2006, which meant the number of college graduates in China quadrupled within 6 years. More important to the supply

Table 2.24 Inflow of skilled labor in China and US (1,000 people)

	1980	1990	2000	2005	2006
Low-skilled (non-college, high-school graduate)					
China		2,614.0	2,571.8	3,605.0	4,201.4
United States	1,565.6	942.4	1,011.5	840.0	915.3
High-skilled (Bachelor and associate graduate)					
Total					
China	146.6	613.6	949.77	3,068.0	3,774.7
United States	1,343.0	1,586.0	1,802.8	2,135.9	2,198.3
Science and engineering degree					
China	52.6	224.8	452.6	1,255.9	1,539.0
United States			297.9	342.9	312.6

Notes: Science and engineering degrees in the United States include architecture and related subjects, biological and biomedical sciences, computer and information sciences, engineering and engineering technologies, mathematics and statistics, physical sciences and science technologies, and transportation and material movement. For associate degrees, construction trades, mechanics and repair, and military technologies are also included.
Source: Author's calculation, based on NBS (various years); US Census Bureau (various years).

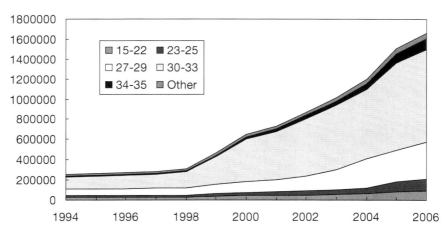

Figure 2.18 Undergraduate admissions in ISIC Review 3 classification
Source: Author's calculation, based on Table 4.5 of Simon and Cao (2009).

of skilled labor for a "world workshop" are science and engineering graduates: even in 2000, China already had 1.5 times as many as the United States, and this gap reached 5 times in 2006.

China has the world's second-largest stock of human resources for science and technology (HRST), just after the United States and ahead of Japan. Its share of university graduates with degrees in science and engineering is 39.2 percent, which is higher than all the OECD countries and almost twice the OECD average (OECD, 2008a). Among all high-skilled laborers, the undergraduate admissions for ICT industry-related subjects (electrical engineering and information) account for more than half the total and reached nearly one million in 2006. This is certainly a strong human-resource basis for China's booming role in world ICT production.

Input–output efficiency—productivity

Single-factor productivity

Capital productivity

Capital productivity, usually measured by its reciprocal capital-output ratio, is quite a stable indicator, with less difference across countries. The OECD *Productivity manual* gives a range from 2 to 4 for the ratio of total capital in service to GDP. If we treat total assets as the capital in service, this ratio for China's industry has kept quite stable, at a little higher than 3, over the past 10 years. China's net industry assets, close to its net capital stock, comprise about half its total assets, and its ratio to output held at around 1.5 during the 1980s and dropped a little to about 1.3 in the 1990s. This therefore shows a small rise in China's industrial capital productivity.

Compared with China, the capital–output ratio of the total assets of the United States' manufacturing rose from 2.72 in 1997 to 3.51 in 2005, which shows that its capital productivity became less than China's after 2001. However, China's ratio of net assets is a little lower than the United States', which means its productivity is higher than the United States'. China's manufacturing ratio followed an inverted U-curve from 1995 to 2005 and almost caught up with the United States at its peak, in 1999.

The productivity of energy is usually measured by consumption intensity, which is energy use per unit of output. China's energy intensity for manufacturing dropped quite fast from 1.6 kg oil equivalent per dollar in 1991 to 0.7 in 2000, and it remained at that level until 2006. China still represents more than double the world's average under exchange rate measurement of manufacturing value added, which is about 0.3 over the past 15 years. The United States has stayed at half the world's average, and Japan has one-third. Unlike China, the manufacturing energy intensity of those industrialized economies held at quite a stable level.

50 *Scale and scope of the "world workshop"*

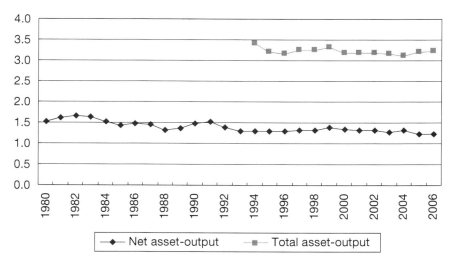

Figure 2.19 China's industrial capital–output ratio, 1960–2006
Notes: The industrial output here is the part in China's GDP accounting. Net asset refers to the net value of fixed capital assets.
Source: Author's calculation, based on Department of Industry and Transport Statistics, NBS (various years).

Table 2.25 Manufacturing capital–output ratio

	1995	1997	1999	2001	2003	2005
Total assets–output						
China		3.10	3.12	2.91	2.87	2.97
United States		2.72	2.94	3.25	3.48	3.51
Net assets–output						
China	0.91	1.06	1.13	1.03	0.93	0.93
United States	1.13	1.15	1.15	1.23	1.22	1.18

Notes: Net assets for China refer to the net value of fixed capital assets; for the United States they refer to the net stock of private fixed assets.
Source: Author's calculation, based on NBS (various years); US Census Bureau (various years).

Under the PPP method, however, China was already close to the world's average by 2000. The world's average manufacturing energy intensity also dropped, from 0.32 kg oil equivalent per international dollar in 1991 to 0.2 kg oil equivalent per international dollar in 2006. The United States has always followed a similar trend to the world's average, with a gap of about 0.3–0.7, but OECD Europe and Japan have followed quite a stable path, about 50 and 40 percent of China's level, respectively, since 2000.

Scale and scope of the "world workshop" 51

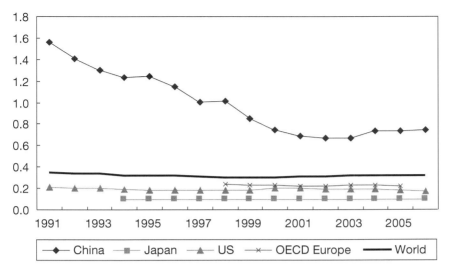

Figure 2.20 Manufacturing energy-consumption intensity (exchange rate)
Source: Author's calculation, based on IEA (2008), World Bank (2008).

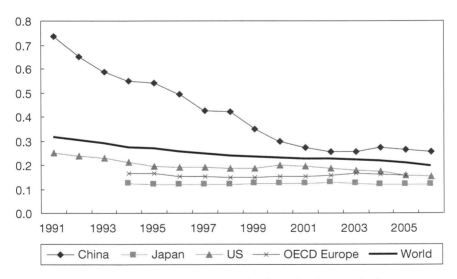

Figure 2.21 Manufacturing energy-consumption intensity (PPP method)
Source: Author's calculation, based on IEA (2008), World Bank (2008).

52 Scale and scope of the "world workshop"

Labor productivity

Compared with capital productivity, labor productivity has appeared quite different from country to country, even in developing ones. Although the two Latin American manufacturers, Brazil and Mexico, have maintained quite stable labor productivity, their relative level has declined from 20 and 25 percent, respectively, of the United States, in 1980, to 5 and 12 percent, respectively, in 2005. Over the same period of time, India almost kept in step with the United States, and its level only dropped from 4.6 percent to 3.9 percent. China, however, has caught up fast in the past 25 years, especially since 1990. Its manufacturing productivity rose from 5 percent of the United States' level to 12 percent in 2005, overtaking Mexico, although the PPP method may have overestimated labor productivity relative to the United States.

Labor productivity is also quite useful to judge the real manufacturing competitiveness of "low-wage" countries. This is mainly because the emphasis on "low wage" actually omits the big labor productivity gap between those countries and "high-wage" countries. Banister et al. (2006) point out that the unit cost of labor may be the "best approximate indicator" of manufacturing competitiveness of all single-factor productivity comparisons, especially for countries such as China and India. Unit cost is labor compensation adjusted by labor productivity and reflects the compensation cost per unit of manufacturing output.

The cross-section comparison in 2002 by Banister et al. (2006) showed that the Chinese and Indian manufacturing industries had kept labor compensation at 2.5–3.0 percent of the U.S. level in 2002. Their labor productivity was also far below the U.S. level, at 12–13 percent. As a consequence, unit labor costs

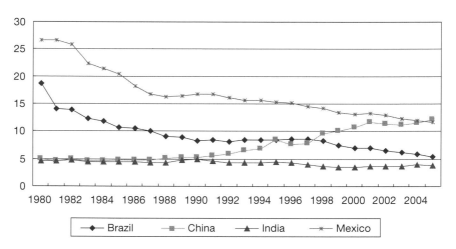

Figure 2.22 Manufacturing labor productivity (US = 100, in 1997 constant international dollars)

Source: Author's calculation, based on ILO (2008).

Scale and scope of the "world workshop" 53

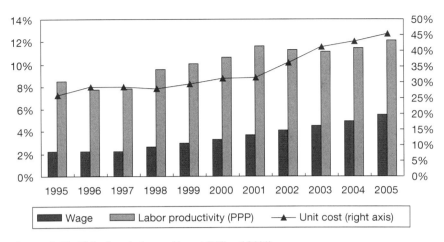

Figure 2.23 China's relative unit cost (US = 100%)
Source: Author's calculation, based on ILO (2008).

in China and India are, on average, 20 percent of unit labor costs in the United States. China and India are the most competitive manufacturers in their sample (Poland amounted to 73 percent; Mexico almost equals the unit cost of the United States).

Following the same methodology, we can estimate the relative unit cost of China. Although the relative wage in China grew by two-thirds, from 2.19 percent in 1995 to 3.67 percent in 2001, its relative unit cost only increased by one-fifth, to 31.51 percent. After that, the relative wage in China rose two-fifths to 5.49 percent in 2005, and its unchanged labor productivity made its relative unit cost increase by half to 45.4 percent in 2005. We believe the PPP method here underestimates China's relative labor-productivity growth, and the wage growth overestimates China's relative labor-compensation growth.

Therefore, if the measurement of labor productivity was changed to use the exchange rate method based on the data from the International Labor Organization (ILO) (2008), we can then establish that China's manufacturing unit cost increased 6.34 percent from 65.3 percent of the United States in 1998 to 71.64 percent in 2001 and then dropped to 54.80 percent in 2004, which is even lower than in 1998. Although relative labor compensation in China's manufacturing industry grew by 75 percent between 1998 and 2004, its relative labor productivity more than doubled and led to a decrease in its unit cost. This trend makes China quite an abstractive processor all around the world.

The estimation from AlixPartners (2009) pointed out that China's low-cost advantage was weakened in 2008: its relative labor cost (the unit cost we defined) rose from 76 percent in 2005 to 81 percent in 2008. However, if we consider changes in the exchange rate and other costs, the overall cost for

Table 2.26 Manufacturing unit costs of China and United States

	1998	2001	2004
Labor compensation (current US$ per hour)			
China	0.44	0.79	0.98
United States	18.63	20.60	23.12
China/United States	2.38%	3.86%	4.24%
Labor productivity (current US$ per employment per year)			
China	3,659	5,662	11,682
United States	100,332	105,205	151,026
China/United States	3.65%	5.38%	7.74%
Unit cost			
China/United States	65.30%	71.64%	54.80%

Note: The annual working hours of China are estimated as 2,224 hours, according to Li (1993).
Source: Author's calculation, based on ILO (2008).

China rose from 78 percent to 94 percent, which resulted in China's costs becoming higher than Mexico's and India's.

Observing sectors in detail, we can establish the source of China's decline in relative unit costs. The decline in all other sectors stems from the rise in relative labor productivity; in fact, among all sectors, only that of the sectors of leather products and furniture rose. The relative unit value of China's petroleum refineries was even 22 percent higher than that of the United States in 1998, but dropped to 90 percent in 2004. The most significant change comes from the transport equipment sector, where the relative unit cost dropped from 96 percent of the United States' value in 1998 to 32 percent in 2004. This is because its relative labor productivity more than doubled, and its relative compensation even dropped from 2.83 percent of the United States' value to 2.13 percent.

Multi (total) factor productivity

The measurement of multi factor productivity, or total factor productivity (TFP), has a long history, dating back to Solow (1956). Although criticized by the old Cambridge School for the heterogeneity of capital, the neoclassical growth accounting method of Denison (1962) and Jorgenson and Griliches (1967) still provides a feasible way to measure multi factor productivity.[3] Using the Cobb–Douglas production function and under the condition of constant return to scale, we can express the TFP (*A* here) as the following:

$$Y = A \cdot L^{\alpha} K^{1-\alpha} \Rightarrow A = Y / L^{\alpha} K^{1-\alpha} \tag{2.1}$$

Here, we first estimate the overall TFP of China's economy. *Data of gross domestic product of China (1952–2004)*, by NBS (2007), provides complete series of gross fixed capital formation and its indices, and we use a linear accelerated depreciation from 4 percent in 1952 to 6 percent in 2004. On the labor input side, we use the data from Nan and Xue (2002) instead of the official data, to avoid the break in 1990 stemming from the data adjustment from the census. An obvious slowdown in China's TFP growth appeared after 1995. Its contribution to economic growth fluctuated between 20 and 40 percent then.

Accounting for China's industrial TFP is more challenging, because of the data quality. We can only use the difference in the net value of fixed assets (which is the original value of fixed assets minus depreciation over the year) as the net capital formation for each year and get the series in constant price using the deflator of the overall GFCF. Furthermore, the missing labor input data after 2002 are estimated by the growth rate of total secondary industry. The value added of all industrial enterprises before 1992 is estimated by the growth rate of the "net output" then, and we find that China's industrial TFP experienced higher growth after 1991 and still a slowdown after 2000.

The estimated result shows that China's industrial TFP growth has experienced higher growth from 1991 to 2003, compared with its overall TFP growth. The gap reached more than 5 percent during the mid 1990s and narrowed after 2001, when China entered the WTO. The decline in industrial TFP partly came, not only from the high growth in capital stock, but also from a recovery of the industrial labor force from the SOE reform, begun in 1998. China's industrial TFP growth has fluctuated between 2 and 3 percent since 2004, and only contributed between one-fifth and one-quarter of its total growth.

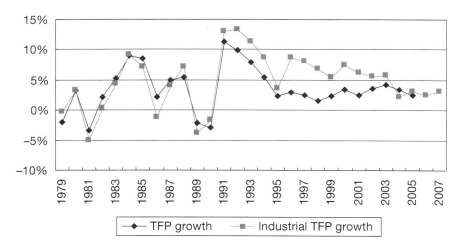

Figure 2.24 Growth of China's TFP

Notes: Labor share is from Bai et al. (2006).
Source: Author's calculation, based on Department of Industry and Transport Statistics, NBS (various years).

Table 2.27 China's relative unit cost by industry (US = 100)

Industrial code (ISIC Revision 2, 3-digit)	1998 Labor compensation	Labor productivity	Unit cost
311 Food products		3.47	
313 Beverages		2.54	
321 Textiles	3.03	3.62	83.78
322 Wearing apparel, except footwear		5.52	
323 Leather products	3.02	4.05	74.59
331 Wood products, except furniture	2.52	4.57	55.00
332 Furniture, except metal	2.97	5.93	50.08
341 Paper and products	1.98	2.33	84.92
351 Industrial chemicals	2.34	1.50	155.45
353 Petroleum refineries	2.93	2.41	121.93
355 Rubber products	3.10	3.50	88.50
356 Plastic products	2.60	4.88	53.27
361 Pottery, china, earthenware		3.01	
362 Glass and products		2.28	
369 Other non-metallic mineral products	2.17	2.24	96.70
371 Iron and steel		3.26	
372 Non-ferrous metals		3.38	
381 Fabricated metal products	2.62	4.68	55.83
382 Machinery, except electrical	2.14	2.11	101.71
383 Machinery, electrical	2.85	4.42	64.54
384 Transport equipment	2.83	2.95	96.11
385 Professional & scientific equipment	2.62	2.63	99.61

Source: Author's calculation, based on ILO (2008) and NBS (2006).

The measurement of relative TFP between two economies is a weighted combination of relative labor and capital productivity, if we use the Cobb–Douglas production function.

$$\frac{TFP_1}{TFP_2} = \frac{Y_1/(L_1^{\alpha_1} K_1^{1-\alpha_1})}{Y_2/(L_2^{\alpha_2} K_2^{1-\alpha_2})} = \frac{(Y_1/L_1)^{\alpha_1} (Y_1/K_1)^{1-\alpha_1}}{(Y_2/L_2)^{\alpha_2} (Y_2/K_2)^{1-\alpha_2}} = \frac{LP_1^{\alpha_1} KP_1^{1-\alpha_1}}{LP_2^{\alpha_2} KP_2^{1-\alpha_2}} \quad (2.2)$$

Here, *LP* refers to labor productivity, and *KP* refers to capital productivity. If we assume the labor share, α, is the same between the two economies, the ratio can be simplified as follows:

	2004		Industrial code (ISIC Review 3, 2-digit)
Labor compensation	Labor productivity	Unit cost	
4.06	7.14	56.95	15 Food products and beverages
4.27	6.84	62.51	17 Textiles
5.79	6.24	92.30	18 Wearing apparel (including fur)
4.26	5.29	81.44	19 Leather products (including footwear)
3.52	7.06	49.42	20 Products of wood, except furniture
4.00	4.90	94.65	36 Furniture; manufacturing n.e.c.
2.89	5.50	52.33	21 Paper and paper products
3.96	3.30	120.18	24 Chemicals and chemical products
4.37	4.82	90.47	23 Coke, petroleum refineries and nuclear fuel
3.89	7.46	53.33	25 Rubber and plastics products
3.17	4.94	64.22	26 Non-metallic mineral products
5.08	10.60	46.05	27 Basic metals
4.08	7.69	52.80	28 Fabricated metal products
4.47	6.53	68.95	29 Machinery and equipment n.e.c.
5.20	6.52	79.29	30 & 32 ICT
4.49	7.52	58.92	31 Electrical machinery and apparatus n.e.c.
2.13	7.72	31.92	34 & 35 Transport equipment
	4.94		33 Medical, precision and optical instruments

$$\frac{TFP_1}{TFP_2} = \frac{LP_1^{\alpha_1} KP_1^{1-\alpha_1}}{LP_2^{\alpha_2} KP_2^{1-\alpha_2}} = (\frac{LP_1}{LP_2})^{\alpha} (\frac{KP_1}{KP_2})^{1-\alpha} \qquad (2.3)$$

Using this method, we can then combine the measurement of China's labor and capital productivity. Because of limited data, we use net assets here as the capital stock in the production function. The result shows that, under the exchange rate method, China's TFP relative to the United States' rose from 14.6 percent in 1995 to 18.4 percent in 2005. Under the PPP method, however, China's relative TFP had already reached 31.0 percent of that of the United States in 2005, which was a rise from 24.6 percent, ten years previously.

Table 2.28 Relative TFP of China's manufacturing

	1995	1997	1999	2001	2003	2005
Relative labor productivity (China/United States, %)						
Exchange rate	2.19	2.24	2.96	3.67	4.56	5.49
PPP method	8.50	7.86	10.05	11.65	11.10	12.09
Relative capital productivity (China/United States, %)						
—	120.90	108.44	101.46	120.20	130.53	127.05
Relative TFP (China/United States, %)						
Exchange rate	14.59	13.33	15.04	17.59	17.66	18.38
PPP method	24.59	22.45	25.34	29.63	29.75	30.97

Note: The labor share we use here is 0.6.
Source: Author's calculation, based on ILO (2008).

Notes

1. Furthermore, China also emitted nearly 30 percent of the world's organic waste water (biological oxygen demand (BOD)) in 2000 (World Bank, 2006), and about half of it comes from the industrial sectors.
2. They also assumed that ten years of investment serve as an adequate proxy for the initial capital stock (Isaksson, 2007).
3. Their calculation of the physical capital stock is usually carried out under the PIM, which treats the aggregation of capital as a sum of investment in real price and deducts the depreciations of each period.

3 Pattern and sophistication of the "world workshop"

China in the world market

China's general trade pattern

Trade volume and type

China's share of the world's merchandise export market doubled after its entry to the WTO, rising from 3.9 percent in 2000 to 9.1 percent in 2008. China overtook Japan in 2004 and the United States in 2007, to become the second-largest exporter of merchandise, 0.2 percent lower than Germany. If we count the intra-regional trade of the EU-15 countries, China's share reached 11.2 percent in 2007, 4.6 percent lower than the total for the EU-15 countries. The slope of its growth curve is much steeper than that from 1980 to 2000, during which time China's share only increased from 0.9 percent to 3.9 percent. This escalation, with an annual growth rate of more than 20 percent, happened between the dot.com bubble and the subprime financial crisis, when China appeared to take the place of the other main economies of the world as they fell.

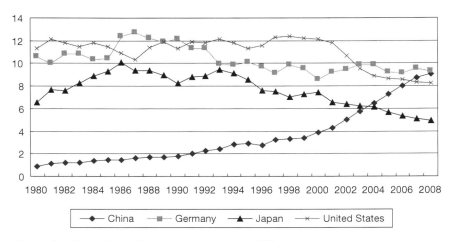

Figure 3.1 Share in world merchandise exports (%)
Source: Author's calculation, based on World Bank (2008) database and WTO (2009).

60 *Pattern and sophistication of "world workshop"*

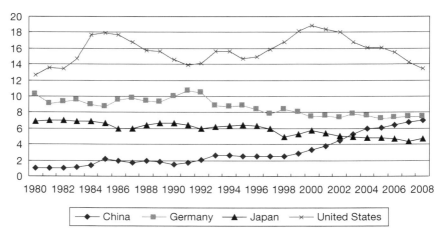

Figure 3.2 Share of world merchandise imports (%)
Note: Intra-EU-15 trade is not included.
Source: Author's calculation, based on World Bank (2008) database and WTO (2009).

China's share of the world's imports rose more slowly than that of exports; it doubled from 3.4 in 2000 to 7.0 in 2008, which was still 0.5 percent lower than Germany. China's share is still half that of the United States, even if its share dropped from 18.9 in 2000 to 13.4 in 2008. If the intra-EU-15 imports are excluded, China's share was 4.3 in 2000 and 8.7 in 2007. The United States still dominate the world market, with a share of 18.3 percent in 2007, higher than the 15.7 percent share of the EU-15 countries.

In fact, the volume of China's merchandise exports became the largest, at product level, around the world in 2005. UN trade statistics show that China had the most products ranking first in 2005: 958 products of the 5,113 items in the six-digit HS catalogue.

Table 3.1 Top ten economies with goods ranking first in world export market

Order	Country	Goods ranking first	Importance in the export market
1	China	958	2
2	Germany	815	1
3	United States	678	3
4	Italy	304	9
5	Japan	280	5
6	France	168	11
7	Belgium	145	7
8	Netherlands	135	13
9	United Kingdom	123	18
10	Hong Kong	116	12

Source: Korea International Trade Association (2007).

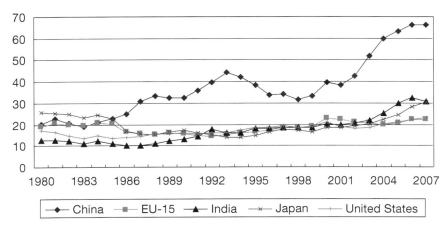

Figure 3.3 Share of merchandise trade in GDP (exchange rate)
Note: The intra-EU-15 trade is not included.

The openness ratio, referring to the proportion of total merchandise trade to GDP, is usually used to reflect the depth to which an economy is integrated into the world market. Surprisingly, China's value is much higher than those of other main economies, especially since 2001, and rose from about 16 percent higher to 36 percent higher than the EU-15 countries in 2007. This ratio seems to overestimate China's extent, which I believe is caused by the underestimation of its GDP using the exchange rate method. Generally speaking, the lower per capita the GDP of a country is, the lower its exchange rate from its PPP converter. Therefore, if we adjust the openness ratio under the PPP method, a different view will appear to reflect the "right" openness ratio.

If we use the GDP in the PPP method, China's openness ratio was about 15 percent before 2002 and then overtook the United States in the following year and doubled to about 31 percent, to catch up with Japan in 2007. Considering the increase in the overall openness ratio of the world, China is the only main economy where the comparative openness ratio rose after 2000, from about 50 percent to nearly 70 percent (India just recovered to its level in 1980).

What needs to be pointed out is that there is a quite different element of China's trade—the processing trade—compared with other main economies (Naughton, 2007). According to the definition of the General Administration of Custom of China (2008), processing trade refers to the practice of importing whole or parts of raw materials, components, elements, and packing materials and re-exporting the finished merchandise after processing or assembly. This kind of trade represented half of China's total exports after the mid 1990s, when China was more deeply integrated into the world economy.

Since the mid 1990s, the processing trade has also accounted for nearly half of China's imports, and China also has a large share of the world's processing

62 *Pattern and sophistication of "world workshop"*

Table 3.2 Share of merchandise trade in GDP (PPP)

	1980	1985	1990	1995	2000	2005	2007
Openness ratio							
China	15.41	13.14	12.74	15.40	15.84	26.66	30.81
EU-15	21.32	13.24	17.92	19.37	19.16	23.15	26.85
India	8.20	5.28	5.60	6.09	6.07	9.93	11.70
Japan	25.98	19.58	22.48	27.52	26.45	28.68	31.14
United States	17.43	13.64	15.82	18.46	20.90	21.27	23.03
Comparative openness ratio (world = 100)							
China	47.29	61.71	46.39	47.91	50.77	70.60	71.99
EU-15	65.41	62.18	65.25	60.26	61.40	61.31	62.74
India	25.16	24.82	20.40	18.95	19.46	26.30	27.35
Japan	79.72	91.97	81.88	85.62	84.78	75.93	72.75
United States	53.47	64.09	57.61	57.45	66.99	56.32	53.80

Source: Author's calculation, based on World Bank (2008).

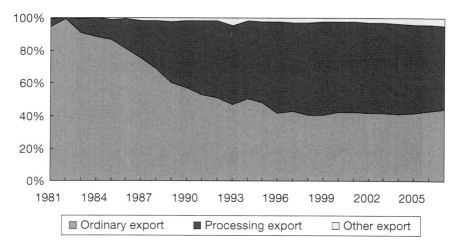

Figure 3.4 Proportions of China's different exports, 1981–2007
Source: NBS (various years).

trade. The estimate from the ILO (Boyenge, 2007) said that, of the 66 million laborers working in 3,500 export processing zones (EPZs) around the world in 2006, 40 million worked in the 169 EPZs in China.[1] The total exports from China's EPZs reached US$145.1 billion (not including the US$101 billion from Hong Kong), followed by US$85.2 billion from Ireland and about US$20–30 billion from several other countries (such as the Philippines, Korea, Indonesia, and Malaysia), which makes China the "processing center" of the world.

The argument from Assche et al. (2008) holds that the processing trade is completely different from ordinary trade, because the country only keeps the difference in value between the import and processed export. Traditional accounting, which only considers the processed export, overestimates China's share of the world's exports. According to Assche et al.'s method, which only counts the surplus of the processing trade, China's adjusted exports only shared 6.1 percent of the world's total in 2007, 2.7 percent lower than the unadjusted figure.

Another argument relates to the source of China's surplus. After 2003, SOEs became net importers, but then, the surplus of private enterprises and foreign-funded enterprises sharply rose to more than US$90 billion. Some researchers think that part of the surplus from affiliations of MNCs in China should be included when China's "real" exports are counted. However, there is no consensus on the proportion of this adjustment. If we followed the estimates of Ferrantino et al. (2007), more than 40 percent of China's trade surplus in 2006 would be excluded, and this adjustment would lead to an even higher reduction in China's trade compared with the developed economies, such as the EU and the United States. For example, in their calculation, almost all advanced-technology products that are surplus in Sino–United States trade are finished by the wholly foreign-owned enterprises or joint ventures in China.

Structure of trade

The trade structure of China has changed a lot over the past 30 years. The share of agricultural products and fuels and mining products dropped from half of total exports in 1980 to less than 7 percent in 2007. However, the share of fuels

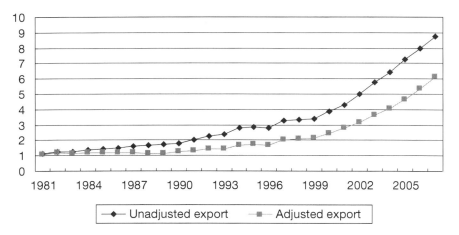

Figure 3.5 China's adjusted share of world merchandise exports, 1981–2005
Note: Adjusted exports = ordinary exports + processing exports − processing imports.
Source: Author's calculation, based on NBS (various years) and World Bank (2008).

64 *Pattern and sophistication of "world workshop"*

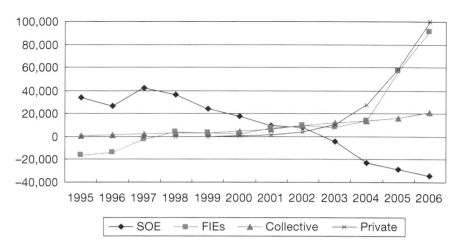

Figure 3.6 China's balance of general merchandise trade with the world, by firm type
Source: Ferrantino, Koopman, Wang et al. (2007).

and mining products in total imports rose very fast, from 5 percent to 22 percent, which kept the import share of manufacturing only 10 percent higher during the same period of time. This, on the one hand, is because of China's oil consumption grows very fast and, on the other hand, is led by the expansion of China's domestic iron and steel industry, which means the share of imported iron and steel dropped from 11.2 percent in 1980 to 2.5 percent in 2007.

Of all manufacturing imports, the share of integrated circuits and electronic components has seen the most significant growth, from 1.4 percent in 1990 to 15.2 percent in 2007. Among all manufacturing exports, electronic data-processing and office equipment and telecommunications equipment both rose very fast and became China's two largest export product groups. The most important part of China's trade has become the processing of office and telecommunications equipment since 2000, instead of the traditional textiles and clothing.

China's export shares of the world market for textiles and clothing reached quite a high level—23.5 percent and 33.4 percent, respectively—in 2007. These have been China's most competitive export products since 1980. The revealed comparative advantage (RCA) index is generally calculated as an industry's share of a country's exports, divided by its share of world exports (Balassa, 1965). We can establish that, although it has fallen since its peak, clothing still has the highest RCA, of about 3.65, which means that the share of China's clothing export in the world's total clothing export is 3.65 times more than China's total export in the world's total.

The RCAs of China's electronic data-processing and office equipment and telecommunications equipment have increased greatly since 2000 and reached 3.35 and 2.85, respectively, in 2007. They become the other two most competitive export product groups and both share 30 percent of the world market.

When we rank the RCA indices for all the three-digit export products in descending order, the characteristics of different economies become quite clear. The steeper the curve, the more the export advantage of an economy is concentrated in higher-RCA products. Korea seems to have the sharpest, with thirteen products that have an RCA greater than 3 (with very high comparative advantage), but only fifty-five products have an RCA larger than 1, which

Table 3.3 China's trade structure

	1980	1990	2000	2007
Export structure				
Agricultural products	24.29	16.51	6.59	3.20
Food	17.33	12.91	5.45	2.73
Fuels and mining products	27.45	10.76	5.00	3.45
Fuels		8.40	3.16	1.64
Manufacturing	48.26	72.73	88.41	93.36
Iron and steel	1.31	2.10	1.77	4.24
Chemicals	6.28	6.16	4.86	4.96
Pharmaceuticals		1.05	0.72	0.49
Machinery and transport equipment	4.67	17.78	33.22	47.47
Office and telecoms equipment	0.38	5.13	17.49	28.56
Electronic data-processing and office equipment		0.62	7.49	13.65
Telecommunications equipment		4.30	7.84	12.03
Integrated circuits and electronic components		0.21	2.15	2.88
Automotive products	0.35	0.42	0.64	1.89
Textiles	14.07	11.85	6.49	4.60
Clothing	9.00	15.87	14.51	9.48
Import structure				
Agricultural products	32.85	14.80	8.75	6.84
Food	16.26	8.70	4.05	3.39
Fuels and mining products	5.25	5.32	15.19	22.09
Fuels		2.37	9.24	11.00
Manufacturing	61.91	79.88	76.06	71.07
Iron and steel	11.27	5.37	4.34	2.53
Chemicals	14.48	12.59	13.53	11.28
Pharmaceuticals		0.79	0.43	0.41
Machinery and transport equipment	26.61	40.54	41.16	43.26
Office and telecoms equipment	2.77	7.65	19.89	23.73
Electronic data-processing and office equipment		1.45	4.86	4.77
Telecommunications equipment		4.78	5.56	3.75
Integrated circuits and electronic components		1.41	9.47	15.22
Automotive products	3.71	3.38	1.70	2.52
Textiles	5.58	9.97	5.74	1.75
Clothing	0.24	0.09	0.53	0.21

Source: Author's calculation, based on WTO (2008).

Table 3.4 Share in world market and RCA of China's exports

	1980	1990	2000	2007
Agricultural products	1.47	2.43	2.96	3.45
	(1.59)	(1.31)	(0.73)	(0.38)
Food	1.40	2.49	3.13	3.63
	(1.51)	(1.35)	(0.77)	(0.40)
Fuels and mining products	0.89	1.34	1.45	1.58
	(0.96)	(0.73)	(0.36)	(0.17)
Fuels		1.41	1.18	0.98
		(0.76)	(0.29)	(0.11)
Manufacturing	0.80	1.85	4.68	11.95
	(0.86)	(1.00)	(1.15)	(1.31)
Iron and steel	0.31	1.21	3.08	10.86
	(0.33)	(0.66)	(0.76)	(1.19)
Chemicals	0.80	1.27	2.07	4.07
	(0.86)	(0.69)	(0.51)	(0.44)
Pharmaceuticals			1.65	1.63
			(0.40)	(0.18)
Machinery and transport equipment	0.16	0.89	3.13	11.64
	(0.17)	(0.48)	(0.77)	(1.27)
Office and telecoms equipment	0.08	1.05	4.49	22.92
	(0.09)	(0.57)	(1.10)	(2.51)
Electronic data-processing and office equipment			5.01	30.69
			(1.23)	(3.35)
Telecommunications equipment			6.77	26.10
			(1.66)	(2.85)
Integrated circuits and electronic components			1.74	8.46
			(0.43)	(0.92)
Automotive products	0.05	0.08	0.27	1.95
	(0.05)	(0.04)	(0.07)	(0.21)
Textiles	4.62	6.92	10.29	23.50
	(4.99)	(3.74)	(2.53)	(2.57)
Clothing	4.00	8.94	18.20	33.37
	(4.33)	(4.83)	(4.47)	(3.65)

Note: The numbers in the brackets are the RCAs.
Source: Author's calculation based on WTO (2008).

means the other 203 groups aren't competitive in the world market. The curves belonging to Japan and the United States are much less steep. Although they have similar groups of products with an RCA greater than 3, Japan has 80 groups where it is larger than 1, and the United States has 117 groups.

China's exports also showed quite strong competitiveness in 2005. China has ninety-one groups of products with an RCA larger than 1, which is eleven more than Japan. The most important thing is that the number of Chinese groups with an RCA larger than 3 was more than double those of Japan and the United States and amounted to twenty-seven groups. This means China already owned a large group of products with high comparative advantage.

Besides the traditional textiles, clothing, footwear, and suitcases, there were also several ICT products, such as office machines and data-processing machines.

Thorbecke and Zhang (2008) divided the world's exports into two main groups and several other miscellaneous groups. According to their estimation,

> the largest category is final electronics goods, defined to include consumer electronics goods, computer equipment, telecommunications equipment, and electrical apparatuses. In 2006, 33 percent of China's exports were in this category. The second largest category is labor-intensive manufactures, defined to include carpets, clothing, fabrics, furniture, knitwear, leather, and yarns. In 2006 21 percent of China's exports were in this second category.

The proportion of China's labor-intensive manufactured goods in the world market overtook Europe's total after 2005 and became close to 30 percent. This share, although quite high, *does* fit the common impression of "made in China."

Lall (2000) classified all export products in three main groups: primary products, manufactured goods based on natural resources, and manufactured goods not based on natural resources. The last group is also divided into low, medium, and high technology. Low-tech products include twenty codes for textile and fashion groups, and another twenty-four codes for simple metal parts, plastic products, pottery, and glass products; medium-tech products

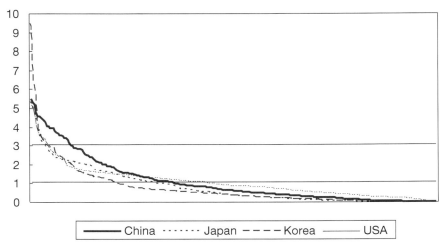

Figure 3.7 RCA in descending order (SITC Revision 3, 3-digit, 2005)
Source: Author's calculation, based on UNSTA (2008).

68 *Pattern and sophistication of "world workshop"*

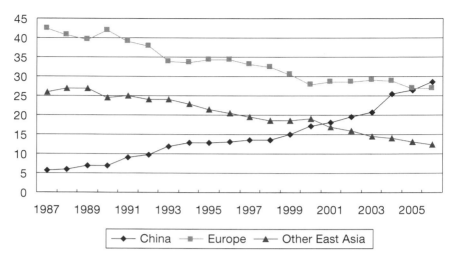

Figure 3.8 Share of the world's labor-intensive manufacturing exports
Source: Thorbecke and Zhang (2008).

include five codes for the automotive industry, twenty-two for processing-industry products, such as chemicals, synthetic fibers, and iron pipes/tubes, and thirty-one for engineering-industry products, such as engines, motors, industrial machinery, and ships; high-tech products include eleven codes for electronics and electrical products, office/data-processing/telecommunications equipment, and power-generating equipment, and seven codes for other products such as pharmaceuticals, aerospace, and optical/measuring instruments. This provides us with a framework to assess the value of the structure of China's exports.

UNCTAD (2002) estimated the structure of China's exports using this classification, which showed that manufactured goods not based on natural resources dominated China's exports, at 86.8 percent in 2005. The most important thing is that the high-tech sector (including the office and telecommunications equipment we have mentioned) increased very fast, from 2.6 percent in 1980 to 33.2 percent in 2005, and its share in the world market also increased to 6.0 percent then. Its share in the world market also doubled from 6.0 in 2000 to 12.3 percent in 2005, which was just less competitive than low-tech manufacturing.

According to the OECD classified manufacturing sectors (Hatzichronoglou, 1997), China's advantage in the high-tech sectors seems even greater. The proportion of exports from high-tech sectors overtook those from low-tech sectors after 2000 and reached 43.25 percent in 2005, completely reversing China's export structure, which was dominated by the low- and medium–low-tech sectors in the 1980s. Correspondingly, China's share of the world market for high-tech-sector exports more than doubled, from 8.64 percent in 2000 to 19.46 percent in 2005, which made China the largest exporter after 2003, 8 percent higher than the United States and the EU in 2005.

Within the high-tech market, the ICT sectors, including ETE and COE, dominate China's exports, contributing nearly 40 percent of China's total manufacturing exports. Since 2002, China has already become the largest exporter in these two industries, where, in 2005, ETE shared 20.5 percent and

Table 3.5 Technological classification of exports

Classification	SITC 3-digit, Revision 2 code
Primary products	
	001, 011, 022, 025, 034, 036, 041, 042, 043, 044, 045, 054, 057, 071, 072, 074, 075, 081, 091, 121, 211, 212, 222, 223, 232, 244, 245, 246, 261, 263, 268, 271, 273, 274, 277, 278, 291, 292, 322, 333, 341, 681, 682, 683, 684, 685, 686, 687
Manufactured goods using natural resources	
Agro-/forest-based products	012, 014, 023, 024, 035, 037, 046, 047, 048, 056, 058, 061, 062, 073, 098, 111, 112, 122, 233, 247, 248, 251, 264, 265, 269, 423, 424, 431, 621, 625, 628, 633, 634, 635, 641
Other resource-based products	281, 282, 286, 287, 288, 289, 323, 334, 335, 411, 511, 514, 515, 516, 522, 523, 531, 532, 551, 592, 661, 662, 663, 664, 667, 688, 689
Manufactured goods not based on natural resources	
Low technology	
Textile/fashion cluster	611, 612, 613, 651, 652, 654, 655, 656, 657, 658, 659, 831, 842, 843, 844, 845, 846, 847, 848, 851
Other low technology	642, 665, 666, 673, 674, 675, 676, 677, 679, 691, 692, 693, 694, 695, 696, 697, 699, 821, 893, 894, 895, 897, 898, 899
Medium technology	
Automotive products	781, 782, 783, 784, 785
Medium-tech process industry	266, 267, 512, 513, 533, 553, 554, 562, 572, 582, 583, 584, 585, 591, 598, 653, 671, 672, 678, 786, 791, 882
Medium-tech engineering industry	711, 713, 714, 721, 722, 723, 724, 725, 726, 727, 728, 736, 737, 741, 742, 743, 744, 745, 749, 762, 763, 772, 773, 775, 793, 812, 872, 873, 884, 885, 951
High technology	
Electronics and electrical products	716, 718, 751, 752, 759, 761, 764, 771, 774, 776, 778
Other high technology	524, 541, 712, 792, 871, 874, 881

Source: Lall (2000).

Table 3.6 China's competitiveness in world trade

Product category	1985	1990	1995	2000	2005
I. Market share	1.6	2.8	4.8	6.1	7.3
1. Primary products	2.4	2.6	2.5	2.3	2.2
2. Manufactured goods using natural resources	1.1	1.3	2.1	2.7	4.1
3. Manufactured goods not using natural resources	1.5	3.4	6.1	7.8	10.2
Low technology	4.5	9.1	15.5	18.7	17.2
Medium technology	0.4	1.4	2.6	3.6	5.5
High technology	0.4	1.4	3.6	6.0	12.3
4. Others	0.7	0.7	1.4	1.8	0.4
II. Export structure	100.0	100.0	100.0	100.0	100.0
1. Primary products	35.0	14.6	7.0	4.7	4.4
2. Manufactured goods using natural resources	13.6	8.2	7.4	6.9	8.3
3. Manufactured goods not using natural resources	50.0	76.2	84.6	87.1	86.8
Low technology	39.7	53.6	53.5	47.6	31.5
Medium technology	7.7	15.4	16.9	17.3	22.0
High technology	2.6	7.3	14.2	22.4	33.2
4. Others	1.4	0.8	1.0	1.1	0.5

Note: Data from 2005 were calculated by the author, based on UNSTA (2008).
Source: UNCTAD (2002).

Table 3.7 Exports of China's industries according to OECD classification

	1985	1990	1995	2000	2005
Export structure					
High-technology	6.87	13.74	18.84	29.79	43.25
COE	0.49	1.03	2.77	9.40	19.05
ETE	2.76	7.18	10.43	14.95	19.66
Medium–high-technology	8.40	16.50	20.33	21.80	23.36
Medium–low-technology	46.86	23.73	19.09	13.17	6.27
Low-technology	37.87	46.02	41.75	35.25	27.12
Total	100.00	100.00	100.00	100.00	100.00
Exports in world market					
High-technology	2.57	5.20	7.15	8.64	19.46
COE	1.57	2.98	5.80	10.29	30.40
ETE	2.86	7.33	8.70	9.74	20.54
Medium–high-technology	0.93	2.26	3.57	4.53	8.39
Medium–low-technology	11.45	7.91	8.33	7.33	6.26
Low-technology	6.35	8.96	10.71	11.38	16.08

Source: Author's calculation, based on National Science Board (2008).

COE shared 30.4 percent of the world market. The shares of the United States, EU-15, and Japan all dropped to about 10 percent in both industries at that time.

The main argument concerns the source of the exports from high-tech sectors in China, because FIEs shared about 90 percent of those exports, and this share was already 86.4 percent when China entered the WTO in 2001. This proportion is quite high because these exports accounted for 70 percent of China's total manufacturing exports, and the high-tech sectors amounted to half of the total exports from FIEs in 2007. In fact, the shares of the other three categories, low-tech, medium–low-tech, and medium–high-tech, were all 10–20 percent lower than the average of all enterprises.

Among the exports from the five main high-tech industries, the export of ICT products was completely dominated by FIEs after 1995. The share of COE even reached more than 99 percent in 2007, which means almost no domestic enterprises contributed to its export. The share of ETE also rose, from 82.4 percent to 90.9 percent in 2005. Furthermore, the share of MEM doubled over 10 years, but then dropped 8 percent from 2005 to 2007.

Yet another argument comes from the processing industry, especially for high-tech products. The most important feature of China's exports is that 90 percent of its high-tech exports came from the processing trade between 1992 and now (Assche et al., 2008). This means only one-tenth of all these products are "made by China," and the others only pass through the country in the course of their assembly or processing. Although the processing shares of the low-tech and medium–low-tech industries declined after 1996, the share of medium–high-tech products still kept half of their total exports.

Table 3.8 Share of exports of FIEs in manufacturing sectors

	2001	2002	2003	2004	2005	2006	2007
Structure of export							
Low-tech	30.71	27.72	24.52	21.49	20.36	18.88	17.53
Medium–low	13.27	12.81	10.96	10.94	10.68	10.55	10.69
Medium–high	18.57	17.70	19.05	19.59	20.17	20.51	21.61
High-tech	37.45	41.77	45.47	47.97	48.80	50.07	50.17
Total	100.00	100.00	100.00	100.00	100.00	100.00	100.00
Share in all enterprises							
Low-tech	56.34	55.90	56.07	59.80	58.39	58.93	59.76
Medium–low	54.74	56.21	54.04	55.55	52.66	50.61	51.25
Medium–high	56.44	56.84	56.40	61.80	59.60	60.05	60.13
High-tech	86.40	86.88	89.06	93.23	91.55	89.21	91.10
Average	64.52	65.96	67.18	72.05	70.28	69.86	70.82

Source: Author's calculation, based on National Science Board NBS (2008) and NBS, NDRC and MOST (various years).

72 *Pattern and sophistication of "world workshop"*

Table 3.9 Share of FIEs in high-tech exports by industry

	1995	2000	2005	2006	2007
Structure of exports from high-tech industries					
AS	2.33	1.25	0.73	0.80	0.82
Ps	0.22	0.24	0.19	0.19	0.23
COE	24.45	29.09	43.49	44.64	45.36
ETE	70.66	66.64	52.99	51.80	51.31
MEM	2.34	2.79	2.60	2.56	2.28
Total	100.00	100.00	100.00	100.00	100.00
Share of exports in all enterprises					
AS	11.19	21.87	38.72	33.54	38.27
Ps	15.22	21.41	26.99	31.06	33.13
COE	92.61	92.72	97.60	93.50	99.05
ETE	82.35	89.01	90.92	89.44	88.78
MEM	38.81	63.07	81.53	78.05	73.26

Source: Author's calculation, based on NBS, NDRC, and MOST (various years).

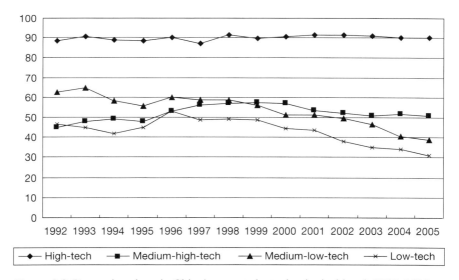

Figure 3.9 Processing share in China's exports by technological level, 1992–2005
Source: Assche et al. (2008).

China's trade sophistication

Export of high-tech products

The *High and New Technology Products (HNTP) Statistics Catalog* has been jointly published by the Ministry of Science and Technology and the Ministry of Commerce and it covers nine technology areas: computers and telecommunications; life-science technologies; electronics; computer-integrated manufacturing; aerospace; opto-electronics; biotechnology; materials; and other technologies. This catalog is compatible with the United States export and import catalogs for advanced technology products (ATPs).

According to China's HNTP catalog, China's high-tech exports reached 28.6 percent of all merchandise exports and 30.1 percent of its manufacturing exports in 2007. This share had doubled from 2000, when China entered the WTO. Although high-tech products account for a higher proportion in both merchandise and manufacturing imports, China changed to become a net high-tech-product exporter after 2004. Until 2007, the surplus had exceeded about 10 percent of the total high-tech trade, which was US$60.84 billion.

Compared with other leading economies, the proportion of high-tech-product exports in China's total manufacturing exports rose quite fast from 6.1 percent in 1992, overtaking Germany in 1998 and Japan in 2003, and reached the level of the United States, at about 30 percent, in 2004 and kept that share after that. It was also in that year that China became a net exporter of high-tech products.

Over the same period of time, China's share of high-tech exports in the world market tripled and reached 14.9 percent in 2006, 1.4 percent higher than the United States. In the year China became a net exporter, it overtook Japan and Germany to become the second largest. As the largest high-tech exporter, China is quite different from other developed economies.

Table 3.10 Current definition of high-tech trade in China

Name	Version	Characteristics	Intended Purpose
China's *High and New Technology Export Products Catalog*	2000	8 fields and 1,900 products	Policy orientation: basis for export value added tax (VAT) rebate benefits
	2003	9 fields and 1,835 products	
	2006	9 fields and 1,601 products	
China's *High and New Technology Product Import and Export Statistics Catalog*	1999	9 fields and 229 HS-6 codes	Statistical orientation: used in Customs' "Monthly statistical report" since 2002

Source: Ferrantino et al. (2007).

74 *Pattern and sophistication of "world workshop"*

Table 3.11 High-tech trade as a percentage of merchandise trade and manufacturing trade

	2000	2001	2002	2003	2004	2005	2006	2007
High-tech trade (US$ billion)								
Export	37.04	46.45	67.86	110.32	165.36	218.25	281.45	347.82
Import	52.51	64.11	82.84	119.30	161.34	197.71	247.30	286.98
Surplus	−15.47	−17.66	−14.98	−8.98	4.02	20.54	34.15	60.84
Share of merchandise trade								
Export	14.9	17.5	20.8	25.2	27.9	28.6	29.0	28.6
Import	23.3	26.3	28.1	28.9	28.7	30.0	31.2	30.0
Share of manufacturing trade								
Export	16.6	19.4	22.8	27.3	29.9	30.6	30.7	30.1
Import	29.4	32.4	33.7	35.1	36.3	38.6	40.9	40.3

Source: MOST (2008).

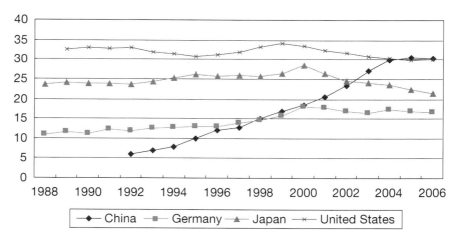

Figure 3.10 Share of high-tech exports in total manufacturing exports
Source: Author's calculation, based on World Bank (2008).

Among all high-tech products, computers and telecommunications dominated China's exports from 1995 and reached 80.4 percent in 2007. Including electronics, the share of ICT products was 93.5 percent. This is also similar to the sum of computers, office machines, electronics, telecommunications and scientific instruments in the classification according to the OECD high-tech products list (95.3 percent in 2007).

The calculation from OECD (2005a) shows that China has become the primary ICT goods exporter since 2004, reaching US$180 billion and overtaking the EU-15 and the United States. China mainly imported electronic components (65 percent of imports in 2004) and mainly exported computers and related equipment (46 percent of total exports in 2004) in its ICT trade. The ICT goods defined by the OECD also include telecommunications equipment, audio and video equipment, and some other ICT goods, most of them belonging to high-tech products.

However, we have to point out that most of China's high-tech-product exports involve the processing industry—nearly 90 percent—just as the high-tech industry exports. General trade exceeded 10 percent for the first time in 2007. Of the total processing industry, exports using supplied materials

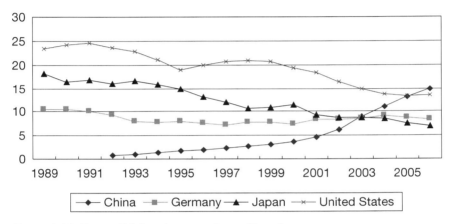

Figure 3.11 Share of high-tech exports in world market
Source: Author's calculation, based on World Bank (2008).

Table 3.12 Structure of high-tech exports (HNTP classification)

	1992	1995	2000	2005	2006	2007
Computers and telecommunications	47.64	60.27	72.91	81.15	79.91	80.39
Life sciences	13.83	9.81	3.71	2.09	2.25	2.56
Electronics	9.25	13.81	15.78	11.22	12.79	13.13
Computer-integrated manufacturing	4.18	4.12	1.35	0.95	1.02	1.42
Aerospace and aeronautics	9.45	1.57	1.87	0.65	0.87	0.72
Opto-electronics	4.40	5.70	2.66	3.29	2.51	1.01
Biotechnology	0.82	0.50	0.34	0.12	0.09	0.08
Materials	0.34	0.51	0.86	0.40	0.45	0.61
Others (nuclear & armaments)	10.07	3.72	0.53	0.13	0.11	0.08

Source: Author's calculation, based on NBS and MOST (various years).

76 *Pattern and sophistication of "world workshop"*

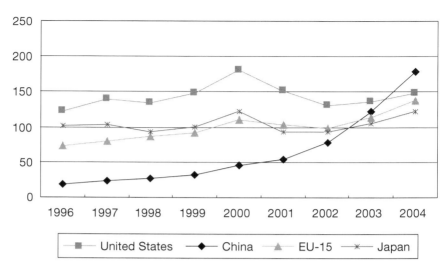

Figure 3.12 Export of ICT goods (US$ billion)
Source: OECD (2005a).

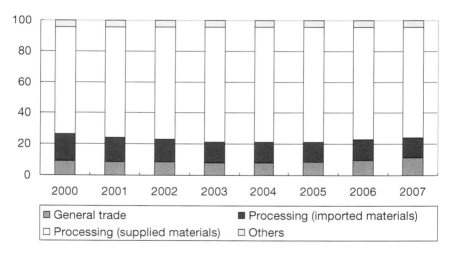

Figure 3.13 Export of high-tech products by trade type
Source: MOST (2008).

dominated China's high-tech exports over the past 8 years—about 70 percent. This means China is almost a processing center, a section of the value chain of the world's high-tech products.

Most of China's high-tech exports are from FIEs, which has led to the share of SOEs dropping from 16 percent in 2000 to 6 percent in 2007. Among all

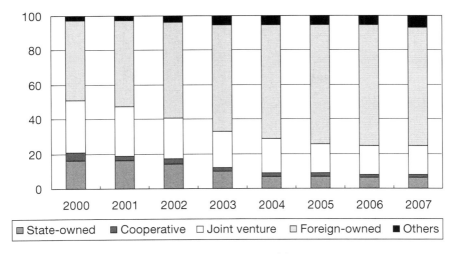

Figure 3.14 Export of high-tech products by ownership
Source: MOST (2008).

FIEs with high-tech exports, joint ventures dropped from 30 percent to 16 percent in 2007, and wholly foreign-owned enterprises rose from less than 50 percent to 70 percent then. This means the MNCs have already been using China as a base for high-tech production, with their own plants located there.

Quality/unit value approach

The unit value approach is introduced to reflect the difference in "quality" of trade products on the world market, and can be traced back to the Linder theory (1961) and Alchian and Allen conjecture (1964). A recent empirical breakthrough came from Schott (2004), who pointed out that export unit values increase together with per capita income and the exporter's relative endowments of physical and human capital. Hummels and Klenow (2005) estimated that an extensive margin (a weighted count of relative categories from two economies) accounts for around 60 percent of the greater exports of larger economies.

Rodrik (2006) and Schott (2006) both brought up the question of why China has such high levels of sophistication compared with its income level and endowment, especially considering China's high proportion of high-tech-product exports in both its own merchandising exports and in the world's market. Fontagné et al. (2008) showed that China's export structure is more similar to those of Japan, the United States, and the EU than to Brazil's and Russia's, according to both sector level and product level. However, judged on unit values, Chinese exports are more likely to be at the low end of the market, like those of Brazil, Russia, and India, than those of the high-income countries.

Table 3.13 Export structure similarity and relative unit values

	Export structure similarity, 2004		Relative unit value (China = 1)	
	Sector level	Product level	1995	2004
EU-25			2.59	2.51
Emerging economy	0.44	0.23		
Germany	0.47	0.30	3.74	3.06
France	0.50	0.30	4.06	3.67
United Kingdom	0.49	0.30	3.39	3.53
Italy	0.60	0.35	3.46	2.83
United States	0.55	0.34	2.34	2.44
Japan	0.56	0.34	3.25	2.89
Brazil			1.38	1.20
Russia	0.30	0.16	1.00	1.17
India	0.56	0.30	1.14	1.27

Source: Fontagné et al. (2008).

Table 3.14 Relative unit value in SITC (Review 3, 3-digit) sectors in 2005 (China = 1)

	Japan[a]	US[a]	India[b]	Russia[b]	Brazil[b]
Total	2.73	2.06	1.33	1.09	1.06
0–1 Food beverages and tobacco	2.67	1.46	1.18	0.86	0.93
2 Inedible crude materials except fuels	1.32	1.00	1.77	0.52	0.41
3–4 Mineral fuels & organic oils, fats	1.12	1.11	1.07	1.14	0.77
5 Chemicals and related products	5.48	3.74	1.80	0.63	0.93
6 Manufacture classified chiefly by material	3.01	2.14	0.95	0.84	1.10
7 Machinery and transport equipment	2.22	1.68	1.34	2.12	1.63
8 Miscellaneous manufactured articles	3.69	2.63	1.83	2.42	1.15

a Several products with ultra-high relative unit price (> 30) are not included.
b Several products with ultra-high relative unit price (> 15) are not included.
Source: Author's calculation, based on UNSTA (2008).

We then calculate the weighted, sectoral relative unit value of five countries' exports to the world, based on the three-digit-coded products of the Standard International Trade Classification (SITC) Revision 3 classification. The sectors with the highest relative unit values for Japan and the United States are both chemicals and related products (especially medicaments and explosives/

pyrotechnics), followed by miscellaneous manufactured articles (especially printed matter and lighting fixtures). The high relative unit value of Russia in sector 8 is mainly for leather/fur clothes and printed matter, and, in sector 7, from power-generating equipment and metal machine tools.

Actually, the unit value itself can be quite an informative basis on which to analyze China's exports. The research by Ferrantino et al. (2007) provides quite an interesting example of color video monitors: the unit values of the exports from enterprises under different ownership and under different regimes are quite varied. The unit value of monitors produced inside high-tech zones,

Table 3.15 Unit value: China's color video monitor exports to the world (US$)

Color video monitor (HS 852821), 2005	
Unit value of G-3 exports	467.4
Unit values in China's exports	
Wholly foreign-owned firms	241.5
Export processing zones	347.8
Processing/high-tech zones	456.7
Processing/outside any zones	56.8
Normal trade/high-tech zones	364.8
Normal trade/outside any zones	73.6
State-owned firms	207.0
Joint ventures	126.3
Private firms	77.2

Source: Ferrantino, Koopman, Wang et al. (2007).

Table 3.16 Relative unit value of ICT exports in 2005 (China = 1)

	US	Japan	India	Korea	Brazil
Total computer equipment (752)	7.74	6.50	7.55	4.84	2.60
7521 Analog/hybrid computers	0.32	0.05	0.21	0.16	0.03
7522 Digital computers	1.21	1.34	1.57	1.49	1.58
7523 Digital processing units	2.10	1.37	2.78	2.61	1.38
7526 ADP peripheral units	4.86	10.27	5.53	4.85	2.39
7527 ADP storage units	7.55	5.13	5.42	4.94	6.43
7529 ADP equipment n.e.c.	20.41	9.83	9.34	12.90	12.39
Total telecommunication equipment (764)	4.75	3.61		2.16	1.15
7641 Telephone equipment	7.41	8.16		6.43	2.54
7642 Microphones/speakers/etc	24.54	16.48		22.47	4.38
7643 Radio/TV transmit equipment	2.81	1.94		1.90	1.06
7648 Telecommunication equipment n.e.c.	3.30	4.17		3.17	15.59
7649 Telecommunication parts/accessory	1.54	3.40		1.47	0.96

Note: ADP = automatic data processing.
Source: Author's calculation, based on UNSTA (2008).

as part of the processing trade of wholly foreign-owned firms, can even reach the level of the G-3 exports, which are six times higher than those outside any zones with normal trade and those from private firms.

Their research also concluded that, "Chinese ATP imports from the United States were dominated by large-scale, sophisticated, high-valued equipment and devices, while Chinese ATP exports to the United States were still mainly small-scale products or components in the low-end of the ATP value-added chain." The relative unit price of the ICT products, which form the main part of China's high-tech exports, is quite low, even compared with other developing countries such as Brazil and India. The high relative unit value of India's computer equipment stems mainly from its automatic data-processing equipment (7529), which shares two-thirds of the total.

China's intra-industry trade

Intermediate goods and parts and component trade

The most general method to describe the international manufacturing sector is the intermediate goods in the broad economic categories (BECs) of the UN. The classification by Hummels et al. (2001) includes primary food and beverages for industry and industrial supplies (111, 21), processed food and beverages for industry and industrial supplies (121, 22), and parts and accessories from capital goods and transport equipment (42, 53). In Lemoine and Unal-Kesenci (2004), only the last two groups (semi-finished goods and parts and components) are included, together with processed fuels and lubricants (31). The first group and primary fuels and lubricants (32) are counted as a separate category of primary goods.

Under the classification of Hummels et al. (2001), intermediate goods always dominated China's imports and also became the largest export product group after 2005. In contrast, consumption goods only shared 4 percent of China's imports but contributed one-third of the total exports, although this

Table 3.17 Classification of intermediate goods by BEC

HIY 1999	UNBEC codes	LUK 2004	
Intermediate goods	111, 21, & 31		Primary goods
	121, 22, & 32	Semi-finished goods	Intermediate goods
	42 & 53	Parts and components	
Capital goods	41 & 521	Capital goods	Final goods
Consumption goods	112, 122, 522, & 6	Consumption goods	

Source: Hummels et al. (2001), Lemoine and Unal-Kesenci (2004).

Table 3.18 Structure of China's trade under BEC classification

	1995	1998	2000	2005	2007
Export					
Capital goods	11.90	15.03	17.27	26.41	27.98
Consumption goods	47.79	47.89	43.75	32.51	29.43
Intermediate goods	36.33	34.27	35.73	38.56	40.67
Import					
Capital goods	25.55	19.40	17.55	19.40	18.23
Consumption goods	4.88	4.08	3.89	3.29	3.52
Intermediate goods	63.80	71.47	68.42	66.72	66.19

Source: Author's calculation, based on UNSTA (2008).

dropped from half of the total. Furthermore, the share of capital goods in China's exports exceeded their share in imports from 2000, so that China became a net exporter then.

Intermediate goods have been the main product group comprising China's trade deficit from the mid 1990s. The deficit of intermediate goods reached US$146 billion in 2004 and kept its level until 2007. Together with the sharp rise in the surplus of consumption goods and the appearance of capital goods, the reduced deficit of intermediate goods meant that the total surplus almost tripled from 2004 to 2005. This shows China's trade pattern has changed, and the increase in its intra-industry trade ratio has reversed, just like its processing export ratio. Overall, China has become a large net producer of consumption goods and capital goods by importing intermediates and fuels.

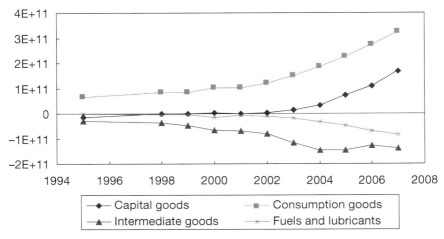

Figure 3.15 Composition of China's trade surplus
Source: Author's calculation, based on UNSTA (2008).

82 *Pattern and sophistication of "world workshop"*

China's intermediate exports formed 8.3 percent of the world's total in 2007, quadrupled from 1995 and close to the share of its merchandise exports at 8.8 percent. However, its imports' share was 2 percent higher, having tripled over the previous 12 years, which made China the second-largest importer of intermediate goods. Although Germany and Japan are net exporters of intermediate goods, the United States became a net importer from 1998, and its deficit reached its peak of 84 billion in 2005.

Among all intermediate goods, industrial supplies (code 2) were still the largest subgroup in both exports and imports in 2007, but the parts and

Table 3.19 Share of intermediate trade in the world market

	1995	1998	2000	2005	2007
Export					
China	2.05	2.49	3.11	6.53	8.29
Germany		10.35	9.04	10.20	10.28
Japan	8.76	7.55	8.54	6.92	6.14
United States	12.88	15.20	16.00	11.40	10.78
Import					
China	3.17	3.84	5.20	9.47	10.41
Germany		8.27	7.12	7.69	8.16
Japan	5.35	4.53	5.04	4.25	4.15
United States	12.18	14.75	15.98	12.82	11.22

Source: Author's calculation, based on UNSTA (2008).

Table 3.20 Structure of China's intermediate goods trade

	1995	1998	2000	2005	2007
Export					
111 & 121	2.89	1.96	1.30	0.67	0.62
2	77.48	69.42	62.80	55.58	56.80
42 & 53	19.63	28.61	35.90	43.76	42.58
Import					
111 & 121	6.57	3.35	2.89	2.98	3.23
2	71.01	66.20	61.69	52.75	52.36
42 & 53	22.42	30.45	35.41	44.27	44.41
Deficit					
111 & 121	13.16	5.70	5.08	7.62	12.64
2	59.44	60.73	60.18	47.07	36.37
42 & 53	27.40	33.56	34.74	45.30	50.99

Source: Author's calculation, based on UNSTA (2008).

components (codes 42, 53) trade represented a larger proportion within the deficit. The share of the parts and components trade doubled from 1995 and was set to surpass the share of industrial supplies in the near future. China's structure change shows intra-industry trade upgraded to the assembly of machinery and transport equipment, especially ICT products.

Actually, the parts and component trade has already become another important structural measurement of intra-industry trade. The method based on SITC classification was mainly from Ng and Yeats (2003) in Revision 2 and Athukorala (2003) in Revision 3. And the method based on HS classification was then brought by Ando and Kimura (2003). There are 79 5-Digit codes in the non-electronic machinery sectors in SITC classification and 73 4&6-Digit codes in HS; 71 codes in electronic machinery sectors in SITC and 37 in HS; 18 codes in transport equipment sectors in SITC and 9 in HS. Besides, there are both 31 codes in the professional/scientific optical/photographic instruments and clock & watch sectors in sectors of SITC & HS.

The estimate from Athukorala (2005) provides us with a basic landscape of China's parts and components industry. Together with the boom in China's manufacturing industry, its parts and components trade also quadrupled from the early 1990s to nearly 6 percent of the world's exports and 10 percent of the world's import in parts and components. As a net importer, the proportion of this trade type doubled, from more than 15 percent of China's imports in 1994 to 34 percent in 2003, but its share in China's exports was still 15 percent, which meant that the deficit in parts and components reached 50 billion that year. According to IMF data (2009), parts and components imports more than doubled, from US$70 billion in 2003 to more than US$160 billion in 2007, which was nearly 40 percent of its total imports.

The parts and components industry represented about 21 percent of the world's manufacturing trade and half the machinery and transport equipment trade (SITC sector 7) in 1992–1993, rising to 24 percent in 2004–2005. The EU-15, Japan, and the United States shared 74 percent of the world's total parts and components exports and 63 percent of imports in 1992–1993, dropping to 55 and 49 percent in 2004–2005. During the same period of time, the export share of the "Four Dragons" (Hong Kong SAR, Taiwan province of China, Korea, and Singapore) and "Four Tigers" (Indonesia, Malaysia, the Philippines, and Thailand) rose 8.3 percent, and the import share rose 3.7 percent. Among them, China's share rose 8.8 and 8.2 percent, respectively, accepting a large proportion of the transfer of the parts and components trade. Furthermore, the parts and components share in China's manufacturing exports rose from 5.3 to 19.5 percent, and the gap between imports rose from 12.4 percent to 19.3 percent, which made the deficit reach US$57.6 billion in 2004–2005.

Of all machinery and transport equipment, electrical machinery goods account for the highest share of parts and components in imports but quite a

Table 3.21 Parts and components trade

SITC Revision 3, 5-digit	HS, 4- & 6-digit
7 Machinery and transport equipment	
71 Power-generating machinery and equipment (14) 72 Machinery specialized for particular industries (28) 73 Metalworking machinery (6) 74 General industrial machinery and equipment, n.e.c., and machine parts, n.e.c. (31)	84 Nuclear reactors, boilers, machinery, and mechanical appliances; parts thereof (73)
75 Office machines and automatic data-processing machines (6) 76 Telecommunications and sound-recording and reproducers, and reproducing apparatus and equipment (4) 77 Electrical machinery, apparatus, and appliances, n.e.c., and electrical parts thereof (61)	85 Electrical machinery and equipment and parts thereof; sound recorders and reproducers, television image and sound recorders and parts and accessories of such articles (37)
78 Road vehicles (13) 79 Other transport equipment (5)	86 Railway or tramway locomotives, rolling stock and parts thereof; railway or tramway track fixtures and fittings and parts thereof; mechanical traffic signaling equipment of all kinds (1) 87 Vehicles other than railway or tramway rolling stock, and parts and accessories thereof (6) Chapter 88 Aircraft, spacecraft, and parts thereof (2)
8 Miscellaneous manufactured articles	
81 Prefabricated buildings; sanitary, plumbing, heating and lighting fixtures and fittings, n.e.c. (6) 82 Furniture, and parts thereof (2) 84 Articles of apparel and clothing accessories (2) 85 Footwear (1)	
87 Professional, scientific, controlling instruments, apparatus, n.e.c. (16) 88 Photographic equipment and supplies, optical goods; watches, etc. (16)	90 Optical, photographic, cinematographic, measuring, checking, precision, medical or surgical instruments and apparatus; parts and accessories thereof (27) 91 Clocks and watches, and parts thereof (5)
89 Miscellaneous manufactured articles, n.e.c. (14)	92 Musical instruments; parts and accessories of such articles (1)

Note: The numbers in brackets are the numbers of the codes within the category.
Source: Athukorala, P. (2003); Ando and Kimura (2003).

Pattern and sophistication of "world workshop" 85

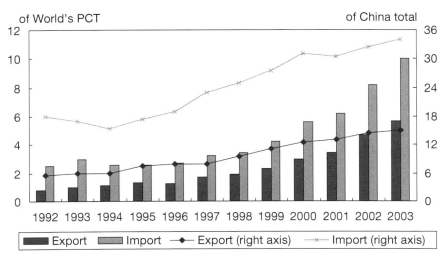

Figure 3.16 China's parts and components trade, 1992–2003
Source: Author's calculation, based on Athukorala (2005).

Table 3.22 Parts and components trade in world market

	Exports		Imports	
	1992–1993	*2004–2005*	*1992–1993*	*2004–2005*
World	100.0 (20.9)	100.0 (24.2)	100.0 (20.9)	100.0 (24.1)
EU-15	38.5 (18.8)	30.4 (19.6)	40.1 (19.1)	30.6 (20.3)
United States	18.8 (30.4)	13.5 (32.2)	19.3 (23.0)	14.2 (19.8)
Japan	16.6 (26.9)	11.1 (32.9)	3.4 (16.5)	4.2 (25.9)
China	1.2 (5.3)	10.0 (19.5)	2.6 (17.7)	10.8 (38.8)
Four Dragons	9.6 (22.0)	13.6 (34.9)	13.0 (25.3)	16.3 (39.2)
Four Tigers	3.4 (23.3)	7.7 (40.1)	5.8 (31.8)	6.2 (50.1)

Notes: Numbers in brackets are the shares of the parts and components trade in the manufacturing industry of the reporter; Four Dragons include Hong Kong SAR, Taiwan province of China, Korea, and Singapore; Four Tigers include Indonesia, Malaysia, the Philippines, and Thailand.
Source: Author's calculation, based on Athukorala (2008).

low share of exports, which means China is almost at the end of the assembly process of these products. This is similar to the situation for China's power-generating machinery, but parts and components for ICT goods and road vehicles also account for quite a high share of exports, which means China is in the middle of their processing and is more vertically specialized in these sectors. Parts and components for the sectors of specialized machinery and metalworking machinery have a much higher share of exports than imports, and this shows China is at the early stages of their processing.

Table 3.23 Share of parts and components of China

SITC	Export			Import		
	1992–3	1999–2000	2004–5	1992–3	1999–2000	2004–5
Total	22.3	34.7	36.7	32.5	56.6	63.4
71 Power-generating machinery	16.5	18.4	22.7	60.0	63.7	55.5
72 Specialized machinery	17.9	27.9	33.0	11.5	14.1	13.5
73 Metal-working machinery	21.8	27.5	28.5	13.1	16.6	16.8
74 General industrial machinery	12.6	29.2	38.5	23.8	31.5	36.8
75 Office machines	25.2	35.5	36.7	51.5	54.7	47.9
76 Telecommunications	40.9	42.6	35.1	48.5	61.4	74.0
77 Electrical machinery	15.0	23.9	24.4	70.3	80.8	87.5
78 Road vehicles	27.3	38.3	52.5	26.3	64.8	57.9
79 Other transport equipment	16.5	18.4	22.7	16.9	23.1	14.5

Source: Athukorala (2008).

Grubel–Lloyd index and vertical/horizontal intra-industry trade

Grubel and Lloyd (1975) first brought out an indicator to describe the intra-industry trade: the Grubel–Lloyd (GL) index was defined as follows:

$$B_k = [1 - \frac{|X_k - M_k|}{X_k + M_k}] \times 100 \tag{3.1}$$

Here, X_k refers to the exports of the industry, and M_k refers to its imports.

The weighted intra-industry trade (IIT) index across industries is as follows:

$$\overline{B}_k = \sum_{k=1}^{n} B_k \left[\frac{X_k + M_k}{\sum_{k=1}^{n}(X_k + M_k)} \right] \times 100 = \frac{\sum_{k=1}^{n}(X_k + M_k) - \sum_{k=1}^{n}|X_k - M_k|}{\sum_{k=1}^{n}(X_k + M_k)} \times 100 \tag{3.2}$$

The weight-adjusted IIT index across industries is as follows:

$$\overline{C}_k = \frac{\sum_{k=1}^{n}(X_k+M_k)-\sum_{k=1}^{n}|X_k-M_k|}{\sum_{k=1}^{n}(X_k+M_k)-|\sum_{k=1}^{n}(X_k-M_k)|} \times 100 \tag{3.3}$$

The descending GL index curve for the 260 three-digit trade groups shows the scope of the IIT of an economy: the convex curve for the United States shows that its trade was most deeply integrated into intra-industry specialization. If we use 50 as the lower limit, two-thirds of its trade groups (174) belong to IIT, and half of the Korean trade group (132) also belong. Even if we use 75 as the lower limit, there are still 106 groups from the United States, followed by 57 groups from Korea and 55 groups from China. Japan has the lowest level of IIT, with 36 groups that have a GL index greater than 75.

We can establish that the gap between China and Korea in the GL index mainly comes from the miscellaneous-manufactured-articles sector, and the adjusted GL index mainly comes from the machinery and transport-equipment sector. They are both separated by a wide gap from the United States in the latter sector in the adjusted GL index. China's mode in sector 8 is quite similar to that of Japan and Korea in sector 7; they have a large surplus in the total trade, leading to much higher adjusted GL indices than unadjusted ones at the sector level. This kind of difference is also the same in sectors 6–8 for the United States, because of the large deficit in total trade.

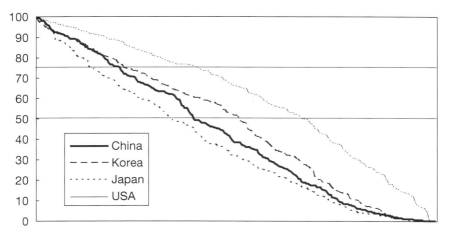

Figure 3.17 Descending GL index in 2005 (SITC Revision 3, 3-digit)
Source: Author's calculation based on UNSTA (2008).

88 *Pattern and sophistication of "world workshop"*

Table 3.24 GL index of China, Japan, Korea, US in 2005 (SITC Revision 3, 3-digit)

	China	Japan	Korea	US
Total	42.85	38.16	48.18	56.17
	(46.16)	(41.09)	(50.32)	(81.88)
5 Chemicals and related products	43.55	61.34	56.65	72.36
	(69.09)	(73.33)	(60.39)	(76.01)
6 Manufacture classified chiefly by material	49.68	43.47	60.03	60.36
	(64.35)	(52.58)	(64.36)	(98.39)
7 Machinery and transport equipment	52.30	43.71	54.33	65.41
	(57.86)	(84.81)	(84.27)	(82.74)
8 Miscellaneous manufactured articles	26.01	44.28	53.15	48.96
	(54.50)	(52.56)	(57.26)	(89.09)

Note: Numbers in brackets are the adjusted GL indices.
Source: Author's calculation, based on UNSTA (2008).

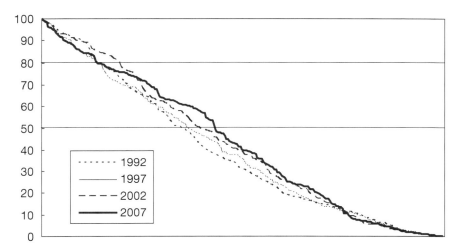

Figure 3.18 China's descending GL index (SITC Revision 3, 3-digit)
Source: Author's calculation, based on UNSTA (2008).

China's descending GL index curve has moved to the upper right gradually over the past 15 years. Interestingly, although the number of groups with a GL index above 50 increased from 90 in 1992 to 112 in 2007, those above 80 reached a peak of 50 in 2002 and returned to 36 in 2007. This meant that the unadjusted GL index of China's total trade dropped from 44.56 to 41.68. However, China's skyrocketing surplus meant that the adjusted GL index still rose 0.44 percent.

The source of this change mainly comes from the machinery and transport-equipment sector, which represents nearly half of China's trade, and its adjusted GL index continuously decreased over the past 15 years. The sharp rise in manufacturing, classified chiefly in the materials sector, and the drop

Pattern and sophistication of "world workshop" 89

in the miscellaneous-manufactured-articles sector from 2002 to 2007 show that China's IIT has expanded into a broader range of sectors that have been integrated into the world manufacturing division.

Another explanation lies with the three main categories under the BEC classification: primary goods, intermediate goods, and final goods. Brülhart (2008) points out that their GL indices all rose over the past four decades, around the world, but the indices of the first two groups remained unchanged after the late 1990s. For China, however, the GL index for its primary goods dropped quite fast, from 75.6 percent in 1998 to 13.6 percent in 2007, equaling the average level for the world, which is the same for China's final goods. However, the GL index for China's intermediate goods is almost double the

Table 3.25 GL index of China, 1992–2007 (SITC Revision 3, 3-digit)

	1992	1995	2000	2007
Total	37.50	40.44	44.56	41.68
	(38.51)	(43.10)	(46.95)	(47.39)
5 Chemicals and related products	34.68	37.86	37.54	50.36
	(61.92)	(54.63)	(65.65)	(70.02)
6 Manufacturing, classified chiefly by material	48.23	54.63	52.79	46.58
	(52.93)	(58.29)	(53.26)	(73.07)
7 Machinery and transport equipment	42.56	50.34	61.71	50.06
	(70.85)	(67.35)	(65.20)	(60.07)
8 Miscellaneous manufactured articles	22.05	20.30	20.86	27.75
	(78.55)	(78.04)	(81.15)	(60.94)

Note: Numbers in brackets are the adjusted GL indices.
Source: Author's calculation, based on UNSTA (2008).

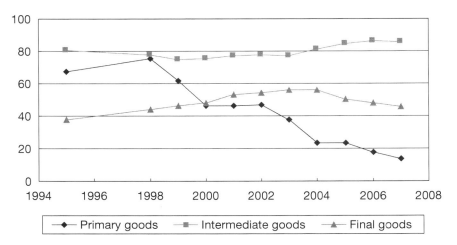

Figure 3.19 GL index of China's merchandising trade groups
Source: Author's calculation, based on UNSTA (2008).

world's average, and this means the materials for processing and parts and components are the main source of China's high GL index.

To classify different types of IIT and other trade modes, Abd-el-Rahman (1991) and Greenaway et al. (1995) developed the classification of vertical and horizontal IIT, based on the relative unit value. Fontagné and Freudenberg (1997) added a division of "one-way trade" in contrast to IIT. We here follow the method of Ando (2006) to first define one-way trade as follows:

$$\frac{Min(X_{kj}, M_{kj})}{Max(X_{kj}, M_{kj})} \leq 0.1 \qquad (3.4)$$

In other words, *horizontal IIT* is defined as the simultaneous export and import of the 3-digit SITC products, where the unit value of exports (measured f.o.b.) relative to the unit value of imports (measured c.i.f.) is within a range of ± 25 percent. Where the relative unit values are outside this range, the IIT is considered to be *vertical IIT*.

$$\frac{1}{1.25} \leq \frac{P_{kj}^X}{P_{kj}^M} \leq 1.25 \qquad (3.5)$$

China's one-way trade dropped from 43.2 percent in 1992 to 27.0 percent in 2007, and most was replaced by vertical IIT, which doubled to 59.4 percent of China's total trade between 1992 and 2007. The sector of miscellaneous manufactured articles has a much higher one-way trade proportion than other sectors, although its vertical IIT rose quite fast and reached the level of the manufacturing sector, classified chiefly by material. The horizontal intra-industry share of sector 6 is the highest, which means nearly half of its exports and imports have quite close unit values. The machinery and transport-equipment sector has a double share of vertical IIT of sectors 6 and 8, which means it was most deeply integrated into the world's section of the value chain.

Compared with other leading economies, China's share of one-way trade in miscellaneous manufactured articles is much higher because China's main export groups in this sector are furniture (82), travel goods (83), apparel and clothing (84), and footwear (85). For other economies, however, their exports consist more of professional instruments (86) and photographic and optical goods (87), which are more intra-industry specialized. Within the IIT of this sector, China's share of the vertical part is similar to Japan's and the United States', and China's share of vertical IIT in the machinery and transport-equipment sector is much higher, which is the result of China's being the processing center for globally outsourced ICT goods (groups 75 and 76).

Table 3.26 China's share of different trade patterns (SITC Revision 3, 3-digit)

	1992	1995	2000	2005	2007
One-way trade					
Total	43.19	39.06	31.87	28.88	27.02
5 Chemicals and related products	40.53	47.07	25.12	12.44	11.19
6 Manufacturing, classified chiefly by material	22.35	21.95	21.27	21.97	17.17
7 Machinery and transport equipment	35.78	26.19	15.88	10.70	7.91
8 Miscellaneous manufactured articles	71.22	70.98	69.27	58.87	57.88
Horizontal IIT					
Total	14.81	12.00	13.75	18.82	13.31
5 Chemicals and related products	7.00	5.43	13.96	10.91	33.23
6 Manufacturing, classified chiefly by material	33.46	31.10	34.95	32.40	42.55
7 Machinery and transport equipment	2.47	2.79	3.86	3.74[a]	4.62
8 Miscellaneous manufactured articles	4.18	5.37	3.99	4.94[b]	3.01
Vertical IIT					
Total	28.68	43.48	53.77	51.97	59.41
5 Chemicals and related products	49.07	40.22	60.92	76.65	55.58
6 Manufacturing, classified chiefly by material	42.98	41.55	43.78	45.63	40.28
7 Machinery and transport equipment	28.19	66.96	80.26	85.56[a]	87.46
8 Miscellaneous manufactured articles	11.36	19.54	26.74	36.19[b]	39.10

a Computer equipment (752) is kept within vertical IIT.
b Optical instruments (871) are kept within vertical IIT.
Source: Author's calculation, based on UNSTA (2008).

Vertical specialization

Hummels et al. (2001) introduced the method of "vertical specialization (VS)," the use of imported inputs in producing goods that are exported. They split the input–output (I–O) matrix into two parts, the imported coefficient matrix A^M and the domestic coefficient matrix A^D. Their sum A is the direct input coefficient matrix, and the VS share in export is:

$$VS = \frac{uA^M * [I - A^D]^{-1} * X^V}{X} \tag{3.6}$$

92 *Pattern and sophistication of "world workshop"*

Table 3.27 Share of different trade patterns in 2005 (SITC Revision 3, 3-digit)

	China	Japan	Korea	USA
One-way trade				
Total	28.88	24.84	27.05	15.36
5 Chemicals and related products	12.44	0.53	10.86	0.00
6 Manufacture classified chiefly by material	21.97	15.26	12.39	9.72
7 Machinery and transport equipment	10.70	6.56	20.48	2.13
8 Miscellaneous manufactured articles	58.87	28.61	5.50	26.99
Horizontal IIT				
Total	18.82	26.48	17.37	43.87
5 Chemicals and related products	10.91	15.09	18.34	38.91
6 Manufacture classified chiefly by material	32.40	20.52	50.68	42.43
7 Machinery and transport equipment	3.74	38.94	6.48	63.01
8 Miscellaneous manufactured articles	4.94	30.38	5.50	25.54
Vertical IIT				
Total	51.97	45.50	55.45	36.70
5 Chemicals and related products	76.65	84.37	70.81	59.48
6 Manufacture classified chieflyby material	45.63	64.22	36.93	47.86
7 Machinery and transport equipment	85.56	54.50	73.04	34.86
8 Miscellaneous manufactured articles	36.19	41.01	89.00	43.65

Source: Author's calculation, based on UNSTA (2008).

where u is a $1 \times n$ vector of 1s; A^M is the $n \times n$ imported coefficient matrix; I is the identity matrix; A^D is the $n \times n$ domestic coefficient matrix; X^V is an $n \times 1$ vector of exports; and X is the total of the country's exports. An element of A^M denotes the imported inputs from sector i used to produce one unit (expressed in any common currency) of sector j's output:

$$a_{ij}^M = \frac{I_{ij}^M}{Y_j} = \frac{I_{ij}^M}{I_{ij}} \cdot \frac{I_{ij}}{Y_i} = \frac{I_{ij}^M}{I_{ij}} a_{ij} = \frac{I_{ij}^M}{I_{ij}^D + I_{ij}^M} a_{ij} \qquad (3.7)$$

Here, a_{ij} is the element of the direct input coefficient matrix A. In practice, two assumption are needed: first is that the shares of imported intermediate goods throughout all sectors that use intermediates from sector i are equal to each other; and the second is that the share of imported intermediate goods equals that of imported final goods (Ping et al., 2005). Then, a_{ij}^M is calculated by the following proportion:

$$\frac{I_{i1}^M}{I_{i1}} = \ldots = \frac{I_{ij}^M}{I_{ij}} = \ldots = \frac{I_{in}^M}{I_{in}} = \frac{I_i^M}{I_i}$$

$$\frac{C_i^M}{C_i^D} = \frac{I_i^M}{I_i^D} = \frac{C_i^M + I_i^M}{C_i^D + I_i^D}$$

$$\Rightarrow a_{ij}^M = \frac{I_i^M}{I_i^D + I_i^M} a_{ij} = \frac{C_i^M + I_i^M}{C_i^D + I_i^D + C_i^M + I_i^M} a_{ij} = \frac{M_i}{Y_i} a_{ij}$$

(for j = 1, 2, 3 ... n) (3.8)

Dean et al. (2007) developed an amended method to calculate this proportion, which equals the share of processing imports and intermediates identified by the BEC classification as non-processing imports to total imports. They believe this definition is "conceptually and economically an improvement over the alternative methods of identifying intermediate imports."

For the categories of "intermediate inputs"(here includes fuels and lubricants) and "capital goods," Koopman et al. (2008) break down imports further into two subcategories: "processing imports" by customs declaration are classified as for processing exports, and the remaining imports are classified as for normal use. Capital goods are part of the final demand in a conventional I–O model. However, this classification can overestimate the import content of exports. They therefore also experiment with classifying a fraction of the capital goods as inputs in production. They use a mathematical programming method to infer an I–O table, with a processing export production account. The idea is to minimize the sum of squared errors in separating

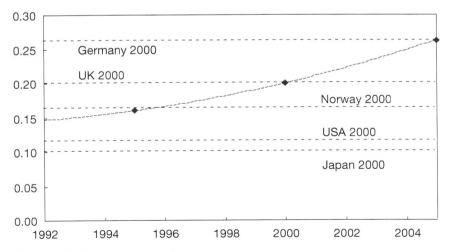

Figure 3.20 VS share of manufacturing
Source: Backer and Yamano (2008) and author's calculation.

the I–O relationships associated with processing exports from an existing I–O table, while maintaining all the logical resource flow constraints.

We think the more the method relies on the detailed split of an I–O table and fit for China's data, the less its results can be compared between countries. The measurement of industries' domestic value added by technology intensity was much more suited to international comparisons, and so here we choose the HYI method and the comparable I–O table of OECD countries and several non-member countries, such as China. The estimate by Ping et al. (2005) calculates the VS share of China's overall exports, which rose from 15.2 percent in 1997 to 21.0 percent in 2002.

Table 3.28 VS share of manufacturing sectors

	China		Japan	Germany	USA
	2000	2005[a]	2000	2000	2000
15–16 Food products, beverages and tobacco	0.05	0.05	0.50	0.09	0.02
17–19 Textiles, textile products, leather and footwear	0.11	0.08	0.13	0.28	0.17
20 Wood and wood and cork products	0.07	0.04		0.40	0.22
21–22 Pulp, paper products, printing, and publishing	0.85	0.16	0.15	0.27	0.08
23 Coke, refined petroleum products, and nuclear fuel	0.29	0.64	0.43	0.70	0.15
24 Chemicals and chemical products	0.70	0.55	0.14	0.35	0.16
25 Rubber & plastics products	0.11		0.10	0.31	0.15
26 Other non-metallic mineral products	0.08	0.05	0.08	0.11	0.20
27 Basic metals	0.72	0.60	0.28	0.69	0.93[b]
28 Fabricated metal products	0.07	0.10	0.04	0.21	0.20
29 Machinery & equipment, n.e.c.	0.31	0.27	0.03	0.12	0.07
31 Electrical machinery & apparatus, n.e.c.	0.40	0.21	0.12	0.23	0.18
30 Office, accounting, & computing machinery	0.16	0.36	0.04	0.30	0.19
32 Radio, television, & communication equipment	0.09		0.15	0.42	
33 Medical, precision, & optical instruments	0.15	0.22	0.06	0.09	
34–35 Transport equipment	0.07	0.15	0.02	0.14	0.12
36 Manufacturing n.e.c.; recycling (including furniture)	0.02	0.02	0.19	0.12	0.07

a Calculated according to 33-sector I–O table for China.
b Iron and steel only.
Source: Author's calculation, based on OECD (2006).

The use of imported inputs in producing goods that are exported, the VS share defined by Hummels et al. (2001), in China's manufacturing rose quite fast. It was about 16 percent in 1995, higher than Japan's 10 percent and the United States' 12 percent in 2000. China's VS share rose to 20 percent in 2000 and 26 percent in 2005, which is the level of the United Kingdom and Germany. This means the imported input share of China's manufacturing exports has reach quite a high level, considering that Germany's VS share includes intra-EU trade, and its manufacturing is deeply integrated into the international division of labor by intra-industry trade.

Observing the detailed manufacturing sectors, we can find out the source of China's high VS share, which is dominated by the raw-material and ICT sectors. The rise in China's VS share mainly comes from the ICT sectors (30, 32), which account for one-third of China's manufacturing exports. Their VS share reached 0.36, a similar level to Germany's and much higher than Japan's and the United States'; this has also happened in China's transport-equipment sector (34–35). China's VS share of medical, precision, and optical instruments (33) even rose to more than double that of Germany.

China's VS share of machinery and equipment (29) dropped from 0.31 to 0.27, but was still more than double that of Germany. Furthermore, although almost all the VS share of resource-related sectors (21–27) dropped to a similar level as that of other main economies between 2000 and 2005, that of chemicals and chemical products (24), which is the largest export sector among them, was still much higher than others, not to mention that petroleum products (23) even rose from 0.29 to 0.64 then.

Note

1. Including 5 Special Economic Zone, 15 Coastal Opening Cities, 56 Economic and Technology Development Zone, 53 National Hi-tech Industrial Development Zones, 12 Free Trade Zone, 14 Border Economic and Cooperation Zone, 10 Tourist and Holiday Resort, and 4 Taiwanese Investment Zone.

4 The competitiveness of the "world workshop"

China's place on the service part of global value chain

Grubel and Walker (1989) divided all industries in the service sector into three categories: consumer services, producer services, and government (social) services. Their producer services include the producer services and circulation (distribution) services defined in Browning and Singlemann (1975), which are also used in early ISIC classifications. Producer services include financial services, business services, marketing and sales, logistics, and communications. The ISIC classification of business services became much more specialized in its Revisions 3 and 4. In Revision 3, the R&D sector and other business appeared as two independent sectors, and other business sectors were then divided into eleven sectors in the newest Revision 4.

Before the economic census of 2004, China's classification of the service sector (GB/T 4754–2002) can hardly be compared with the ISIC one, especially as there were no other business services, and catering and communications were still not independent sectors. The overall value added of the service sector accounted for 40 percent of China's GDP, of which three-quarters were producer and consumer services. The independent scientific-research and business-research sectors (sharing 8.8 percent of the GDP of the United States) were still the two smallest ones, which shows that these activities were still deeply embedded in the production sectors.

R&D and technology standards

Research and development activity

A general indicator to measure the input of the R&D of a country is the proportion of its expenditure in GDP. Gao and Jefferson (2007) pointed out that China began its science and technology take-off after the late 1990s, and its R&D expenditure reached 1.5 percent of its GDP in 2007, which was the level of the United States in the mid 1950s, of Germany and Japan in the mid 1960s, and of Korea and Taiwan (China) in the mid and late 1980s. This proportion for all of them, except Taiwan (China), has doubled to nearly 3 percent today, following two different paths: the steep slope of the United

States and Korea and the shallow slope of Germany and Japan. China seems to be following the latter path.

A more important indicator for our analysis is the expenditure of business R&D, other than that from government, research institutions, and higher education. The total scale of China's business R&D expenditure increased tenfold from 1995 to 2006 and reached 50.2 billion international dollars (PPP method), which is half that of Japan and a quarter that of the United States.

Table 4.1 Evolution of the classification of business services sectors

ISIC Revisions 1 & 2	ISIC Revision 3	ISIC Revision 4
83: (Real estate and) Business services	71: Renting of machinery and equipment without operator and personal and household goods	77: Rental and leasing of activities
	72: Computer and related activities	60: Programming and broadcasting activities 62: Computer programming, consultancy, and related activities 63: Information service activities
	73: Research and development	72: Scientific research and development
	74: Other business activities	69: Legal and accounting activities 70: Activities of head offices; management consultancy activities 71: Architectural and engineering activities; technical testing and analysis 73: Advertising and market research 74: Other professional, scientific, and technical activities 75: Veterinary activities 78: Employment activities 79: Travel agency, tour operator, reservation service, and related activities 80: Security and investigation activities 81: Services to buildings and landscape activities 82: Office administrative, office support, and other business support activities

Source: UNSTA (various years).

Table 4.2 Structure of China's service sector

GB2002 (and ISIC Revision 3)	2004		2005		2006	
Wholesale and retail trades (50–52)	152.03	(7.79)	169.79	(7.39)	203.46	(7.30)
Hotels and catering services (55)	44.74	(2.29)	52.60	(2.29)	63.02	(2.26)
Transport, storage, and post (60–63)	113.58	(5.82)	135.93	(5.91)	164.14	(5.89)
Information transmission, computer services, and software (64 & 72)	51.71	(2.65)	59.81	(2.60)	70.08	(2.51)
Financial intermediation (65–67)	65.83	(3.37)	79.12	(3.44)	111.65	(4.01)
Real estate (70)	87.58	(4.49)	103.41	(4.50)	127.09	(4.56)
Leasing and business services (71 & 74)	32.07	(1.64)	36.53	(1.59)	43.14	(1.55)
Scientific research, technical services, and geologic prospecting (73)	21.47	(1.10)	25.73	(1.12)	31.68	(1.14)
Public services (75–99)	219.10	(11.23)	258.25	(11.24)	299.89	(10.76)

Note: Numbers in brackets are their share in GDP.
Source: Author's calculation, based on NBS (various years).

Table 4.3 Total business enterprise R&D (billions of international dollars)

	1981	1985	1990	1995	2000	2005	2006	2007
China				4.75 (43.68)	16.21 (59.96)	41.69 (68.32)	50.21 (71.08)	
EU-15	59.79 (62.38)	73.50 (64.15)	91.34 (64.95)	89.95 (62.16)	113.65 (64.59)	122.08 (63.39)	128.94 (63.89)	132.44
Japan	28.30 (60.68)	41.95 (66.81)	60.80 (70.86)	58.86 (65.21)	70.09 (70.96)	87.98 (76.45)	92.87 (77.16)	
Russia			27.43 (77.15)	6.01 (68.51)	8.31 (70.78)	10.92 (67.98)	11.61 (66.65)	13.58 (64.24)
United States	85.37 (69.31)	118.25 (71.50)	131.62 (70.48)	140.98 (70.53)	199.96 (74.58)	200.05 (69.83)	212.25 (71.04)	221.32 (71.91)

Note: Numbers in brackets are the share of business R&D in total R&D expenditure.
Source: Author's calculation, based on OECD (2008b).

Although this may have overestimated the business R&D of China, its escalation is also a result of its proportion of total R&D having caught up with other economies, from 43.7 percent in 1995 to 71.1 percent in 2006.

The intensity of business enterprise research and development (BERD) is measured by its share of total business value added. The data for China are estimated by using the total value added of secondary and tertiary industry (some tertiary industry, mainly government, education, and healthcare, is excluded) as the business value added. China's ratio rose from 0.3 percent in the early 1990s to 1.4 percent in 2007, overtaking Russia in 2004. However, its gap with the United States and Japan was even larger than that of the total R&D intensity.

The human resource input into China's R&D activity also increased quite fast: the total personnel (full-time equivalent, FTE) increased from 206,000 to nearly 1 million in 2006, overtaking Japan and Russia and close to the total of EU-15 countries; and the number of business researchers (FTE) in China had already doubled from 2000 to 0.78 million in 2006 and became the second largest, reaching two-thirds of the United States' figure in that year. China has accumulated a large-scale business research team, and it will certainly form the basis of its science and technology catch-up.

In China, the number of business researchers per total of employees had also caught up with the EU-15 countries in 2006: about 4.5 researchers per 1,000 employees. During the same period of time, the proportion in Russia dropped from 6.9 in 1995 to the same level in 2006. These levels only equal 40 percent of those in Japan and the United States, and this is the source of their technological advantage. China's business employment here is estimated by using the total employment of secondary and non-public tertiary industry

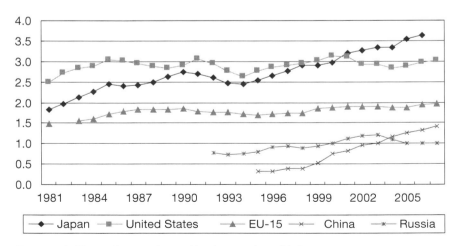

Figure 4.1 Share of BERD in total business value added
Source: Author's calculation, based on OECD (2008b).

100 *The competitiveness of the "world workshop"*

(employment in the sectors of social services, healthcare, education, and government are excluded).

Among the human-resource base of researchers, graduates with doctoral degrees certainly form an important part. In the early 1980s, China had almost no doctoral graduates, but the number grew very fast after 2000, nearly

Table 4.4 Total business personnel and researchers (1,000 FTE)

	1981	1985	1991	1995	2000	2005	2006
Total personnel							
China			206.0	317.5	480.8	883.1	987.8
Russia				787.6	628.9	524.0	515.3
OECD							
EU-15	732.9	785.6	871.1	845.2	976.3	1,052.0	1,102.9
Japan	363.9	451.3	563.0	573.7	581.7	609.8	619.2
US							
Researchers							
China			126.0	192.9	353.8	696.4	777.0
Russia				368.3	289.9	238.0	236.8
OECD	965.0	1,231.8	1,500.7	1,740.8	2,161.0	2,492.7	2,590.7
EU-15	244.2	289.2	374.8	388.6	483.5	582.7	612.9
Japan	192.9	251.8	340.8	384.1	421.4	481.5	483.3
United States	498.8	646.8	776.4	789.4	1,041.3	1,097.7	1,135.5

Source: Author's calculation, based on OECD (2008b).

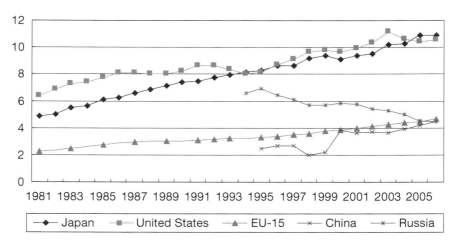

Figure 4.2 Number of business R&D researchers per 1,000 employees
Source: Author's calculation, based on OECD (2008b).

Table 4.5 Doctoral degree graduates (persons)

	1980	1990	2000	2005	2006
Total					
China			11,004	27,677	36,247
United States	32,615	38,371	44,808	52,631	56,067
Science and engineering degrees					
China			7,019	14,885	19,371
United States	10,160	14,630	16,547	18,767	20,645

Source: Author's calculation, based on NBS (various years) and US Census Bureau (various years).

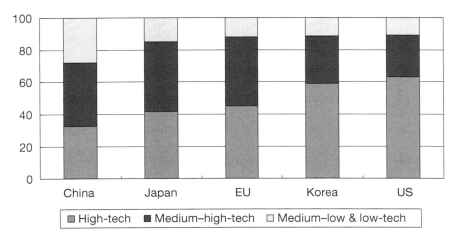

Figure 4.3 Structure of manufacturing business R&D by technological intensity, 2004
Note: The data for China are from the 2004 census.
Source: OECD (2007).

quadrupling within 6 years from 11,000 to 36,000 in 2006. Among them, those who have science and engineering degrees are closer to manufacturing development. In China, the number of these graduates tripled during that period, to 19,000 in 2006, catching up with the United States.

If we divide the R&D expenditure by technology intensity, we find that China's structure is still quite different from that of other main economies. Its proportion of medium–low and low-tech sectors reached 27.8 percent, which is close to the share of high-tech sectors (32.7 percent). The proportion of high-tech sectors in Japan and the EU is higher, nearly 45 percent of total R&D expenditure, and close to the share of their medium–high-tech sectors. However, the R&D expenditure of the high-tech sectors in Korea and the United States dominated their expenditure with about 60 percent.

The OECD classification of the manufacturing sector by technology intensity is actually divided by the R&D intensity, measured by the share of R&D expenditure in the industrial value added. Interestingly, although the R&D expenditure in several of China's sectors (such as 32, 35, and 33) has a higher intensity, their intensity is still quite low (about a quarter) compared with that of the United States, Germany, and Japan (sector 35 of Japan is lower than China, in contrast). This explains the low proportion of the high-tech sectors in China's overall manufacturing R&D expenditure.

China's R&D researcher intensity shows the same pattern. Its ICT sectors (30 and 32) and sectors 33 and 35 also have a higher intensity within its manufacturing sectors. However, the intensity of China's ICT sectors is only one-tenth that of Japan and one-twentieth that of the United States—much higher than the gap in overall manufacturing.

Across all high-tech industries, China only has similar R&D expenditure intensity in the aircraft and spacecraft industry. The two healthcare-related industries have a similar intensity to Korea. The two ICT industries have quite low intensity, because FIEs dominated their production, and China only controlled the assembly, not the R&D in the home countries of those enterprises. The intensity in the office-, accounting-, and computing-machinery industry is only 2.77 percent of its value added, which is the lowest in China's machinery and electronic-equipment industries (29–35).

Although FIEs are only 10.40 percent of the total number of industrial enterprises, they share about 21 percent of China's GIO, 19 percent of R&D expenditure (but only 11.2 percent of R&D personnel FTE), and one-quarter of China's invention-patent applications. In contrast, although private enterprises represent 43.17 percent of total industrial enterprises, they only share 17.43 percent of the GIO and 7.65 percent of R&D expenditure. Interestingly, they share 17.73 percent of invention-patent applications, compared with SOEs, which share 11.96 percent of the R&D expenditure but only contribute 4.92 percent of invention patents.

The variation in R&D intensity among different types of enterprise is based on their expenditure structure. For China's domestic enterprises, nearly half of their R&D expenditure is in the medium–high-tech sectors, such as machinery or general electronic equipment, and one-quarter is in the high-tech sectors, which represent only one-seventh for the SOEs. However, the high-tech sectors share nearly half of the expenditure of non-domestic enterprises.

Patent

Patents are usually treated as an important output of R&D activity. The volume of patent applications and grants in China (by office) and from China (by country of origin) "exploded" after its entry into the WTO, being called a "great wall of patents" by Hu and Jefferson (2009). China's patent office has become the third-largest filing office, sharing 11.93 percent of the world's patent applications and 7.95 percent of patent grants in 2006. As the originator

Table 4.6 R&D intensity across sectors, 2004

	Expenditure in value added (%)					Researchers (FTE) per 1,000 employees				
	China	Germany	Japan	Korea	US	China	Germany	Japan	Korea	US
Total manufacture	1.90	8.19	10.24	4.96	7.22	6.33	52.82	36.30	53.19	
15–16 Food, beverages, and tobacco	0.63	0.74	2.40	0.96	0.95	3.05	11.05	12.01	10.29	
17–19 Textiles, fur, and leather	0.85	2.07	2.85	0.51	1.13	0.94	9.93	2.46	8.60	
20–22 Wood, paper, printing, publishing	0.88	0.66	1.27	0.21		1.75		6.64	2.00	
23–25 Coke, petroleum, nuclear fuel, chemicals and products, rubber, and plastics	2.02	9.99	11.57	3.23	9.52	6.97	82.71	38.62	75.55	
26 Non-metallic mineral products	0.91	2.18	3.47	1.10	1.21	2.01	22.54	9.85	13.52	
27 Basic metals	1.85	1.43	4.85	1.36	0.97	6.73	43.13	9.52	10.67	
28 Fabricated metal products, except machinery and equipment	0.75	1.37	1.41	0.64	1.15	2.02	10.04	4.64	11.07	
29 Machinery and equipment, n.e.c.	4.39	5.96	8.47	3.15	4.17	13.26	46.72	19.57	51.59	
30 Office, accounting and computing machinery	2.27	12.83		4.19	17.07	16.65		71.59	359.35	
31 Electrical machinery and apparatus n.e.c.	2.73	3.69	25.10	2.26	4.04	8.45	122.09	18.50	34.69	
32 Radio, TV, and communications equipment and apparatus	6.65	29.85	28.69	12.72	25.61	18.50	198.90	154.05	328.16	
33 Medical, precision, and optical instruments, watches and clocks (instruments)	4.44	15.50	20.97	8.88	15.89	17.52	99.40	65.54	122.51	
34 Motor vehicles, (semi-) trailers	3.52	19.81	15.19	8.30	10.40	12.44		64.79	32.89	
35 Other transport equipment	5.02	27.53	3.38	4.58	16.57	18.44		33.27	27.88	

Source: Author's calculation, based on OECD (2008b) and NBS (2006).

of patents, China is still the fourth-largest applicant, after Korea, and fifth-largest grantee, after Germany.

Even if we just consider China's resident patents (their share of China's total patent applications rose from 38.8 percent in 1997 to 62.4 percent in 2007, and their share of patent grants also rose, from 27.3 percent in 2002 to 48.0

Table 4.7 R&D intensity in high-tech industries, 2003

	China	Japan	Korea	EU-11	US
Total high-tech industry	5.50	25.74	19.47	24.19	29.01
Aircraft and spacecraft	16.17	12.47	26.90		30.82
Pharmaceuticals	4.02	23.75	5.12	26.50	20.71
Office, accounting, and computing machinery	2.77	95.67	14.67	20.89	32.99
Radio, television, and communication equipment	6.40	15.19	23.00	34.57	26.87
Medical, precision, and optical instruments	6.40	32.71	7.28	12.86	42.10

Notes: Data for China are data for large and medium enterprises; EU-11 refers to EU-15, excluding Austria, Greece, Luxembourg, and Portugal, and the data are for 2002.
Source: Author's calculation, based on NBS, NDRC, and MOST (various years).

Table 4.8 Share of non-domestic and foreign-funded enterprise, 2004

	Enterprise number	GIO	R&D expenditure	R&D personnel (FTE)	Invention-patent application
Domestic	79.32	67.27	72.88	82.00	66.38
State-owned	8.47	11.62	11.96	15.17	4.92
Private	43.17	17.43	7.65	9.75	17.73
Non-domestic	20.68	32.73	27.12	6.79	33.62
Foreign-funded	10.40	20.95	19.06	11.20	25.37

Note: Non-domestic enterprise includes foreign-funded enterprise and enterprises with funds from Hong Kong, Macao, and Taiwan.
Source: Author's calculation, based on NBS (2006).

Table 4.9 R&D expenditure structure

	Total	Domestic	State-owned & holding	Non-domestic
Low	9.05	8.83	6.54	9.59
Medium–low	16.32	19.88	23.68	7.42
Medium–high	44.03	46.78	56.66	35.87
High	30.61	24.50	13.12	47.12

Note: Non-domestic enterprise includes foreign-funded enterprise and enterprises with funds from Hong Kong, Macao, and Taiwan.
Source: Author's calculation, based on NBS (2006).

Table 4.10 Share of total invention patents

	By office				By country of origin		
	1985	1995	2000	2006	1995	2000	2007
Application							
China	0.93	1.77	3.81	11.93	1.00	1.94	9.27
Germany	4.81	4.38	4.56	3.43	6.71	8.34	7.52
Japan	32.51	35.00	30.77	23.16	39.04	35.87	28.94
Korea	1.15	7.45	7.48	9.42	6.41	6.28	10.10
United States	12.50	21.65	21.70	24.14	17.86	20.11	23.51
Grant							
China	0.01	0.80	2.56	7.95	0.41	1.27	4.72
Germany	4.93	3.77	2.88	2.89	7.22	7.92	7.20
Japan	12.67	25.72	24.64	19.44	34.09	32.89	32.74
Korea	0.57	2.95	6.84	16.61	2.13	5.80	15.05
United States	18.12	23.91	30.83	23.89	24.19	26.15	19.86

Source: Author's calculation, based on WIPO (2008).

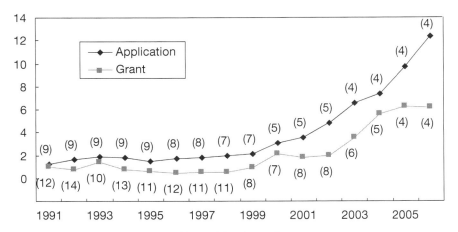

Figure 4.4 China's share of world's resident invention patents
Note: The numbers in brackets are China's ranking in the world.
Source: Author's calculation, based on WIPO (2008).

percent in 2007), its tripling from from 2000 to 2006 is certainly an "explosion," which has made China the fourth largest in the world. Its applications reached 12.3 percent of the world's total in 2006, and its grants also reached 6.2 percent, taking into consideration the general pendency time lasting from 20 to 40 months.

Enterprises have come to dominate applications for resident patents, together with grants, especially with regard to invention patents. Their share in invention-patent applications tripled from 13.99 percent in 1990 to 48.28 percent in 2007, and their share in grants also rose, from 17.93 percent to 40.23 percent. This shows that enterprises have already became the main source of R&D output. In addition, among all enterprises, manufacturing enterprises particularly dominated invention-patent applications. The 2004 census shows that, of all 27,029 applications, manufacturing enterprises applied for 20,077, or three-quarters of the total.

Interestingly, within the manufacturing sectors, medium–high-tech industries presented more patent applications than high-tech industries. Among all manufacturing enterprises, these industries were responsible for 45.4 percent of triadic-patent applications and 39.34 percent of invention-patent application. Furthermore, they also owned 46.35 percent of all the invention patents in force. This may relate to the structure of R&D expenditure, where medium–high-tech industries also have the largest proportion.

Table 4.11 Share of enterprises in resident patents

	1990	1995	2000	2005	2007
Application	16.28	17.21	32.68	33.25	38.10
Invention	13.99	10.84	32.81	43.00	48.28
Utility	13.93	10.91	21.78	28.71	35.21
Design	40.12	39.08	48.64	31.37	34.02
Grant	15.82	13.06	32.89	34.44	36.08
Invention	17.93	13.40	16.45	37.25	40.23
Utility	13.43	8.70	23.56	31.67	36.02
Design	42.38	26.82	50.45	36.63	35.05

Source: Author's calculation based on NBS (Various Years).

Table 4.12 Total manufacturing patents by technological intensity, 2004

	Triadic application		*Invention application*		*Invention owned*	
	Total	LME	Total	LME	Total	LME
Low-tech	9,149	5,115	2,213	3,637	1,002	1,917
	(14.49)	(12.50)	(11.02)	(7.40)	(12.37)	(11.21)
Medium–low-tech	8,530	5,217	2,741	5,261	1,629	3,366
	(13.51)	(12.75)	(13.65)	(12.02)	(17.89)	(19.68)
Medium–high-tech	28,675	19,256	7,899	13,630	5,134	7,237
	(45.41)	(47.05)	(39.34)	(37.90)	(46.35)	(42.32)
High-tech	16,792	11,337	7,224	6,877	5,782	4,582
	(26.59)	(27.70)	(35.98)	(42.68)	(23.39)	(26.79)

Notes: Total enterprises mean all enterprises with revenue above 5 million yuan. LME = large and medium enterprises.
Source: Author's calculation, based on NBS (2006).

Table 4.13 High-tech-related patent applications by field of technology (2001–2005 average)

	ISIC	Japan	United States	Germany	Korea	China
I: Electrical engineering						
Computer technology	30	256,879	195,085	26,145	45,345	19,186
Audio-visual technology	32	278,958	65,750	15,550	52,953	10,561
Telecommunications	32	206,626	110,999	20,679	66,682	19,960
Digital communication	32	63,195	77,898	12,516	20,860	12,497
Semiconductors	32	219,804	70,207	19,165	63,183	8,478
II: Instruments						
Optics	33	287,600	58,981	16,438	41,536	8,642
Medical technology	33	104,453	181,798	44,478	10,098	22,472
III: Chemistry						
Pharmaceuticals	2423	36,521	134,682	30,887	5,290	26,730

Note: Fields of technology overlap and cannot be summed up directly.
Source: Author's calculation, based on WIPO (2008).

Compared with the patent giants, China still has a big gap in high-tech-related patent applications. Those of the ICT industries are less than one-tenth of Japan's (except for digital communications), about one-fifth of those of the United States, and one-third of Korea's. China's disadvantage mainly relates to semiconductors and optics, which are used more in parts and components than in assembly. The United States has a higher number of patent applications in medical technology and pharmaceuticals, and China only has one-eighth of the former and one-fifth of the later. However, China has overtaken Korea in these two industries.

A more generally accepted measurement is the Patent Cooperation Treaty (PCT), because the patents it covers will be accepted by its 141 member countries. China's applications rose from 1,706 (1.4 percent of the world's) in 2004 to 6,089 (3.7 percent) in 2008, which advanced its ranking to sixth in 2008, just after France. According to the OECD (2008a), the annual growth of China's PCT filing was the highest around the world from 1997 to 2007, at about 44 percent (46 percent of those from high- and medium–high-tech industries, and 33 percent from medium–low- and low-tech industries). Huawei overtook Philips to become the largest PCT patent applicant in 2008 (with 1,737 applications, having been fourth largest in 2006, with 1,365 applications). ZTE overtook GE and rose to thirty-eighth (with 329 applications, from fifty-first in 2006, with 235 applications).

Table 4.14 PCT international applications by country of origin

	2004		2005		2006		2007		2008	
US	43,350	(1)	46,803	(1)	50,941	(1)	54,086	(1)	53,521	(1)
Japan	20,264	(2)	24,869	(2)	27,033	(2)	27,744	(2)	28,744	(2)
Germany	15,214	(3)	15,984	(3)	16,732	(3)	17,818	(3)	18,428	(3)
Korea	3,558	(7)	4,688	(6)	5,944	(5)	7,061	(4)	7,908	(4)
China	1,706	(13)	2,503	(10)	3,951	(8)	5,441	(7)	6,089	(6)

Note: The numbers in brackets are the ranking of the country in the world.
Source: Author's calculation, based on WIPO (2009).

Technology standards

Technology standards are actually located in the upper end of the value chain, compared with R&D, which are still at the enterprise level. Technology standards are accepted throughout an industry's producers and developers, nationally or even internationally. They are the baseline for entering an industry, but are also a barrier at the same time. In today's international market, 99.8 percent of all technology standards used are established by the leading developed economies (Zhao, 2008).

China began to earn its position on the Technical Committee/Subcommittees and the Working Groups from 2002. Its secretariats in the former rose from six in 2002 to seventeen in 2007, and its convenorships in the Working Groups also increased, from thirteen to twenty-seven. In addition, China was elected one of the eighteen council members in 2008. However, the International Standard Organization (ISO) as a whole is still dominated by leading developed economies, such as the United States, the United Kingdom, Germany, France, and Japan, who share two-thirds of all the positions.

Furthermore, compared with the ISO, the national standards of China, Guo Biao (GB), still have a 10 percent higher share in agriculture and food technology, but 5 percent lower transport and distribution of goods. This is related to China's industrial structure, which still has a high proportion in agriculture and a low proportion in (producer) services. However, China's structure within manufacturing-related sectors is quite interesting, being 10 percent lower in engineering technologies but similar in electronics and ICT. This is related to the comparative lack of traditional engineering and the large-scale ICT outsourcing in China.

Today, private technology standards, especially in the ICT sectors, are more the output of leading companies' R&D. When their patent (group) becomes an industry standard, great rewards will be generated by the royalties and license fees. The fierce competition for the next-generation video disk, between the Blu-ray group (Sony, Philips, and Panasonic) and high-definition DVD (Hitachi and NEC), from 2002 to 2008, became a classic case of this kind of standard. Each side has invested huge amounts in R&D expenditure, but the winner will benefit from a huge market and enjoy billions of license fees in the future.

China has already begun to set up several important technical standards in ICT-related fields since 2000, when Time Division Synchronous CDMA was accepted as one of the three main standards for 3rd-generation mobile telecommunications. However, its standard for the next-generation wireless

Table 4.15 ISO member bodies' contribution

	2002	2003	2004	2005	2006	2007
Number of secretariats (Technical Committee/Subcommittees)						
Total	721	715	720	717	713	728
USA	138	135	130	124	124	126
United Kingdom	104	98	99	100	92	87
Germany	121	123	124	126	128	134
France	84	81	79	77	77	76
Japan	39	41	45	47	49	54
Republic of Korea	5	5	9	10	13	12
China	6	7	9	9	12	17
Number of convenorships (Working Groups)						
Total	2,055	2,060	2,057	2,071	2,137	2,173
USA	494	473	469	472	473	487
United Kingdom	345	347	338	339	335	340
Germany	349	358	351	348	367	378
France	188	183	181	174	175	182
Japan	113	115	118	121	140	142
Republic of Korea	5	8	12	13	14	18
China	13	14	16	16	20	27

Source: ISO (various years).

Table 4.16 Pattern of standards in force

International classification for standards	GB		ISO	
Generalities, infrastructures, and sciences (01–07)	977	(4.67)	1,544	(8.69)
Health, safety, and environment (11–13)	2,216	(10.59)	699	(3.93)
Engineering technologies (17–27)	3,727	(17.81)	4,829	(27.18)
Electronics, ICT (29–39)	3,629	(17.34)	2,990	(16.83)
Transport and distribution of goods (43–55)	1,244	(5.94)	1,896	(10.67)
Agriculture and food technology (59–67)	3,284	(15.69)	1,023	(5.76)
Material technologies (71–87)	5,122	(24.47)	4,264	(24.00)
Construction (91–95)	495	(2.37)	376	(2.12)
Special technologies (97)	236	(1.13)	144	(0.81)

Source: Author's calculation, based on China National Knowledge Infrastructure (2009) and ISO (various years).

intranet, the WLAN Authentication and Privacy Infrastructure, experienced a long period of debate and freezing on the ISO/IEC joint technical conference, after it was announced as a national standard in China from June 2004. In June 2009, it was finally accepted as an independent part of the international standard.

In 2002, China began to draft its own coding standard for audio-video and tried to get a position in the next generation of video disks. The Advanced Video-coding Standard has been accepted as one of the coding standards within the Blu-ray group, but its main achievement has been its role in the establishment of the international standard for Internet Protocol Television: China finally contributed a third of the total document for that standard for the International Telecommunication Union (ITU). In May 2007, it became one of the four video-coding standards within the overall standard.

The established standards, such as Digital Multimedia Broadcast-Terrestrial or Intelligent Grouping and Resources Sharing, now mainly rely on policy support and compulsory use within China. However, other standards aiming to catch up with mature international standards meet more of a challenge from the market than policies. For example, the attempt to set up China's own Blu-ray disk, on the one hand, faced the license fee from the Blu-ray Group and, on the other hand, faced the charge of infringement from its predecessor,

Table 4.17 China's current ICT standards

Chinese standard	International standard
Adopted standards	
1. Time Division Synchronous CDMA	Wideband CDMA CDMA2000
2. WLAN Authentication and Privacy Infrastructure	IEEE 802.11i
3. Advanced (Audio-) Video-coding Standard	ISO/IEC Advanced Video Coding, ITU-T H.264
Establishing standard	
1. Intelligent Grouping and Resources Sharing; ITopHome	Universal Plug and Play Digital Home Work Group
2. China Radio Frequency Identification Tagging	Ubiquitous Identification Electronic Product Code—Global
3. Digital Multimedia Broadcast—Terrestrial	Advanced Television Systems Committee Digital Video Broadcasting—Terrestrial
Catching-up standards	
1. China Blue High-definition Disk	Blu-ray Disk
2. Dragon Chip	Intel, AMD

Source: Author's design, based on Zhao (2008) and Hu and Jefferson (2008).

The competitiveness of the "world workshop" 111

China's own DVD standard (Enhanced Versatile Disk). There is also still a big gap between China's own CPU, the "dragon chip," and the products of Intel and AMD, even if it is based on a different instruction set from them.

China and the outsourcing of R&D and business services

The definition and coordination of the services sector are carried out by the UN System of National Accounts and the IMF's *Balance of Payment Manual*. Until 2007, China was the fifth-largest service importer and the seventh-largest exporter, and its share of the world totals rose from 0.5 and 0.7 percent, respectively, in 1982, to 4.2 and 3.7 percent, respectively, in 2007. However, since 1992 (except 1994), China has become a net importer of commercial services, and its deficit reached its peak, US$0.95 billion, in 2004. Furthermore, the peak of the service trade within the total goods and service trade appeared before China's entry into the WTO.

The service trade has varied proportions between different countries. Interestingly, developed countries such as Japan and Germany had similar shares of exports as Brazil and China before 2000. However, the shares of China and Mexico (even from 1995) both dropped after that, because of their deep integration into the global production division, which also made the share of services in their import the lowest among all the main economies. In contrast, India has quite a high share of service trade, like the United Kingdom and the United States, especially after the boom of the "dot.com" economy, and has become an offshore outsourcing center for computer and information services.

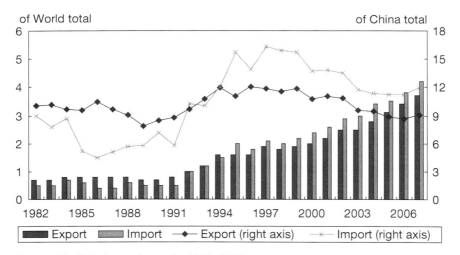

Figure 4.5 China's service trade, 1982–2007
Source: Author's calculation, based on Bureau of Service Trade, MOC (2008).

112 The competitiveness of the "world workshop"

Table 4.18 Service trade in total goods and service trade

	Export				Import			
	1982	1990	2000	2006	1982	1990	2000	2006
Brazil	7.94	10.55	13.99	11.52	18.78	23.01	20.87	22.07
China	9.99	8.47	10.79	8.62	8.82	7.16	13.74	11.25
India	23.21	20.42	27.44	38.31	18.69	20.13	26.83	26.46
Mexico	13.68	15.07	7.54	6.14	24.91	18.77	8.38	7.69
Russia			8.31	9.22			26.65	21.01
France	26.48	25.71	19.61	19.17	19.00	20.26	14.95	16.48
Germany	11.65	10.72	12.61	13.09	18.20	18.97	21.45	19.04
Japan	12.75	12.58	12.47	15.11	20.40	26.37	23.36	18.77
United Kingdom	22.92	22.52	29.35	33.96	18.41	16.70	21.78	22.28
United States	19.02	25.24	26.23	27.73	12.72	15.93	14.17	13.85
World	16.97	19.02	19.07	18.64	17.55	19.04	18.30	17.34

Source: Author's calculation, based on World Bank (2008).

Table 4.19 China's commercial services trade, 2006 (US$100 million)

	Total			From FIEs		
	Export	Import	Surplus	Export	Import	Surplus
Transportation services	210.15	343.69	−133.54	76.73	61.87	14.86
Travel	339.49	243.22	96.27	10.44	5.56	4.88
Other commercial services	364.56	416.35	−51.79	166.92	158.77	8.15
Communications services	7.38	7.64	−0.26	3.19	1.4	1.79
Construction	27.53	20.5	7.03	4.26	4.32	−0.06
Insurance services	5.48	88.31	−82.83	1.55	2.32	−0.77
Financial services	1.45	8.91	−7.46	0.04	1.47	−1.43
Computer and information services	29.58	17.39	12.19	25.92	13.94	11.98
Royalties and license fees	2.05	66.34	−64.29	0.72	55.25	−54.53
Other business services	289.72	206.05	83.67	131.15	80.03	51.12
Consulting	78.34	83.89	−5.55	53.92	55.78	−1.86
Advertising	14.45	9.55	4.9	10.24	4.43	5.81
Other business service n.e.c.	196.93	112.61	84.32	66.99	19.82	47.17

Source: Author's calculation, based on Bureau of Service Trade, MOC (2008).

Of all the service trade of China, other business service (R&D activity was included, based on the classification of the Balance of Payment (BOP)) is the third-largest group, after transport and travel, and the second-largest source of the surplus. Unlike transportation and travel, FIEs share 40 percent of the other business service trade and more than half of its surplus. FIEs here are the main bodies importing royalties and licenses and exporting their services of information and R&D.

The competitiveness of the "world workshop" 113

Since 2002, China has become the second-largest net importer of royalties and licenses in Asia and in the world, just after Singapore. China's deficit doubled from about US$3 billion in 2002 to US$6.4 billion in 2006. Among all imports in 2006, the United States (14.4 billion), EU (13.6 billion), and Japan (11.7 billion) were the three main sources in China. We can also establish that the largest deficit in the commercial service trade of China's FIEs comes from royalties and license fees, which also share 85 percent of China's total (Bureau of Service, MOC, 2008).

Among all other business service trade, only consulting (legal, accounting, management, and public relations, according to the BOP classification) and advertising (advertising, market research, and public-opinion polling) can be defined as independent sectors in China. The WTO (various years) treated all the remaining parts of China's other business service trade in 2007 as merchandising and other trade-related services, which shared 68 percent of exports and 55 percent of imports of other business trade.

UNSTA, EC, IMF et al. (2002) enriched the BOP classification into the Expanded Balance of Payment Service Classification (EBOPS) and Foreign Affiliates Trade in Services (FATS).[1] According to their definition,

> Data on the activities of majority-owned foreign affiliates in the compiling economy are usually referred to as inward FATS, and those relating to majority-owned foreign affiliates of the compiling economy that are established abroad are referred to as outward FATS.

FATS is in fact the commercial presence of FDI. According to the UNCTAD (various years), the FDI of the service sector as a share of total FDI rose from

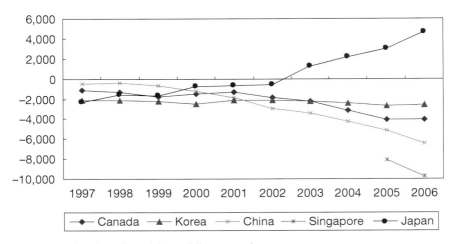

Figure 4.6 Surplus of royalties and license trade
Source: Author's calculation, based on OECD (2008c) and WTO (various years).

50.1 percent in 1990 to nearly 70 percent in 2005. Its share of inward FDI stock rose from 49.27 percent to 62.83 percent in 2004, and the share of outward FDI stock also rose from 46.59 percent to 68.73 percent. The WTO estimated that the service trade realized by commercial presence is about 1.5 times that supplied across the board.

According to the Bureau of Service, MOC (2008), the non-financial FDI in China's service sector reached US$12.08 billion in 2005 (7,428 new enterprises, which represented 16.85 percent of all newly founded FIEs), after the transitional period of China's entry to the WTO finished at the end of 2004. This type of FDI rose 25.8 percent to US$14.69 billion in 2006 (7,129 new enterprises, representing 17.17 percent of all newly founded FIEs). Until the end of 2006, there had been 44,128 non-financial foreign affiliates in China, whose total revenue reached US$91.32 billon (23.5 percent higher than in 2005).

Among all these FDIs, the scientific-research sector tripled, from US$0.29 billion in 2004 to US$0.92 billion in 2007, which is one of the fastest-growing sectors. The inside impetus comes from the convenience of having an R&D center close to the production base. A survey carried out by UNCTAD of the largest companies around the world showed that 61.8 percent of them were willing to expand their R&D activities in China between 2005 and 2009, which was the top destination country (Bureau of Service, MOC, 2008). This is why there were twenty-four of this type of R&D center in China in 1997, but 1,140 10 years later. Almost all the activities of the R&D centers founded by MNCs in China should be considered as importing FATS.

According to the estimate by McKinsey (2007), the potential global market of offshore service outsourcing reached US$465 billion in 2005, including

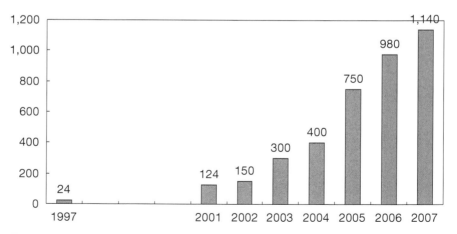

Figure 4.7 Foreign corporate R&D centers in China
Source: Simon and Cao (2009), p. 32.

The competitiveness of the "world workshop" 115

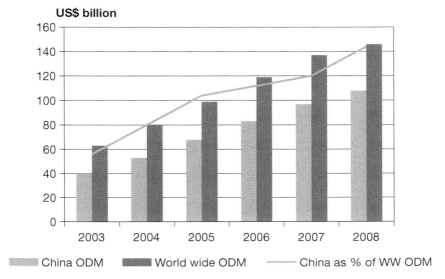

Figure 4.8 China's ODM revenue from electronic systems, 2003–2008
Source: Wang (2004).

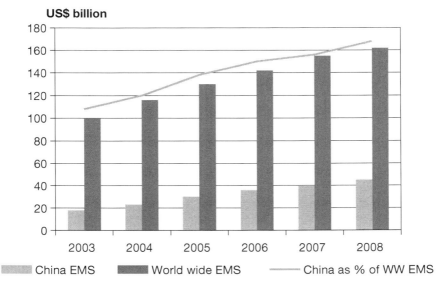

Figure 4.9 China's EMS revenue from electronic systems, 2003–2008
Source: Wang (2004).

US$9 billion of IT application services, US$8.5 billion of IT infrastructure services, US$17 billion of business process outsourcing (BPO), and US$12 billion of engineering services (including design and R&D). Since entering the WTO, China has played a more and more important role in global ODM of electronic systems. For example, its ODM revenue for electronic systems exceeded US$100 billion in 2005 and was nearly 70 percent of the world's total, just as India acounts for 70 percent of the world's software offshore outsourcing.

Asia had 45.9 percent of the world's total EMS in 2004, the United States had 31.1 percent, and the EU had 23 percent (Technology Forecasters, 2006). Although the total revenue from China's EMS was less than half that of its ODM, China still shared half of Asia's EMS revenue, which was 23 percent of the world's in 2005. This share rose from 18 percent in 2003 and was predicted to reach 28 percent in 2008.

Sales and brands: "made in China" and "made by China"

Sales "made in China"

The most impressive part of China as the "world workshop" for the global consumer is the label of "made in China" all around the world. However, more than half of these goods are not "sold" by Chinese enterprises, and FIEs still shared 52 percent of all exports from the industrial sector in 2007. Within the top 500 enterprises by export from China in 2005, 60.8 percent were FIEs, 28.3 percent were SOEs, and all other enterprises only shared 11.0 percent (Xinhua Net, 2006). These FIEs account for the real "made in China" sales in the world market.

Although the wholesale and retail sector became the largest sector in the outflow of FDI from China in 2007 (growing sixfold, from US$1.1 billion in 2006 and overtaking the leasing and business sector), there were still small overseas retail branches in the main economies. However, there appeared to be a large number of foreign-invested wholesale and retail enterprises after the end of the transition period of China's entry to the WTO at the end of 2004. The newly founded enterprises reached 1,027 in 2005, which was more than three times the total from 1992 to 2004 (324).

Compared with the manufacturing sectors (FIEs share one-fifth of both the revenue and profit), these foreign-invested wholesale and retail enterprises have enjoyed double proportion of profit than their revenue and employment from 2002. In contrast, their contribution to sales tax and extra charges kept a stable level nearly than 6 percent and became less than that of the revenue after 2003 and less than that of employment after 2005. The sectoral difference between the enterprises above designed scale may be even wider.

Among all sectors, the Hong Kong, Macau, and Taiwan FIEs have a large profit advantage in both wholesale and retail of textiles and garments and wholesale of culture and sports appliances together with integrated retail. The

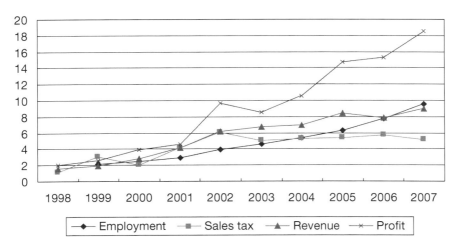

Figure 4.10 Share of FIEs in wholesale and retail enterprises
Notes: The statistical range for a wholesale enterprise is that it employs more than 20 people and has revenue above 20 million yuan; a retail enterprise employs more than 60 people and has revenue above 5 million yuan.
Source: Author's calculation, based on NBS (various years).

FIEs have quite a large share in culture, sports appliances (20.29 percent), machinery and electronic equipment (38.35 percent)— which are both double their revenue—and medicines and medical appliances (18.79 percent)—which quadruples its revenue. Besides, they also have 30.12 percent of the profits from the retail of food, beverages, and tobacco and 17.46 of household electric appliances, where their revenues are only 0.85 and 1.23 percent of the sectors. Even considering the tax preference they enjoyed, their share of tax for these sectors was still quite low.

In China, distribution enterprises should pay value added tax as turnover tax, like industrial enterprises, but not business tax, like service enterprises. The big difference between the sales tax and extra charge (value added tax as base) and the profit raised a big question about MNCs' sales in China. According to the estimate by Lehmann (2002), the return on equity of U.S. FDI in China was about 13.4–14.2 percent between 1995 and 1998, which is about 6 percent higher than the traditional estimate under International Financial Statistics (IFS) data, which is based on BOP. The program "Research on China's using FDI and Foreign Invested Enterprises" by NBS (2006) thinks that FIEs mitigate tax through false losses, which has become a general phenomenon throughout industrial sectors. It believes that two-thirds of these loss-making enterprises show false losses, and this has brought China a loss in tax of about 30 billion yuan per year, because of "transfer pricing," which was one-tenth of its total profit in 2004. Obviously, MNCs occupy much higher positions in the sales part of the value chain of "made in China" than in the production part.

Table 4.20 Share of wholesale and retail FIEs across sectors, 2004[a]

	HK, Macau & Taiwan			Foreign Invested		
	Total revenue	Sales tax[a]	Total profit	Total revenue	Sales tax[a]	Total profit
Wholesale trade						
15–17 Food, beverages, and tobacco	0.28	0.91	0.08	2.88	0.73	0.81
18–20, part of 36 Textiles, garments, and daily consumer articles	1.58	2.08	8.46	4.52	1.11	−0.44
21–22, part of 36 Culture, sports appliances, and equipment	2.92	0.59	7.06	9.37	3.93	20.29
23–27 Mineral products, building materials and chemical products	0.50	0.17	0.71	1.57	0.80	3.52
Part of 24 & 33 Medicines and medical appliances	0.69	0.59	3.77	4.25	1.16	18.79
28–35 Machinery, hardware, and electronic equipment	3.02	0.80	2.96	18.92	5.35	38.35
Trade broker and agency	0.44	0.30	−0.34	2.72	4.75	9.70
Other, not classified elsewhere	1.99	0.50	3.10	8.16	1.63	12.08
Retail Trade						
15–17 Food, beverages, and tobacco	0.23	0.49	3.70	0.85	1.74	30.12
18–20, part of 36 Textiles, garments, and daily consumer articles	3.34	0.71	26.45	3.83	2.23	−3.50
21–22, part of 36 Culture, sports appliances, and equipments	0.21	0.14	−0.13	0.49	0.20	−8.43
Part of 24 & 33 Medicines and medical appliances	1.32	0.53	−14.35	0.19	0.16	−2.21
29–33 Household electric appliances and electronic products	2.74	0.75	8.26	1.23	0.50	17.46
34–35 part of 23 Motor vehicles, motorcycles, fuel, and parts	0.29	0.04	0.22	0.35	0.19	0.58
36 part of 24–28 Hardware, furniture, and decoration materials	0.21	0.49	0.22	5.50	0.52	0.63
Integrated retail	4.04	2.01	12.29	12.25	1.79	17.21
Non-shop and other retail	0.54	0.24	0.83	2.07	1.01	1.91

a Should be sales tax and extra charge.
Source: Author's calculation, based on NBS (2006).

Branding

Another important problem with the competitiveness of FIEs in sectors such as food, beverages, and tobacco concerns the brands they own. The MNCs have an overwhelming advantage in branding over China's domestic enterprises. Until 2009, there were no Chinese firms with a world-famous brand in *Business Week*'s 100 Top Brands, but the United States continued to have more than half of them. Considering giant consumer groups in China, the BrandZ Top 100 brand ranking by Millward Brown Optimor (2009) still included four Chinese firms in their list, China Mobile as number 7, Industrial and Commercial Bank of China as number 12, and China Construction Bank, Bank of China, and China Merchants Bank as numbers 24, 27, and 80, respectively.

In China's own ranking of the world's top 500 brands (World Brand Laboratory, 2010), Chinese enterprises held seventeen of them in 2009, rising from four in 2005. Among these seventeen brands, only four of them belong to competitive manufacturers, Haier (household appliances), Lenovo (IT), Chang Hong (household appliances), and Tsingdao Beer (brewing). Among them, Lenovo became world famous mainly because it acquired the PC department of IBM (the "Thinkpad") at the end of 2004.

Actually, if only China's enterprises owned their own brands in the world market, those "made in China" could then be turned into "made by China." However, the real challenge for Chinese enterprises is that many brands have merged with MNCs when they became locally famous, and among them many are already the domestic leaders. This happened throughout almost all industries and makes them dominated by foreign brands.

The role of big business: national champions of China

The role of big business in the national economy

The importance of big business was brought out by Chandler (1977, 1990) in his famous work *The visible hand* and later the *Scale and scope*. He called the

Table 4.21 Country distribution of *Business Week*'s 100 Top Brands

	2001	2002	2003	2004	2005	2006	2007	2008	2009
United States	62	66	60	57	52	51	53	52	51
United Kingdom	7	5	6	4	5	6	5	3	4
Germany	7	6	6	9	9	9	10	10	11
France	3	5	7	8	7	8	8	8	8
Japan	6	6	7	8	7	8	8	7	7
Korea	1	1	1	1	3	3	3	2	2

Source: Author's calculation, based on Interbrand (various years).

Table 4.22 Incomplete statistics for China's acquired national brands

	Brand	Acquirer
15–17 Food, beverages, and tobacco	Robust	Danone (2000)
	Ta Ta	Wrigley
	Shuanghui[a]	Goldman Sachs
	Huiyuan	Coca-Cola
	Tsingtao Beer	Asahi Beer (Japan)
	Harbin Beer	AB Group (Budweiser)
	Dali Beer	Carlsberg
21 Paper products	Shuermei	Kimberley-Clark (1994)
23 Oil	Tongyi PrteoChem.	Shell
24–26 Chemicals	Zhonghua & Maxam	Unilever (1994)
	Panda	P&G
	Huoli 28	Reckitt Benckiser (1996)
	Sanxiao	Colgate
	Xiaohushi	L'Oréal (2003)
	Dabao (2008)	Johnson & Johnson
	Huarun Paints	Valspar (US)
31 Machinery	Jiamusi Combine Harvester[b]	John Deere (US) (2004)
	Xibei (Luoyang Bearing Group)	FAG (Germany)
32–33 Household appliances	Supor[c]	SEB (France)
	Five Star[d]	Bestbuy (US)
	Nanfu[e]	Gillette (2003)
34–35 Transportation	Weifu[f]	Bosch (Germany)
36 Other	GoodBaby Group[g]	PAG (private equity)

a Number 1 meat food brand of China.
b The only producer of large combine harvesters in China.
c Number 1 cooking-pot brand in China.
d Number 4 household-appliance retailer in China.
e Number 1 battery producer in China.
f Number 1 diesel fuel-injection system producer in China.
g Number 1 baby-carriage producer in China.
Source: Author's collection using Chinese Internet sites.

integration of mass production and mass distribution a "visible hand" in the market, and modern industrial enterprises played key roles in the industrialization of the United States, making it a "world workshop" after the United Kingdom in the late nineteenth century. Nolan (2001) points out that this trend continued in the twentieth century, showing as the rising concentration of leading firms in manufacturing. Except that the United Kingdom's lead was interrupted by the Great Depression, from 1929 to 1935, all ratios increased steadily from 1909 to 1963.

A group of forty-five of Europe's biggest industrial companies, including Eon, Philips, BP, and Total, has spent a year attempting to quantify its members' contribution to Europe's economy. The survey will argue that, together, the forty-five companies sustain 6.6 million jobs, or 5 percent of total employment, fund 14 percent of European research spending, and employ 11 percent of the continent's researchers. Their contribution to Europe's GDP "exceeds that of 21 of the 27 member states" (Hollinger, 2009).

After the Second World War, a widely accepted measurement for modern industrial enterprises was founded by the Fortune Global 500, from 1955 onwards. Over the past 30 years, we can see the comparative drop of the United States, from 241 in 1975 to 140 in 2009; the inverted "U" shape of Japan, with its peak of 147 in 1995, and the rise of China, which quadrupled from 2000 to 2009 and caught up with the three leading European countries.

Big business has already played important roles in the economies of the leading economies. If using GDP as a basis, the share of the revenue of the Fortune 500 firms shows quite a big difference between China and them. China's share rose from 25.7 in 2000 to 36.3 in 2007. Although 14 percent higher than India, it is still has at least a gap of 20 percent with the United States, United Kingdom, Japan, and Germany, not to mention France's high figure. However, in 2008, China's share jumped 10 percent higher and was

Table 4.23 Net share of manufacturing output of the top 100 firms, 1909–1963 (%)

	1909	1929	1935	1963
United States	22	25	26	33
United Kingdom	16	26	23	38
France	12	16		26

Source: Nolan (2001).

Table 4.24 Country distribution of Fortune Global 500

	1975	1980	1985	1990	1995	2000	2005	2007	2009
United States	241	217	212	164	150	179	177	162	140
United Kingdom	49	51	48	43	33	38	35	32	26
Germany	38	38	33	30	43	37	36	37	39
France	29	29	23	30	40	37	39	38	40
Canada	17	20	22	12	5	12	13	16	14
Japan	54	66	82	111	147	108	81	67	68
Korea		6	9	11	8	11	11	14	14
China[a]		0 + 1	0 + 1	0 + 1	2 + 2	10 + 1	18 + 2	24 + 6	37 + 6
India	2	2	4	6	1	1	8	10	7

a Taiwan enterprises are included.
Source: Data from 1975 to 1990 are from Hopkins and Wallerstein (1996); data from 1995 to 2009 are from Fortune (2009).

122 *The competitiveness of the "world workshop"*

just 10 percent lower than that of the United States. The financial crisis has begun to change the landscape of global business.

Another measurement of big business today is the market value of the *Financial Times* Global 500, as against the revenue method of the Fortune Global 500. Mainland China had no *Financial Times* 500 before 2006, but overtook Germany, Canada, and France within 3 years. Including Hong Kong and Taiwanese firms, China has almost caught up with Japan. Among the top ten largest, China owned three of them: PetroChina, the second largest, China Mobile, the fourth (fifth in 2008), and the Industrial and Commercial Bank of China as the fifth (sixth in 2008).

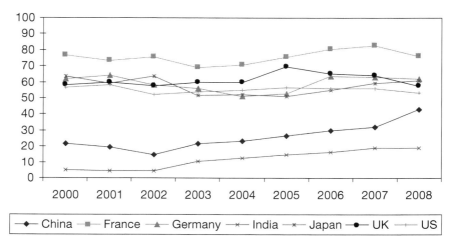

Figure 4.11 Revenue of Fortune Global 500 firms to GDP
Source: Author's calculation, based on Fortune (2009) and World Bank (2008).

Table 4.25 Country distribution of *Financial Times* Global 500

	2000	2005	2006	2007	2008	2009
United States	218	219	196	184	169	181
Japan	77	43	60	49	39	49
United Kingdom	46	33	34	41	35	32
France	26	28	30	32	31	23
Germany	20	19	19	20	22	20
Canada	10	22	22	23	24	27
China:						
Mainland				8	25	27
Hong Kong	7	8	7	8	10	16
Taiwan	4	5	4	5	4	4
India	3	5	8	8	13	10

Note: All numbers are from the fourth quarter of the year.
Source: Author's calculation, based on *Financial Times* (2009).

Table 4.26 Market value of *Financial Times* Global 500

	Total market value (US$ trillion)			Share in market capitalization	
	2007	2008	2009	2007	2008
United States	10.59	9.62	6.15	54.49	48.21
Japan	2.09	1.60	1.11	44.24	35.95
United Kingdom	2.50	2.24	1.16	65.78	57.95
France	1.75	1.75	0.80	72.23	63.28
Germany	1.03	1.20	0.62	63.03	57.07
Canada	0.77	0.87	0.53	45.40	39.62
China					
Mainland	0.86	1.96	1.37	35.46	31.51
Hong Kong	0.39	0.61	0.44	43.91	52.04
Taiwan	0.15	0.14	0.09	24.51	21.13
India	0.24	0.42	0.21	29.40	23.13

Note: Market capitalization of Taiwan comes from the Taiwan Stock Exchange website: www.twse.com.tw/en/statistics/statistics_week.php.
Source: Author's calculation, based on *Financial Times* (2009) and World Bank (2008).

Although the number of enterprises in mainland China is still lower than in the United Kingdom and Japan, their total market value has already overtaken that of the United Kingdom, in 2009, to take second place. Even if mainland China had a 30.3 percent downturn from US$1.96 trillion in 2008 (number 3 in that year), its decline is still one of the smallest of all the main economies. Furthermore, the market values of mainland China and India both have a comparatively low proportion in their total market capitalization. The financial crisis also brought them drops of 3.95 and 6.27 percent, respectively. The concentration proportion of Chinese big businesses in the capital market still shows a gap with the leading economies.

Compared with their competitors, big businesses in mainland China are still quite locally oriented. Until 2007, only the China International Trust and Investment Company group had entered the top 100 non-financial transnational companies (TNCs) of the world, as number 88. It is ranked seventh of the top 50 non-financial TNCs in developing countries, where the vast Chinese region dominates the list. This situation may have changed since 2008, because of the boom of big business in mainland China.

Another disadvantage of the big businesses of mainland China is their R&D expenditure. The survey of top businesses expanded from 500 in 2001 to 1,000 in 2009. The United States, Japan, and the three leading European economies still dominate the top business R&D firms of the world, with 740 out of a total of 1,000 firms in 2009. The share of the United States dropped from 45.8 percent in 2002 to 36.8 percent in 2009, and all other economies doubled from 12.5 percent to 26 percent over the same period of time. However, their proportion of expenditure was still only 19.6 percent in 2009.

124 *The competitiveness of the "world workshop"*

Table 4.27 Country distribution of Top 50 non-financial TNCs in developing countries[a]

	2000	2001	2002	2003	2004	2005	2006	2007
China								
Mainland	3	1		5	7	7	6	6
Hong Kong	11	11	11	10	10	10	11	10
Taiwan	2	5	3	8	5	7	6	5
Korea	5	5	4	3	4	4	5	5
Singapore	6	6	9	9	7	6	4	5
Malaysia	5	4	3	3	3	3	3	4
India				1	1	1	1	2
Brazil	4	2	3	3	3	3	3	3
Mexico	5	7	7	4	4	3	4	2
South Africa	4	5	7	4	5	5	4	5
Others	5	4	3	0	1	1	3	3

a The "developing countries" here are only the analyzed group of UNCTAD, and Hong Kong, Taiwan, and Korea should be divided into "developed region/countries," according to their GDP per capita.
Source: Author's calculation, based on UNCTAD (various years).

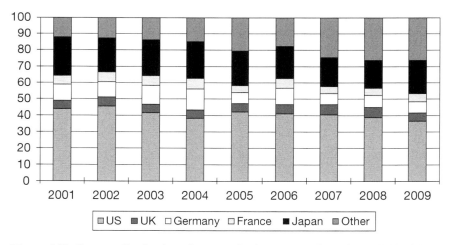

Figure 4.12 Country distribution of DTI top business R&D firms (by individuals)
Source: Author's calculation, based on DIUS and BERR (various years).

Twelve firms from mainland China entered this list in 2009 and formed the thirteenth-largest group. However, only five of the thirty-seven Fortune Global 500 firms from mainland China (PetroChina, China Petroleum & Chemical, China Railway Construction, China Communications Construction, and China Telecom) were ranked on this list in 2009. This shows that these gaint Chinese companies are still behind in R&D capacity.

The Taiwan province of China had thirty-two firms on the list that year, and they became the sixth-largest group from 2006. However, their total expenditure is still less than the leading firm in Korea, Samsung Electronics, which shares half of Korea's total expenditure.

These big businesses also dominate the business R&D expenditure of the leading economies. In France, Germany, and the United Kingdom, the share fluctuated from more than 80 percent to almost all business R&D expenditure (the overseas R&D activity of these companies is not excluded). The share of Japan and the United States also rose, from more than 60 percent to about 80 percent. Along with the enlargement of the scope of the survey, the share of big businesses in Korean business R&D expenditure rose sharply, from 40.6 percent in 2003 to 71.5 percent in 2005. However, the share of mainland China is still quite low, and was still lower than 6 percent in 2006.

Table 4.28 Number of top business R&D firms (individuals)

	2001	2002	2003	2004	2005	2006	2007	2008	2009
Total	500	600	700	700	1,000	1,250	1,250	1,400	1,000
China Mainland		1	1	2	3	5	7	9	12
Hong Kong			1	1	3	4	3	4	5
Taiwan	3	4	8	8	22	44	40	41	32
India				1		1	3	7	15	7
Korea	2	4	6	9	11	20	21	21	21

Source: Author's calculation, based on DIUS and BERR (various years).

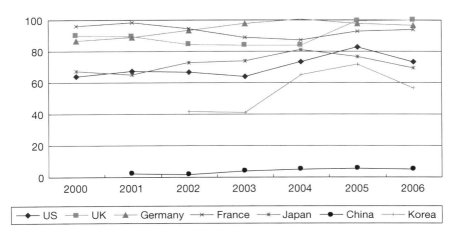

Figure 4.13 Expenditure of R&D scoreboard firms to BERD

Source: Author's calculation, based on DIUS and BERR (various years) and OECD (2008b).

Role of national champions in China

The big difference between the big businesses of China and other main economies is that most of them are SOEs. Among all the Fortune Global 500 firms from China, there has only been one non-SOE, which newly entered the list in 2009, the Sha-steel Group. All the 2009 *Financial Times* Global 500 from China are state-owned or state-holding enterprises (at least relative holding), except for Ping An Insurance Group[2] and Minsheng Bank. Among all the top 500 enterprises in China (by revenue) in 2006, there were 349 SOEs (69.8 percent), which shared 94.9 percent of the total assets and 88 percent of the total profits.

This is one of the main results of China's reform of SOEs to "Grasp the large," intended to invigorate large enterprises while relaxing control over small ones, dating back to 1991. The reform was accelerated from 2003 when the State-owned Assets Supervision and Administration Commission

Table 4.29 Patterns of national champions

	2003	2004	2005	2006	2007
Total[a]	189	178	169	159	151
Fortune 500	6	8	10	16	19
Financial Times 500[b]				2	14
Total assets > 100 billion yuan	17	23	27	34	44
Total revenue >100 billion yuan	9	10	15	21	27
Total profit > 10 billion yuan	6	9	11	13	19

a Number at year end.
b Author's calculation, based on *Financial Times* (2009)
Source: SASAC (2009).

Table 4.30 Main indicators of national champions

	2003	2004	2005	2006	2007
Of all SOEs					
Total assets	42.23	41.01	41.44	42.02	42.06
Revenue	41.69	45.43	47.68	51.21	49.94
Profit	60.71	64.84	65.86	62.75	57.05
Tax	43.96	46.06	48.49	48.95	51.06
Of all business enterprises[a]					
Total assets		25.11	23.91	23.53	23.94
Revenue		18.39	17.19	17.05	16.39
Formal sector employment	16.65	16.51	16.02	15.78	15.76
Science & technical input		22.07	26.99	30.28	34.17

a The data for leasing and business services sectors and scientific research, technical services, and geological prospecting sectors are not included in all business enterprises.
Source: Author's calculation, based on SASAC (2009) and NBS (various years).

Table 4.31 National champions in China's capital market (year end 2007)

	National champions	All listed companies	Proportion
Mainland China stock market			
Individuals	228	1,530	14.90
Total capital stock (100 million shares)	5,902.96	16,954.72	34.81
Total capitalization (100 million Yuan)	128,442.53	327,140.02	39.26
Negotiable capitalization (100 million Yuan)	22,475.69	93,064.18	24.15
Hong Kong stock market			
Individuals	68[a]	1,215	5.60
Negotiable capital stock (100 million shares)	2,698.89	10,059.22	26.83
Negotiable capitalization (HK$100 million)	58,465.29	208,135.60	28.09

a Includes 30 red chip shares.
Source: SASAC (2009).

(SASAC) was founded. The SASAC took charge of the non-financial, state-owned and state-holding big businesses of China, which came from the two trial group batches in 1991 and 1997 (Sutherland, 2003). Almost all the non-financial Fortune Global 500 (except Lenovo Group, in 2007) and *Financial Times* Global 500 (except Kweichow Moutai, China Vanke, and Shanghai International Port Group, in 2007) firms from China are members of this national group. Furthermore, their own scale expanded quite fast.

These national champions played quite important roles in the SOEs and even in all business enterprises in China. Although the total number declined from 189 in 2003 to 151 in 2007, through internal mergers and acquisitions (M&A), they share 42 percent of the total assets of SOEs and nearly a quarter of all business enterprises. The proportion of their revenue in SOEs rose from 42 percent to 50 percent, but the proportion in all business enterprises dropped 2 percent to 16.4 percent. Furthermore, the national champions also contributed nearly two-thirds of the SOEs' profits and half their tax. The key indicator is that their share in the science and technology input (including R&D activities) rose 10 percent, from 22 percent in 2004 to 34 percent in 2007.

The national champions also have big share in China's capital market. They owned 228 listed companies in the A and B shares of mainland China and shared 40 percent of the total capitalization and a quarter of negotiable capitalization. Furthermore, although they only hold 5.6 percent of all listed companies on the Hong Kong stock market, their market value exceeded one-quarter of the negotiable capitalization.

The sector structure of China's national champions is concentrated on manufacturing, from the setting up of fifty-seven trial business groups in 1991, where forty-five of them remain. In 2002, the SASAC included more business groups under its administration, and there then were 115 groups in the manufacturing sector out of all 189 groups. In 2008, they merged into 142 groups,

Table 4.32 Industrial distribution of national champions

ISIC Revision 3	1991	1997	2003	2008
Primary industry	4	9	10	6
01 Agricultural		5	8	4
02 Forestry	4	4	1	1
05 Fishing			1	1
Secondary industry	46	82	121	94
Mining				
10 Coal mining	1	3	5	4
13 Mining of metal ores			1	1
Manufacturing	45	79	115	89
15–22 (except 17), 36 Light industry	3	10	5	
17 Textiles	1	4	5	3
23–25 (except 2423) Chemicals	4	7	13	8
2423 Pharmaceuticals	2	5	4	3
26 Non-metal materials	4	5	4	2
27 Basic metals materials	4	8	18	15
28, 29, 31 Machinery & electrical	10	14	11	10
30, 32, 33 Electronics (ICT included)	3	10	13	12
34 Automobiles	3	6	5	4
35 Other transportation equipment	6	6	6	6
Utility & construction				
40 Electricity generation	8	8	16	14
45 Construction		3	10	7
Tertiary industry	7	29	58	42
50–52 Foreign trade	2	8	10	8
50–52 Domestic trade/service	6	3	2	
60–61 Transportation	2	5	6	5
62 Civil aviation	3	3	7	6
63 Travel			4	2
64 Communication			6	5
65–67 Financial intermediation			6	5
70 Real estate activities			6	4
Other (business etc.)		7	10	5
Total	57	120	189	142

Source: Data for 1991 and 1997 are from Sutherland (2003, p. 50); data for 2003 and 2008 have been compiled by the author from the SASAC website.

The competitiveness of the "world workshop" 129

and the manufacturing groups merged into 89, which still represent nearly two-thirds of the total.

Within the manufacturing sector, most of these national champions are still in the low-tech and medium–low-tech industries, such as basic metals, which still represented one-sixth of them in 2008. Nevertheless, there are also just fifteen groups that have evolved in high-tech manufacturing, including three in pharmaceuticals, eight in ICT, and four in aircraft/spacecraft. The selection of these groups is mainly according to their scale, and their distribution is then decided by the structure of China's domestic manufacturing, which is quite different from overall manufacturing, balanced by FIEs.

The "going out" of China's national champions

The most abstractive activities of China's national champions after the financial crisis that began in 2007 have been their M&A around the world. This is the main part of China's outward FDI, which boomed from US$3 billion in 2003 to US$25 billion in 2007 and then US$42 billion in 2008 (non-financial sectors). China's share of the FDI outflow also rose from less than 1 percent to 2.81 percent in 2008, but its stock, about US$147 billion, only shared 0.91 of the world's total.

In 2009, the FDI outflow for M&A from China exceeded the FDI inflow from overseas to acquire Chinese enterprises for the first time (Xinhua Net, 2006). In fact, the outflow for M&A from China reached US$20.5 billion (non-financial sectors) in 2008, which had tripled from US$6.3 billion in 2007.

Table 4.33 Share of outward FDI of the world

	1980	1985	1990	1995	2000	2005	2008
Share in FDI outflow (%)							
China		1.01	0.35	0.55	0.08	1.39	2.81
France	6.09	3.59	15.15	4.36	14.62	13.08	11.84
Germany			10.14	10.80	4.66	8.63	8.42
Japan	4.63	10.41	20.08	6.26	2.60	5.21	6.89
Russian				0.17	0.26	1.45	2.82
United Kingdom	15.29	17.86	7.51	12.04	19.23	9.20	6.00
United States	37.30	21.60	12.96	25.46	11.75	1.75	16.78
Share in FDI outward stock (%)							
China		0.12	0.25	0.60	0.46	0.54	0.91
France	4.54	5.16	6.30	6.95	7.33	8.19	8.62
Germany			8.49	9.12	8.93	8.75	8.95
Japan	3.57	5.86	11.28	8.11	4.59	3.65	4.20
Russian				0.11	0.33	1.38	1.25
United Kingdom	14.65	13.36	12.84	10.36	14.79	11.30	9.32
United States	39.24	31.75	24.11	23.76	21.68	21.14	19.51

Source: UNCTAD (2009).

The outflow in the M&A of the financial sectors also rose, from US$1.3 billion in 2006 to US$9.7 billion in 2008.

Within the outward FDI, the manufacturing sector has become dominated in the amount of both source enterprises and founded enterprises overseas (see Figure 4.14). Although the figure has dropped, about half the enterprises that have FDI outflow are from the manufacturing sector. Of Chinese enterprises overseas, which doubled from 3,439 in 2003 to 6,264 in 2005, and to about 12,000 in 2008, more than 30 percent of them are manufacturing firms, but these enterprises only contributed less than 10 percent of the FDI outward stock, and their share in the outflow also dropped, from 21.9 percent in 2003 to 4.2 percent in 2008. This shows their sizes are much smaller than the average.

In contrast, the leasing and business services sector contributes nearly 40 percent of China's FDI outward stock, and its share in the outflow also rose to 51.9 percent in 2008. However, in overseas Chinese enterprises, the sector only has about 15 percent of the total amount and only 5 percent in source enterprises. This big differential with the manufacturing sector shows that their average sizes are much larger, and this is related to the investment body, the National Champions of China, which are building their own sales and service branches, rather than the small production basis.[3]

Although the national champions, managed by China's central government, only founded 19.6 percent of all China's oversea enterprises in 2008, their share in the total FDI outward stock kept a proportion of 80 percent from 2004. If we measure by ownership, the purely SOEs share 70 percent of the total stock. The second-largest group comprises the limited liability

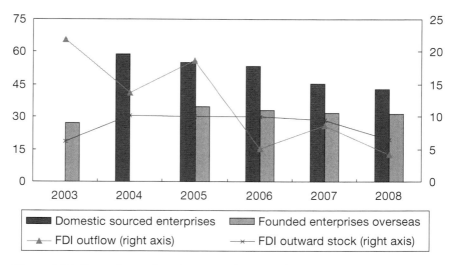

Figure 4.14 Share of manufacturing sector in outward FDI
Source: MOC, NBS, SAFE (various years).

The competitiveness of the "world workshop" 131

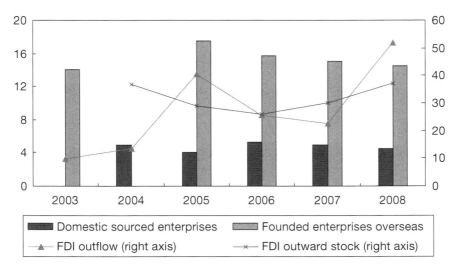

Figure 4.15 Share of leasing and business services sector in outward FDI
Source: MOC, NBS, SAFE (various years).

Table 4.34 China's FDI outward stock structure of sourced enterprises

	2003	2004	2005	2006	2007	2008
By ownership						
State owned				81.0	71.0	69.6
Limited liability					20.3	20.1
Shareholding limited					5.1	6.6
Shareholding cooperative					1.2	1.2
Private				1.0	1.2	1.0
Other					1.2	1.7
By management body						
Central government	> 90	83.7	81.8	82.0	78.5	81.3
Local bodies	< 10	16.3	18.2	18.0	21.5	18.7

Source: MOC, NBS, SAFE (various years).

corporations,[4] and some of them are also under the management of China's central government.

In 2004, the top thirty enterprises owned 80.4 percent of China's all outward FDI stock, and this proportion didn't change too much until 2008. Among the top thirty enterprises, only Lenovo, Huawei, and ZTE (not in the list in some years) are not SOEs. In that year, fourteen of the top twenty private enterprises ranked by FDI outflow are in the manufacturing sector. However, their average investments are obviously smaller than those of the leading national champions, which focused on building business-services branches overseas.

The purchase of the PC division of IBM by Lenovo at the end of 2004 may still be one of the most impressive cases of the "going out" strategy of China's enterprises. If the purchase of Volvo by Geely succeeds, it will become another milestone of that strategy, together with the acquisition of Saab Automobile by Beijing Automotive Works, because the two companies are even not leading car producers in China. However, the M&A of China's national champions are facing stricter restrictions in their relationship with the Chinese government, especially in the resource industry. Leading deals, such as the purchase of Unocal by China National Offshore Oil Corporation (about US$15.6 billion) in 2005 and the capital injection into Rio Tinto by China Aluminum Cooperation (about US$19.5 billion) in 2009, have all failed.

China's total outward FDI stock is still just on the scale of the overseas assets of two or three of the largest MNCs, such as GE. The "going out" of China's national champions still has a long way to go if they want to compete with these global leaders. They need to climb further up the global value chain, from resource and asset purchase to sales channels and R&D capacity, and then to brands and intellectual property in the future.

Notes

1. The General Agreement on Trade in Service (GATS) of WTO divided all service trade into four kinds, the Cross-border supply (about 35% in 2005), Consumption Abroad (about 10–15%), Commercial Presence (50%) and Presence of Natural Persons (about 1–2%) in 1995. FATS belongs to the Commercial Presence in the GATS classification but not included in the BOP classification.
2. It should be also included in the 2008 Fortune Global 500 and ranked No. 440, higher than the No. 499 of Lenovo Group.
3. Joint Ventures only shares 4 percent of all Chinese enterprises overseas (MOC, NBS, SAFE, Various Years).
4. Limited liability corporations refer to economic units registered in accordance with the Regulation of the People's Republic of China on the Management of Registration of Corporations: with capitals from 2 to 49 investors, each investor bears limited liability to the corporation depending on his/her holding of shares, and the corporation bears liability to its debt to the maximum of its total assets.

5 Comparative study of three of China's industries in the international manufacturing division

The comparative analysis of this chapter is about both the selected manufacturing industries and the firm cases within them. The three industries are the ceramics industry, steel industry, and photovoltaic industry, which are representative of the different stages of the industrialization of the past centuries. The ceramics industry has quite a long history before the industrial revolution, but as a craft production and mainly using manpower. Today, it is still quite a labor- and resource-intensive industry. The steel industry has been the typical pillar industry of the "industrialized" economies and one of the best examples of mass production. It has always been an extremely resource- and capital-intensive industry. The photovoltaic industry is now treated as an emerging industry with the revolution of "new energy," which should provide an opportunity for China to catch up. It is also an industry in the capital- and technology-intensive mode. These three industries, on one hand, have been dominated by China, at least in terms of physical output, and, on the other hand, can provide a broad view of its position in the global value chain.

The methodology we use here is a structural analysis among different industries and cases, following the framework in Chapter 1, from production, trade, R&D, and sales, even to the standards and brands. The advantage of this method is that it can provide a platform for comparison and let the industries and cases easily correspond to the analysis of the preceding chapters. However, the lack of details of the cases is inevitable, because some of the topics in this research, such as the source of key technology and standard "know-how," the real situation, and strategies in marketing and branding activities, usually comprise core information held by these enterprises that is hard to obtain in interviews. This makes the method a second-best choice, based on the limited materials obtained from the interviews.

The ceramics industry

The ceramics industry may be one of the oldest industries of humankind, with a history as old as 10,000 years. China may be one of few countries with the name of a kind of product. Over the past thousand years before the Industrial Revolution, it was always one of China's most competitive products.

From the fifteenth century to the nineteenth century (late Ming Dynasty to Middle Qing Dynasty), porcelain was always China's main "high-value-added" export product. An impressive case is a sunken ship named the SS *Gothenburg*, which sailed from China to Sweden in 1745. The total shipment of the 700 tons of products on board were worth 250–270 million Swedish silver coins, which was equal to the GDP of Sweden that year, and a majority of its goods were porcelain from China (Arensberg, 2005). Another historical record said that, over the 200 years of the late Ming Dynasty, half of the silver from South America gained by the Netherlands, Spain, etc., was used in the trade with China, which reached about 353 billion liang just during the 70 years from 1572 to 1642 (Wikipedia, 2009).[1] Most of them were used to buy ceramic products, and this was also the main source of China's trade surplus.

At that time, China was the center for high-value-added ceramic products. The center of its production was a town called Jingdezhen, in Jiangxi Province of China, which was to ceramics what today's Silicon Valley is to the world ICT industry. For example, the Gui Gu Zi blue and white porcelain pot, which reached a record auction price (£15.688 million at Christie's in London on July 12, 2005) for porcelain items around the world, was produced in this town during the Yuan Dynasty (the one before the Ming Dynasty).

Gunder Frank (1998) points out that, before 1800, although only 16 percent of Chinese ceramic products were exported to Europe, they contributed about half of the total export value. Those products were the high-value-added export products of China at that time. After the mid 1800s, however, the high-value-added ceramic products from China began to be replaced by those from domestic producers in the United Kingdom, France, Austria, etc., when they had achieved technological breakthrough. Chinese producers then could only expand in the market for low-value-added, commonly used products. This also resulted in the relative decline of China's economy.

Ceramic production was traditionally a labor-intensive industry, and only changed to a capital-intensive one when it became widely used as a construction material. Today, even many complex, daily used ceramics can be formed using high-tech equipment, but a large quantity is still made by Chinese laborers, using very simple equipment, and is sold to the world at a low "Chinese price."

On the other hand, the highest-value ceramic products today are made in the United Kingdom, Germany, and Italy, with an average price ten or twenty times higher than those from China. This means the global value chain is quite uneven throughout the world, and the ceramics industry is a very good example of China's position. What we need to find out is why China is still quite low down the chain, but contributes more than half of the world's physical output of daily used ceramics.

Before we look at the ceramics industry in more detail, its definition and related classification must be clarified. In Revision 3 of the ISIC, there are two industrial groups related to ceramic products, non-structural (non-refractory) ceramic ware (2691), which comprises mainly household products such as kitchen and tableware, furnished artwork, or toilet articles, and structural (non-refractory) clay and ceramic products (2693), which are mainly products used in construction, such as tiles and bricks. The latter are included in the group of structural clay products (3691 in ISIC Revision 2), together with the group of refractory products (2692).

However, in China's classification, structural clay products are not included in the ceramics industry. In the old version of industrial classification (GB1994), structural ceramic products (called "construction ceramics") were still included in the ceramics industry (315) and shared the same code (3151) with ceramic toilet articles (called "sanitary ceramics" in China). However, they are excluded in the new version (GB2002), which makes the ceramics industry of China equal to the non-structural (non-refractory) ceramic ware in ISIC Revision 3. Structural ceramic products were then given a new code, 3132, and the original one was left to ceramic toilet articles.

Within the coding of SITC Revision 3, the main group is pottery (666), which has two subgroups: household (mainly kitchen and tableware) ceramics (6661) and ornamental (mainly statuettes and furnished artwork) ceramics (6662). The former correspond to daily used ceramics (3152) in China's GB2004 classification,[2] and the latter then correspond to gardening and art ceramics (3159). Ceramic plumbing fixtures (8112) correspond to sanitary ceramics (3151). However, industrial ceramics (3153) then correspond to the other two SITC codes: ceramic wares for laboratory, chemical, or other technical uses (66391), and ceramic electrical insulators (77323). Structural clay and ceramic products come under the group of non-refractory ceramic bricks, tiles, pipes, and similar products (6624) in SITC.

The classification we use in this chapter consists of two main groups: non-structural ceramics—group 2691 in ISIC Revision 3 and group 666 in SITC Revision 3—and structural ceramics—group 2693 in ISIC and group 6624 in SITC.

Table 5.1 Scope of the classification of the ceramics industry

		GB1994	GB2002	ISIC Rev3	ISIC Rev2	SITC Rev3
Non-structural ceramic	Ornamental	3159	3159	2691	361	6662
	Industrial	3155	3153	2691	361	66391, 77323
	Used daily	3153	3152	2691	361	6661 + ?
	Sanitary	3151	3151	2691	361	8122
Structural ceramic		3151	3132	2693	3691	66244–5
Structural clay products		3131	3131	2693	3691	66241–3
Refractory products		3169	3169	2692	3691	6623, 6637

Source: Author's design, based on NBS (2008b) and UNSTA (2002).

Production and productivity

Under the above definitions, we can establish that China overtook Japan (it overtook the United States in 2001) to become the number 1 producer of non-structural ceramic products in 2002; and that its GIO reached nearly US$7 billion in 2005. It was still at the level of Japan in 2000, but the GIO almost doubled to US$13 billion two years later (China National Light Industry Council, 2008), which is even higher than Japan's peak in 1995 in nominal price. On the other hand, China's industrial value added in 2005 was still only two-thirds that of Japan, which is again the problem we pointed out in Chapter 2, that China's manufacturing has quite a low value-added ratio (to gross output) compared with countries such as Japan.

China's structural ceramics industry also began its catch-up after 2000, and overtook the United States in 2001 and Spain in 2003. What we should point out is that the data for all other countries here include the share of structural clay products, which for China was US$2.3 billion in 2004. This means China's total GIO had already caught up with Italy's in 2004 and also became number 1, as it had for non-structural ceramic products. If we use the measurement of value added, China was still a little lower than Spain and the United States in 2004, and, if we include structural clay products, China is also nearly 20 percent lower than Italy.

If we turn to the physical output of the ceramics industry, China completely dominates world production. The census data show that China's total output of daily used ceramics reached 15 billion pieces in 2004, which was nearly 60 percent of the world's total; the output of structural (construction) ceramics

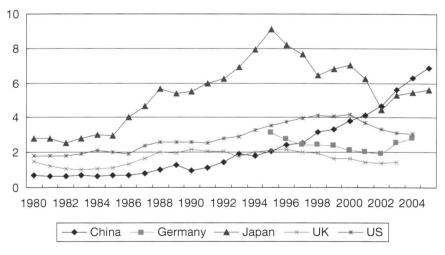

Figure 5.1 GIO of main non-structural-pottery producers (US$ billion)
Source: Author's calculation, based on UNIDO (2008).

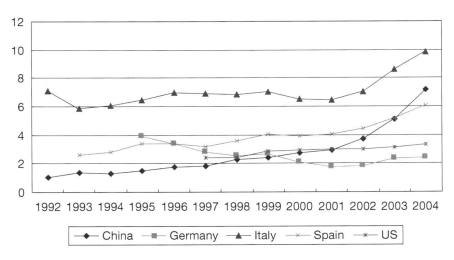

Figure 5.2 GIO of main structural-pottery producers (US$ billion)
Source: Author's calculation, based on UNIDO (2008).

Table 5.2 Physical output of China's ceramics industry [a]

	1986	1990	1995	2000	2005	2006
Physical output						
Construction ceramics (million m^2)	82.9	197.2	1,584	1,357	3,500	4,200
Sanitary ceramics (million pieces)	9.49	17.83	49.00	30.46	79.90	84.75
Daily used and ornamental ceramics[b] (billion pieces)			8.36	6.76	9.91	12.02
Weight equivalent (million tons)						
Construction ceramics	1.66	3.94	31.68	27.14	70.00	84.00
Sanitary ceramics	0.14	0.27	0.74	0.46	1.20	1.27
Daily used and ornamental ceramics			2.09	1.69	2.48	3.01
Total			34.50	29.29	73.67	88.28

a Data from 2000 are the output of upper-scale enterprises.
Source: China National Light Industry Council (2008).

reached 3 billion m^2—half the world's total; and even sanitary ceramics shared 30 percent of the world's total (about 75 million pieces).

The weight equivalent physical output is counted by the following rules: the daily used ceramics are estimated at 0.25 kg per piece; sanitary ceramics at 15 kg per piece; and construction ceramics at 20 kg per m^2, assuming a standard tile to have a thickness of 8 mm. According to these estimations, we can then establish the total output of China's ceramics industry to have been 96 million tons in 2005, which was 52 percent of the world's. Among them, upper-scale enterprises (with revenue above 5 million yuan, according to the definition of the National Bureau of Statistics of China) contributed nearly 74 million tons. In addition, construction ceramics shared more than 90 percent of the total physical output, and so they also dominate the consumption of raw materials.

Despite consuming such a large volume of raw materials, the gross output of structural ceramics was less than double that of non-structural ceramics. This led to its material intensity reaching 11–13 times that of non-structural ceramics. For example, in 2006, structural ceramics needed to produce 6.65 kg of products to obtain output worth US$1, but non-structural ceramics only needed 0.57 kg of products. Fortunately, the gap in their energy intensity was not as large, but was still about twice the average of China's manufacturing (see Figure 2.24).[3]

The problem related to its dominant position is that structural ceramics actually overuse the raw material of the daily used and ornamental ceramics, the kaolin (china) clay. This kind of white clay is quite rare compared with generally used red clay, but, in China, the proportion of kaolin clay in the raw material of construction ceramics (about 30–40 percent) is even closer to

Table 5.3 Physical indicators of different ceramics products of upper-scale enterprises[a]

	2003	2004	2005	2006
Structural ceramics				
Gross output (US$ billion)	5.07	7.16	9.92	12.64
Physical output (million tons)	47.26	60.22	70.00	84.00
Material intensity (kg/US$)	9.31	8.41	7.06	6.65
Energy consumption (mtoe[b])	8.60	10.96	12.74	15.29
Energy intensity (kgoe[c]/US$)	1.69	1.53	1.28	1.21
Non-structural ceramics[d]				
Gross output (US$ billion)	4.51	5.09	5.53	7.54
Physical output (million tons)	3.08	3.43	3.67	4.28
Material intensity (kg/US$)	0.68	0.67	0.66	0.57
Energy consumption (mtoe)	2.59	2.88	3.09	3.59
Energy intensity (kgoe/US$)	0.57	0.56	0.56	0.48

a Those with revenue above 5 million yuan, according to the definition of the National Bureau of Statistics of China.
b Million ton oil equivalent.
c Kilogram oil equivalent.
d Industrial ceramics are excluded.
Source: Author's calculation, based on China National Light Industry Council (2008).

Table 5.4 China's kaolin clay trade

	Export			Import		
	Amount (10,000 ton)	*Value (US$10,000)*	*Price (US$/ton)*	*Amount (10,000 ton)*	*Value (US$10,000)*	*Price (US$/ton)*
1996	88.2	1,927	21.85	3.7	959	257.80
1997	82.0	1,850	22.56	5.4	1,326	244.20
1998	88.2	1,766	20.02	6.4	1,473	229.08
1999	89.2	1,807	20.49	10.5	2,538	241.71
2000	87.1	2,070	23.77	18.3	3,545	231.93
2001	77.7	1,931	24.85	19.1	4,430	231.93
2002	70.8	2,236	31.58	23.3	5,091	218.50
2003	83.9	2,742	32.68	27.4	5,803	211.78

Source: China National Light Industry Council (2008).

that actually in them (about 45 percent), which is much higher than in the construction ceramics of Italy or Spain. According to this proportion, we can then estimate that the consumption of kaolin clay in 2006 for the three main groups was 21.1 million tons for construction ceramics, 0.39 million tons for sanitary ceramics, and 1.56 million tons for daily used and ornamental ceramics (China National Light Industry Council, 2008).[4] The limited resource of kaolin clay should be used with much lower material intensity to produce non-structural ceramics.

Another problem with the kaolin clay resource is that China mainly exports the raw clay and imports high-value-added finished clay products. In 2003, 0.84 million tons were exported, with a total value of US$27.4 million, but imports reached US$58.0 million with only 0.27 million tons. This means the export unit value is only one-seventh of the import unit value. Even given that this gap had narrowed from one-twelfth in 1996, its trade balance has changed from a surplus of about US$9 million to a deficit of about US$20 million in the same period of time.

Another important input of China's ceramic industry is its large labor force. Over the past 10 years, China's labor force input maintained a level of nearly half of the world's total. This is the same as its physical output of the world, which means physical-labor productivity (ton per person per year) is just about the average level of the world, which is about half that of the leading economies (China National Light Industry Council, 2008). However, under the measurement of GIO, China's productivity was only one-seventh to one-twelfth of that of other leading countries in 2004, but the nominal productivity quadrupled from 1995, which meant that China's gap narrowed a lot. China's structural ceramics industry had a higher comparative productivity, about one-fifth of the other main producers, apart from Italy, but that of the non-structural industry was about one-tenth.

Table 5.5 Employment and productivity of main ceramic producers

	Employment (persons)			Labor productivity (US$/person/year)		
	1995	2000	2004	1995	2000	2004
Total ceramics						
China	985,000	698,900	800,800	3,578	9,297	16,485 (100)
Italy	83,172	76,916	68,251	121,346	123,512	194,528 (1,180)
Japan	72,046	60,690	43,036	153,764	136,998	147,975 (898)
Spain	61,953	63,378	57,192[a]	101,114	92,929	121,660[a] (738)
United States		62,408	45,037		114,296	142,727 (866)
Structural ceramics						
China			269,600			26,560 (100)
Italy	46,396	45,531	42,370	139,541	143,428	232,555 (876)
Japan	12,017	8,751	6,581	162,787	144,213	140,446 (529)
Spain	29,144	37,075	38,488[a]	117,382	104,773	157,202[a] (592)
United States		25,018	20,511		118,318	162,547 (612)
Non-structural ceramics						
China			531,200			11,881 (100)
Germany	36,776	31,385	25,881	84,812	66,924	109,055 (918)
Japan	60,029	51,939	36,455	151,958	135,782	149,334 (1,257)
United Kingdom	32,809	26,303	18,704[a]	64,214	61,876	76,962[a] (648)
United States	44,000	37,390	24,526	80,273	111,605	126,152 (1,062)

a Data for 2003.
Note: Numbers in brackets are the relative level of labor productivity.
Source: Author's calculation, based on UNIDO (2008).

Export and its sophistication

With regard to the export side, the market of China's total non-structural and structural ceramic products reached US$5 billion in 2005, which represented 17 percent of the world's total, just behind Italy. Concerning the production structure, China's export structure experienced an important change after 2000, when structural ceramic products began to have an increasingly larger share of China's exports. Before 2000, its share remained at 5 percent, but, by 2007, it had already reached nearly half (46.54 percent) of China's export of ceramic products.

China became the biggest exporter of non-structural ceramics in 1994, and its exports reached US$2.7 billion in 2006, but dropped to US$2.4 billion in 2007. Among all exports in 2006, household ceramics reached US$1.9 billion, and ornamental ceramics accounted for US$0.8 billion, all of which were world leaders. The physical output reached 15.53 billion pieces in 2006, which was nearly 70 percent of the world's total (China National Light Industry Council, 2008).

However, China's export of structural ceramic products is still the third largest in the world, after Italy and Spain. Since 2000, China has seen its exports catch up, rising more than tenfold from US$0.15 billion in 2001 to US$2.13 billion in 2007. China's physical output overtook that of Italy and Spain in 2005 and reached 0.6 billion m^2 in 2007.

The difference between China's export value and physical exports comes from the latter's export unit value. Measured by area, the unit price of China's structural ceramic products is only one-quarter of Italy's and half Spain's. However, the unit price per kilogram is just the same as Spain's and half

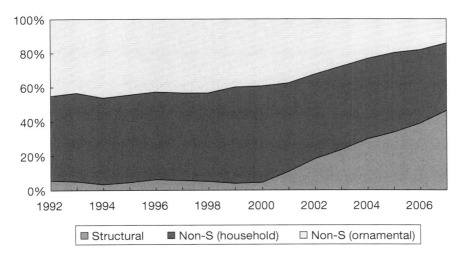

Figure 5.3 Export structure of China's ceramics products
Source: Author's calculation based on UNSTA (2008).

142 *Comparative study of three of China's industries*

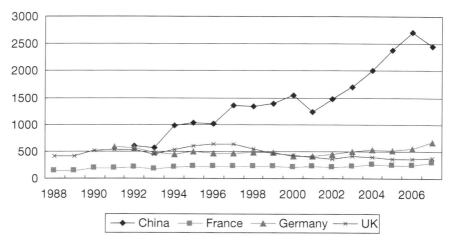

Figure 5.4 Export of non-structural ceramics (666) (US$ million)
Source: Author's calculation, based on UNSTA (2008).

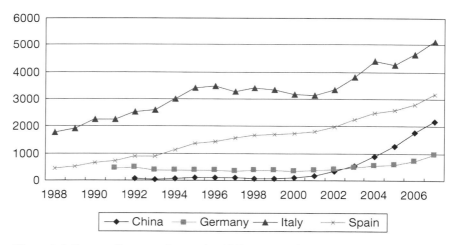

Figure 5.5 Export of structural ceramics (66244-5) (US$ million)
Source: Author's calculation, based on UNSTA (2008).

Italy's. This difference comes from the export product form. The average weight per square meter of China's export tiles and bricks is only 7–8 kg, but that of Italy's or Spain's reached 16–18 kg, although their level of production is similar to China's overall production. This may mean that China follows the mode of "export the good apples first."

The gap between China's export unit price of non-structural ceramic products and that of other leading producers is much larger. China's export unit values of both household and ornamental ceramics in 2007 were only about one-ninth those of other leading producers (one-sixth of Germany's ornamental ceramics). From 1996, the export unit value of China's household ceramics remained almost unchanged, but that of ornamental ceramics dropped from 1.59 per kilogram to 1.16. Even its relative unit value to the other three leading producers has dropped slightly over the past ten years.

China's low unit value is related to its low R&D intensity. China's R&D expenditure for the whole non-metallic mineral products industry is only 0.91 percent of its industrial value added, much less than the 2.18 percent Germany reached and France's 2.76 percent. The intensity of China's non-structural ceramics industry is 0.75 percent, higher than that but still lower than the average of China's total manufacturing. It is similar for the ratio of researchers to employees, but we can image the main contributor to either this ratio or the expenditure intensity for the non-structural ceramics industry is industrial ceramics, not daily used or ornamental ceramics.

Table 5.6 Export unit value of structural ceramics

	1999	2000	2001	2002	2003	2004	2005	2006	2007
US$/m²									
China	3.26	3.15	2.92	2.60	2.53	2.65	2.86	3.14	3.61
Italy		7.47	7.63	8.33	10.08	11.53	11.99	13.53	14.72
Spain	5.58	5.70	5.86	6.02	6.09	7.51	7.42	6.62	6.72
US$/kg									
China		0.37	0.37	0.38	0.46	0.41	0.41	0.41	0.44
Italy	0.52	0.47	0.47	0.50	0.60	0.66	0.68	0.73	
Spain	0.38	0.34	0.32	0.33	0.39	0.43	0.40		

Source: China National Light Industry Council (2008) and UNSTA (2008).

Table 5.7 Export unit value of non-structural ceramics (US$/kg)

	1991	1996	2001	2006	2007
Household (6661)					
China		0.87	0.63	0.91	0.91
France	8.79	11.17	6.74	9.43	9.36
Germany	7.59	8.68	6.47	8.18	9.01
United Kingdom	8.56	9.12	8.29	6.09	9.85
Ornamental (6662)					
China		1.59	0.98	1.28	1.16
France	10.30	14.01	7.76	8.36	9.53
Germany	9.55	5.50	5.03	5.61	6.30
United Kingdom	13.17	11.62	10.76	9.28	9.20

Source: Author's calculation, based on UNSTA (2008).

144 *Comparative study of three of China's industries*

Table 5.8 R&D intensity throughout sectors, 2004

	R&D expenditure in value added (%)	Number of researchers (FTE) per 1,000 employers
Total manufacturing	1.90	6.33
31 Non-metallic mineral products	0.91	2.01
315 Non-structural Ceramics	1.66	2.65

Source: Author's calculation based on OECD (2008b).

Main case: Sanhuan Group—top daily-used-ceramics producer

Sanhuan Group is based at the Beiliu Stoneware Porcelain Factory (located in Yulin City, in Guangxi Province), a joint venture between the state-owned Third Ceramic Factory of Beiliu City and Hong Kong investors, built up from 1988. In 1992, a new, shareholding cooperative enterprise, Sanhuan Industry Co. Ltd., was founded, with contributions from all employees.[5] Shareholding cooperation had just become legal for companies after the 15th Chinese Communist Party National Congress in that year. This new cooperation focused on more technology-intensive products, and until 1996, its revenue had grown fifteenfold. It then became the fifth-largest producer of daily used ceramics in China, with a physical output of 50 million pieces per year, revenue of nearly 100 million yuan (about US$12 million), and exports worth US$10 million.

In 1995, Sanhuan acquired the largest state-owned ceramics enterprise, the Ceramics Factory of Beiliu. During this M&A, Sanhuan used a "splitting, leasing, and buying" method to avoid ownership problems if it directly let the enterprise be bankrupted. It then, first, bought all shares belonging to non-state shareholders and leased the two worst production lines. The other four, better-performing lines were leased by the new shareholding company, Xinshiji Co. Ltd., founded by Sanhuan (51 percent share) and the employees of the Ceramics Factory of Beiliu. Two years later, it used the "offsetting-debts-with-assets" (*yizi dizhai*) method to pay back its bank loan and finally hold the majority share of the Ceramics Factory of Beiliu.

Sanhuan Industry Co. Ltd. first transited its ownership to limited liability cooperation in 1997, then to a shareholding cooperation in 1998, according to the requirements of the Cooperation Law of China. It then had four branch companies for kiln furniture, packing paper products, refractory materials, and mechanical engineering. Including the shareholding companies of Beiliu Stoneware Porcelain and Ceramics Factory, its physical output reached 100 million pieces, with revenue of 180 million yuan, and it became the third-largest ceramics producer in China.

After China entered the WTO in 2000, Sanhuan Group experienced quite fast growth: its revenue became the highest among China's daily-used-ceramics

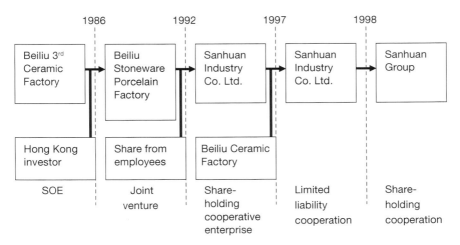

Figure 5.6 History and ownership transition of Sanhuan Group
Source: Author's design.

producers in 2002 and then doubled by 2007; its exports become number 1 among all Chinese daily-used-ceramic producers in 2003 and doubled over the next 4 years. The most important feature is that exports represented between 70 and more than 80 percent of its revenue, which is typical of export-oriented production. However, during the same period of time, its profits followed an inverted-U curve, and those of 2007 were even lower than those of 2003. Its profit–revenue ratio, 5.42 percent in 2004, was much higher than the average of China's daily-used-ceramics industry of about 1.41 percent in 2004, but it was seriously damaged by the influence of the appreciation of RMB and the decrease in export tax refunds in 2007 and dropped to 2.56 percent in 2007.

The comparatively high profit ratio is related to the production mode of the Sanhuan Group. The share of OEM mode in revenue dropped from 86.72 percent to 72.79 in 2004, but the ODM mode skyrocketed from 0.99 percent to 15.18 percent within these two years. From 2005, the share of OBM even reached nearly 10 percent of the revenue. Generally speaking, the profit ratios of these three modes are quite different: the OEM products have an average export unit price of US$0.3 per piece, which is a little higher than the average in China of about US$0.21 per piece. However, the unit price of stoneware porcelain products, designed by Sanhuan and marked with their "GXKC" brand (the OBM mode), reached nearly US$2 per piece, close to that of Germany, but the costs of these two kinds of product are not so different.

Even within the OEM production, the mode with the lowest profit ratio, the share of foreign companies doubled from 11.24 percent in 2002 to 21.39 percent in the first half of 2005. Two world-famous brands, IKEA and TOGNANA had become the third- and fourth-largest OEM clients of Sanhuan,

Table 5.9 Main economic indicators of Sanhuan Group (10,000 yuan)

	2002	2003	2004	2005	2006	2007
Physical output (pieces)	16,276.16 (1)	17,837.44 (1)	17,970.87 (1)	19,033.10 (1)	17,600.00	17,500.00
Revenue (10,000 yuan)	39,000.00 (1)	43,198.02 (1)	49,373.91 (1)	63,191.37 (1)	70,743.50	78,200.00
Export (US$10,000)	2,281.22 (2)	4,228.67 (1)	5,119.29 (1)	6,303.96 (1)	6,321.61	7,155.43
Export in revenue (%)	72.75	82.12	84.40	81.72	71.24	69.58
Tax & profit (10,000 yuan)		7,652.21 (3)	8,365.76 (3)	9,749.08 (2)	7,969.07 (2)	6,131.40
Profit (10,000 yuan)	1,513.95 (6)	2,217.98 (5)	2,677.48 (3)	(3)	3,065.13	2,000.00
Profit–revenue ratio (%)	5.42	5.13	5.42		4.33	2.56

Notes: Numbers in brackets are the ranking among China's daily-used-ceramics producers.
Source: Author's calculation, based on Sanhuan Group (2005, 2007).

Table 5.10 Distribution of different production modes of Sanhuan Group (10,000 yuan)

	2002	2003	2004	2005 (01–07)
OEM	24,238.07 (86.72)	32,930.06 (76.23)	35,939.5 (72.79)	21,640.91 (60.00)
ODM	276.75 (0.99)	3,796.04 (8.79)	7,493.32 (15.18)	4,094.39 (11.35)
OBM	923.19 (3.30)	2,321.39 (5.37)	1,839.88 (3.73)	3,478.2 (9.64)
Total	25,438.01 (91.02)	39,047.49 (90.39)	45,272.7 (91.69)	29,213.5 (81.00)

Note: Numbers in brackets are the shares of the mode of total revenue.
Source: Author's calculation, based on Sanhuan Group (2005).

Table 5.11 Main OEM brand of Sanhuan Group

Sourcing corporation	OEM brand	Share in revenue (%)			
		2002	2003	2004	2005 (01–07)
Mainland China		14.89	16.64	13.68	10.26
Wangfang Industry	ROYAL	5.14	4.73	3.20	3.84
	BYGOLDA	0.38	0.45	0.49	1.06
Dongchengxin Industry	MF	4.30	6.05	5.07	1.64
Guolin Industry	TOP CHOICE	5.07	5.41	4.92	3.72
Hong Kong & Taiwan		31.19	27.78	32.21	32.62
HK: Jianyi	VANWELL	22.12	20.53	15.11	1.34
HK: Lianhe Ceramics	ARC			1.95	12.18
	MIKASA				8.12
HK: Fengli Supply	NPX	5.50	1.79	2.67	1.74
HK: Yongda Mingji	HOME	2.06	0.44	0.26	0.24
HK: Changfa Industry	RICH FINE	0.82	1.22	1.28	1.86
HK: Fujia Industry	SAKURA	0.69	3.80	5.49	1.35
Taiwan: Tangcai	SNOOPY			4.17	4.40
	LENOXX			1.28	1.39
Foreign countries		11.24	14.16	20.46	21.39
Germany: Dezhonghang	R&B	11.24	14.16	11.73	8.19
Sweden: IKEA	IKEA			4.45	6.98
Italy: TOGNANA	TOGNANA			4.08	4.99
USA: LENOX	GORHAM			–	0.76
UK: BT				0.20	0.47
Total		57.32	58.58	66.35	64.27

Source: Author's calculation, based on Sanhuan Group (2005).

148 *Comparative study of three of China's industries*

Table 5.12 Total input of technical activity

	2003	2004	2005
Technical Development (10,000 yuan)	2,250.74	2,949.57	3,938.97
	(5.21)	(5.91)	(6.23)
R&D expenditure (10,000 yuan)	230.17	508.93	
	(0.53)	(1.03)	(0.97 [a])
Technical renovations (10,000 yuan)	4,177.53	2,255.47	1,880.90
	(9.67)	(4.52)	(2.97)
Total technical activity (10,000 yuan)	6,428.27	5,205.04	5,819.87
	(14.88)	(10.43)	(9.20)

Notes: All numbers in brackets are their share in revenue.
a Data for the first half of 2005.
Source: Author's calculation, based on Sanhuan Group (2005).

and their outsourcing had already accounted for 12 percent of its revenue. This shows Sanhuan's advantage as the leading daily-used-ceramic producer and processor in China.

Sanhuan's competitiveness partly comes from its high-technology input. The R&D expenditure had a 1.03 percent share of its revenue in 2004, which is double the average of the ceramics industry, which was about 0.54 percent that year. The overall expenditure on technical development shared nearly 6 percent of its revenue, which was five times the industrial average in 2004. Furthermore, Sanhuan's technology center had 533 employees, which was 6.94 percent of its total employees, but the average of China's ceramic industry was only 1.37 percent in 2004. This center was already the enterprise's technology center of Guangxi Province and may become the national center in the near future, which will be the first among all daily-used-ceramic enterprises.

Based on this large technical input, the Sanhuan Group's new products doubled each year, from 300 in 2000 to 574 in 2002, and to 1,294 and 1,336 in 2004 and 2005. Of them, Sanhuan already has ninety-seven design patents in China and fourteen in the European Patent Office. Furthermore, Sanhuan adopted twenty-five national technology standards and also contributed to the establishment of three, the "Measurement method for lead (cadmium) release by daily used ceramics" (GB/T3534–2002), the "Permitted limit for lead (cadmium) release by ceramics in contact with food" (GB/T12651–2003), and the ceramics-related China Compulsory Certification (CCC). These have all provided Sanhuan Group with a strong competitive advantage over all the other ceramic producers in China.

Their main trademark, "GXKC," has also been registered at the Trademarks and Designs Registration Office of the European Union and the United States Patent and Trademark Office. This trademark already had a good reputation in the EU and U.S. markets, which means that Sanhuan can outsource some production to other domestic producers. These are mainly the daily-used-ceramics companies in Chaozhou City of Guangdong Province, and their products contribute one-quarter of Sanhuan's total revenue (about 200 million yuan).

Furthermore, Sanhuan already had a trademark group, including "Sanhuanci," "Yuci," "Guici," "Guiyu," and "Nanyu," and some of these brands are used when Sanhuan outsources low-quality ceramic products to other small producers. This kind of outsourcing is called "colorful ceramic processing," which means those enterprises only provide blank ceramic items, which are glazed and marked by the Sanhuan Group. The physical output with these trademarks reached 185 million pieces, which was 10 million pieces more than the output of products with the "GXKC" brand in 2007.

In other words, more than 60 percent of Sanhuan's products were not produced by the company itself, either partially or totally. The license fees from its outsourcing also brought Sanhuan large amounts of profit. Its advantage mainly comes from having a strong R&D capacity and brand reputation. This shows that Sanhuan has already moved to a higher position on the value chain, but, compared with the world market leaders, such as Royal Doulton (United Kingdom), Wedgwood (United Kingdom), Villeroy & Boch (Germany), and Tognana (Italy), only Sanhuan's top OBM products can be likened to theirs in terms of export unit price.

Contrast case: New Zhongyuan—top construction-ceramics producer

Foshan City of Guangdong Province has been China's production base since the late 1990s. By 2006, the production capacity of all the construction-ceramics companies in Foshan had reached 1.6 billion m^2, which was 90 percent of that of Guangdong Province and half the total capacity of China. In addition, 83.6 percent of the total exports of China's construction-ceramic products in 2005 were from Guangdong, and Foshan produced a large majority of the exports (China National Light Industry Council, 2008). Of all the construction-ceramics companies in Foshan, New Zhongyuan is the largest, contributing one-fifth of the total production capacity—about 300 million m^2 per year. Furthermore, its exports also represented one-tenth of the total of China's construction-ceramic products, worth US$80 million in 2004.

The New Zhongyuan Ceramics Co. Ltd. was founded in 2001, and its main brand was set up by its predecessor, Nanyue General Factory, for its ceramic products, in 1995. During New Zhongyuan's 20-year history, the main strategy has been to expand its production capacity by building factories throughout China, from Foshan to many hinterland cities outside Guangdong Province. From 2001, New Zhongyuan built branches in Jiajiang City in Sichuan Province (southwest China), Hengyang City in Hunan Province (central China), Gaoan City in Jiangxi Province (southeast China), and Faku City in Liaoning Province (northeast China). The aim was to seek the lowest production costs and be close to the forefront of the domestic market.

New Zhongyuan's R&D capacity makes it the leading company within China's construction-ceramic industry. For example, the largest polished tile (1,800 × 1,200 mm) can be only formed under a 10,000-ton hydraulic press, and its equipment advantage means that New Zhongyuan dominates the market for this high-value-added product. Furthermore, New Zhongyuan also has quite a lot of technological capacity in new products. Over 1,000 of New Zhongyuan's products have been granted the National Patent (design patent included).

A large number of franchised stores all around China formed its powerful sales network, which strengthened the brand marketing of New Zhongyuan compared with many other producers that joined the integrated retail of construction materials. At the very least, New Zhongyuan has already become a well-known brand through the boom in consumption, together with that of the real-estate industry in China. However, during recent years, global giants such as Marcacorona (Italy) have begun to enter the Chinese market. Marcacorona's exhibition center in Shanghai is its second-largest center in the world, and there were due to be between five and eight more in the main cities of China by 2010. This will certainly increase competition greatly.

The challenge for New Zhongyuan comes more from outside restrictions, because the construction-ceramic industry is highly energy and raw-material intensive (see Table 5.3). In 2006, it only contributed 7 percent of Foshan's total gross industrial output but consumed 20 percent of total energy used (30 percent of all fuel) and emitted 13 percent of total sulfur dioxide. New Zhongyuan must certainly be one of the largest energy consumers in Foshan. The construction-ceramic companies in Foshan also consumed 36.8 million tons of clay material, which was 43.8 percent of China's total.

The physical energy intensity of New Zhongyuan dropped 9.6 percent to 0.31 ton coal equivalent per ton of product in 2007, which was 23.8 percent lower than the average for China's construction-ceramic industry. The energy consumption per 10,000 yuan GIO also dropped 15.9 percent and reached 2.2 tce, already meeting the energy-saving policy in the eleventh Chinese Five-Year Plan, which brought strict targets for these kinds of company (China National Light Industry Council, 2008).

However, according to the new catalogue of export tax refunds in July 2007, construction ceramics was classified as "high energy and resource use products," and the tax refund for its exports was also adjusted, from 13 percent to 5 percent. Besides, the compulsory indefinite contracts for labor and related compensation required by China's new labor law from 2008 also increased the costs of migrant labor in Guangdong Province. Together with the appreciation in RMB, these new changes certainly brought New Zhongyuan big challenges.

International comparison

Today, high-end non-structural-ceramic products are dominated by the producers from West Europe, such as Waterford Wedgwood from the United Kingdom and Villeroy & Boch from Germany. These two emerged from the Industrial Revolution, and their brands have enjoyed a long-lasting, world-class reputation since then. Today, they have expanded greatly through a series of M&A to become the two leading producers in the world's daily-used-ceramics market.

Waterford Crystal purchased Wedgwood Porcelain for US$360 million in 1986, held the majority of shares of Rosenthal AG in 1997, and then acquired Royal Doulton in 2005 for US$77.5 million, all of which are world-famous, fine-porcelain producers. Villeroy & Boch became publicly listed on the German stock market in 1990 and then expanded to all European countries through about ten different M&As after that. Villeroy & Boch also changed its structure through the purchase of the leading Swedish sanitary-ware producer, AB Gustavsburg, in 2000, and the sale of its tile factory in 2004.

Compared with Wedgwood and Villeroy & Boch, Sanhuan Group is still quite small in terms of either revenue or total assets, which were still only one-tenth in 2007. Its operating income is even smaller when compared with Villeroy & Boch. However, the physical output of Sanhuan Group might be even larger than theirs, if we consider the low unit price of its products, but its exports represent a large proportion of the total sales of all three, varying from nearly 70 percent to 90 percent.

Table 5.13 Main indicators of daily-used-ceramics producers

	2001	2002	2003	2004	2005	2006	2007
Revenue (US$ million)							
Sanhuan		33.8	52.2	59.7	77.1	88.7	102.8
Wedgwood	1,019.3	900.7		1,036.9	1,023.2	952.4	934.8
Tableware			527.2	539.0	574.0	638.6	672.0
Villeroy & Boch	916.7	870.0	1,192.6	1,306.0	1,057.0	1,074.3	1,248.8
Tableware	276.6	263.9	359.2	431.4	377.4	429.4	480.3
Export (US$ million)							
Sanhuan		22.8	42.3	51.2	63.0	63.2	71.6
Wedgwood			899.8	909.6	814.6	779.6	828.5
Villeroy & Boch	605.9	606.4	828.9	917.3	732.4	706.9	988.9
Operating income (US$ million)							
Sanhuan		1.8	2.7	3.2		3.8	2.6
Wedgwood	−1.0	−9.1	−23.5	−18.2	−254.4	−158.3	−22.9
Villeroy & Boch	25.4	24.0	−22.3	46.0	28.8	43.9	57.1
Total assets (US$ million)							
Sanhuan		42.3	47.3	57.3	63.7		
Wedgwood	884.2	838.6	953.5	1,043.3	940.4	824.9	898.7
Tableware			528.4	633.3	750.0	648.1	707.5
Villeroy & Boch	828.0	783.5	1,059.4	1,068.2	911.3	1,040.5	1,184.5

Source: Author's calculation, based on Sanhuan Group (2005, 2007), Waterford Wedgwood (various years), and Villeroy & Boch (various years).

Table 5.14 Operating indicators of main daily-used-ceramic producers

	2001	2002	2003	2004	2005	2006	2007
Operating margin (%)							
Sanhuan		5.4	5.1	5.4		4.3	2.6
Wedgwood	−0.1	−5.1	−2.3	−1.8	−26.7	−16.9	−2.3
Tableware			−4.1	−5.1	−26.7	−18.8	−3.8
Villeroy & Boch	2.8	2.8	−1.9	3.4	2.7	3.4	4.6
Tableware	5.1	7.3	0.5	6.4	3.4	1.9	5.4
Labor productivity (US$1,000/person/year)							
Sanhuan					9.5		
Wedgwood			116.1	127.0	91.5	97.3	114.3
Villeroy & Boch	84.6	79.0	110.3	135.6	111.0	116.3	135.4
Tableware	87.1	81.2	108.7	130.1	117.5	142.6	168.7
R&D expenditure to revenue (%)							
Sanhuan			0.53	1.03	0.97		
Wedgwood			0.98	0.73	1.05		0.73
Villeroy & Boch	1.35	1.32	1.13	1.39	1.48	1.10	1.22
Tableware		0.76	0.74	0.75	1.03	0.89	0.73

Source: Author's calculation, based on Sanhuan Group (2005, 2007), Waterford Wedgwood (various years), and Villeroy & Boch (various years).

The labor productivity of Sanhuan Group was also only one-tenth of that of Wedgwood and Villeroy & Boch, but its R&D intensity was similar to theirs. The operating margin for Wedgwood has been negative since 2001. Even after its largest loss in 2006, Wedgwood increased its investment in Indonesia from US$75 million to more than US$100 million, through Royal Doulton, in 2007, and doubled the production capacity from 6 million pieces per year to 12 million pieces per year, which made Indonesia its largest production base overseas. Finally, Wedgwood went into administration in January 2009.

Distribution of value added to the value chain

Comparing the two cases, they show different patterns on the generalized value chain. Overall, the two companies have quite low value added to the whole value chain, especially the production parts, and this is also characteristic of China's ceramics industry. The difference between them comes from the higher ends.

Sanhuan Group has stronger R&D capacity, based on an independent technology center that can be self-sufficient and provides technical solutions and designs for new products for the group. This makes the value added of the R&D part of Sanhuan Group higher than that of New Zhongyuan. Although the Sanhuan Group has had no role in the establishment of international technology standards, the technology standard it was involved in gave an advantage to China's daily-used-ceramic industry. However, the New Zhongyuan shows almost no activity in this field, and this makes its value chain show an absence on the left-hand side, which corresponds to a potential loss in real value added on the value chain.

In contrast, New Zhongyuan has advantages in sales in the domestic market, as one of the only construction-ceramic companies that has its own franchised-store network all across China. The value added of this part for New Zhongyuan is certainly higher than that for Sanhuan Group, whose main sales come under OEM or ODM. Besides, even if Sanhuan Group has some OBM products with higher value added on the international market, it cannot compete with the domestic reputation of New Zhongyuan in terms of brand value added.

Wedgwood has even lower value added in the processing segment than Sanhuan Group, but this is greatly compensated for by its ultrahigh value added in its branding. Overall, however, Villeroy & Boch has more balanced value added in all parts of the value chain, from a stronger R&D capacity to a more effective sales system, and this should be the future model for China's firms in the ceramics industry.

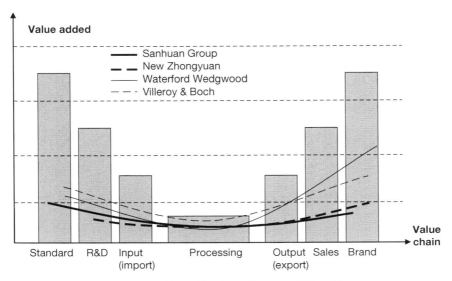

Figure 5.7 Pattern of value added of Sanhuan Group and New Zhongyuan
Source: Author's design.

154 *Comparative study of three of China's industries*

Steel industry

From a wider historical perspective, China's share in the world's total crude steel production has reached the level of Russia's in the mid 1980s and that of the United Kingdom at the beginning of the twentieth century. The peak of the United Kingdom's share exceeded half the world's total in the mid nineteenth century, when it was the "world workshop." The peak of the United States' share was about 50 percent in the inter-war period (except for the time of the Great Depression, when the United States still produced one-third of the world's steel), which also made it a "world workshop" at that time. Among the three catch-up countries, China has the highest growth rate when compared with Russia and Japan.

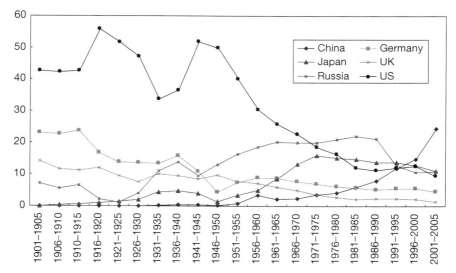

Figure 5.8 Shares of major steel producers from a historical perspective
Note: The points are 5-year averages.
Source: China Iron and Steel Industrial Association (2006).

Table 5.15 Length of time taken by major steel producers to expand production from 1 to 100 million tons

	Time scale	*Output scale (million tons)*	*Duration (year)*	*Average growth (%)*
China	1950–1996	0.158–101.24	47	14.7
Japan	1909–1973	0.154–119.32	64	10.9
Russia/Soviet Union	1885–1967	0.193–102.22	82	7.9
United States	1872–1953	0.145–101.25	81	8.4

Source: Chen and Zhao (2005).

By 1996, the first year of the Ninth Five-Year Plan period, China's crude-steel output exceeded 100 million tons, making it the world leader. It took China only 48 years to bring the annual steel output up to 100 million tons, which is half the output of the United States and the former Soviet Union. It took Japan, known as a miracle of growth, 64 years to raise its steel output from 154,000 tons to more than 100 million tons.

Production and export

China has passed through three different stages since 1980, in terms of the proportion of its steel output in the world's total. The first stage was the period of the 1980s, when its steel output was close to that of Germany and the Republic of Korea (ROK, 5 percent of the world's total), and it became the third-largest steel producer after overtaking Russia in 1992. The second stage was the period from 1992 to 2000, when the proportion of China's steel output of the world's total rose steadily to reach 15 percent. The breakthrough, in 1992, was price reform of crude steel and its products. Market pricing greatly enhanced the development of China's iron and steel industry. The third stage was the period since 2000, when the proportion doubled within five years and reached one-third of the world's total output.

This growth was prompted by both internal and external factors. The housing reform of 1998 greatly stimulated steel consumption in construction, so that its proportion of total consumption has risen from one-third to more than half over the past ten years. The expansion of steel production from appointed enterprises to all enterprises with a foreign trade license, after

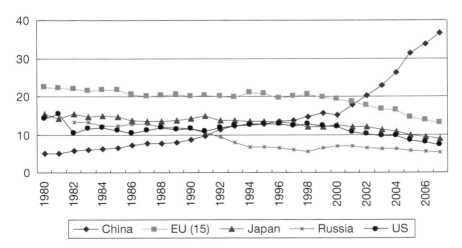

Figure 5.9 Shares of main steel producers in the world's physical output

Source: Author's calculation, based on China Iron and Steel Industrial Association (2006) and IISI (various years).

156 *Comparative study of three of China's industries*

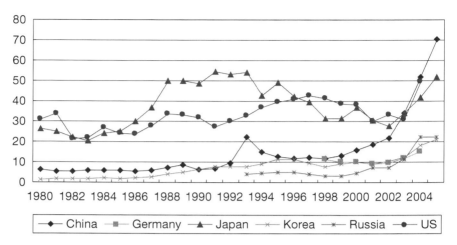

Figure 5.10 Industrial value added of the iron and steel industry (3710/2710 + 2731; US$ billion)
Source: Author's calculation, based on UNIDO (2008).

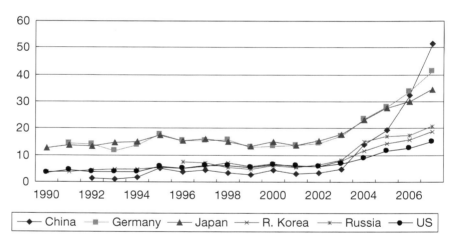

Figure 5.11 Exports of main steel producers (US$ billion)
Source: Author's calculation, based on UNSTA (2008).

China entered the WTO in 2000, provided a great opportunity for China's steel production to boom. In 2006, China's iron and steel industry became the largest in the world, measured in terms of industrial value added, and surpassed Japan's peak in the early 1990s.

The production boom of China's iron and steel industry was accompanied by a sharp rise in its exports. The exports of the six main producers all increased from 2003, and China's growth rate was much higher, with the result that its exports overtook those of the United States, Korea, and Russia two years later, and it became number one in 2007. In fact, the nominal growth rates of other main steel producers were between about 17.8 percent (Japan) and 26.0 percent (Russia), which were quite fast. That of China, however, reached 80.9 percent between 2003 and 2007, and this made it possible for China to catch up within a very short period of time.

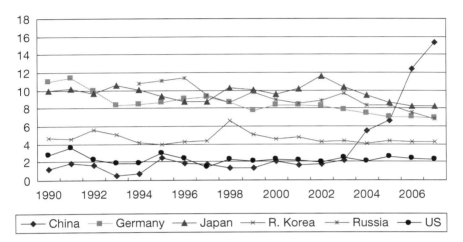

Figure 5.12 Shares of main steel producers in the world's physical exports
Source: Author's calculation, based on UNSTA (2008).

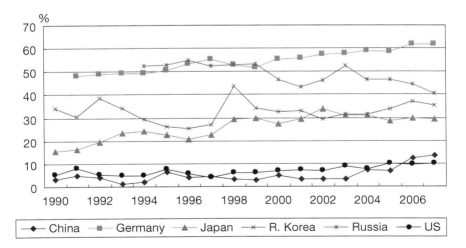

Figure 5.13 Export share of physical output
Source: Author's calculation, based on UNSTA (2008) and IISI (various years).

Interestingly, however, the physical exports of the other five main producers hardly increased after 2003. The shares of Germany, Japan, and Russia of world exports even dropped 2–3 percent. China's share rose nearly eightfold, from 2.1 percent in 2003 to 15.4 percent in 2007. The reason for these differences was that China's increases alone were driven by the quantity of physical exports, whereas all the others were driven by rises in export prices. Whether or not the cause of this problem is decided by product structure can only be clarified by analysis of the details of China's export products.

Speaking overall, the share of exports in the total output of the six major steel producers can be divided into three groups. Germany and Russia are in the first group, exporting about 50 percent of their steel products (they diverged after 2000). Korea and Japan form the second group, exporting around 30 percent of their production. China and the United States belong to the third group, where exports are just 10 percent of their total output, which may be because of their huge domestic consumption.

Structure and sophistication

The Steel Industry Production Statistical Classification of China was revised by the China Iron & Steel Association in 2002 and can be compared with the classification of the International Iron and Steel Institute (IISI). In IISI classification, the group of wide strip, plate, and sheet in coil and length equals the groups of thick and medium wide strip, ultra-thick, thick, and medium-thick plate, all sheets in length and wide sheet in coil, as in China's.[6] However,

Table 5.16 Steel product classification

IISI Classification	SITC Revision 3
Flat products	673–5
Wide strip, plate, and sheet in coil and length	63311–5, 63321–5, 67331–8, 67341–8
Narrow strip and universal plate	67316–9, 67326–9, 67339, 67349
(Tinmill or other) metallic coated sheet and strip	6742, 4–5
Non-metallic coated sheet and strip	6743
Electrical sheet and strip	6751
Long products	676–8
Concrete reinforcing bars	6761–4
Hot-rolled bars (other than concrete reinforcing bars)	6761–4
Heavy sections	6768
Light sections	6768
Railway-track material	677
Wire rod (drawn wire)	678
Tubes and tube fittings	679
Seamless tubes	6791
Welded tubes	6793–5

Source: Author's work, based on IISI (various years) and UNSTA (1986).

Comparative study of three of China's industries 159

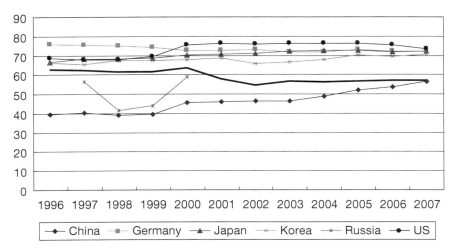

Figure 5.14 Share of flat and tube products in physical output
Source: Author's calculation, based on IISI (various years).

Table 5.17 Steel consumption by end-use sector, 2008 (%)

	China	OECD (2007)	World
Construction	49.5	50	48.1
Machinery	25.4	28	27.1
Automotive	5.6	12	11.3
Electronic equipment	2.3	5	4.6
Oil, gas, & petro	1.3		3.3
Shipbuilding	2.3	3	1.7
Other	13.6	2	3.8

Source: Data for China from China Commodity Market (2009); OECD Steel Committee (2009); Metals Consulting International Ltd. (2009).

universal plates are included in the group of narrow strips in IISI classification, but are counted as plates in China's.

The proportion of flat and tube products in China's production rose from 39.5 percent in 1996 to 56.5 percent in 2007 and has just caught up with the world average. However, it is still far lower than that of developed countries (more than 70 percent). Here, the proportion is only for the physical output. If we consider the significant difference between the prices of the high- and low-value-added products, the gap is much larger. Generally speaking, long products involve lower-tech production than flat and tube products, and so this ratio means that China still stands on a low rung of the "quality ladder" of the world's steel industry.

160 *Comparative study of three of China's industries*

The production structure of China's iron and steel industry is related to the consumption structure by the end-use sector. The share of China's high-value-added sectors, such as automotive and machinery (metal goods included), is lower than the world's average and also that of OECD countries. In particular, the share of its automotive sector is only half of theirs. In contrast, other Chinese sectors, which mainly consume low-value-added products, have quite a high proportion.

Among China's physical exports, the proportion of flat and tube products even dropped, from 75.6 percent in 2000 to 54.7 percent in 2003, and reversed to 62.4 percent in 2007, which was 8 percent lower than the world average. The proportions of the leading producers, such as Japan and Korea, varied between 82.8 and 85.8 percent that year. This is one of the main reasons for China's low export unit value.

The difference between these three groups of products is quite clear. The export unit value of long products hardly changed during that period of time, and, although that of tube products rose, its level relative to other main producers dropped. The export unit value of China's flat products, however, doubled between 2000 and 2007, following the trend of all the other leading steel producers. Among flat products, several higher-tech products, such as coated steel sheet (for car and household electronics), played a more and more important role in China's exports, and this is the case we would like to discuss later.

If we examine the detailed export unit value, there is much more variance among them than in the three groups above. The highest one for China, other stainless-steel tube and pipe fittings (67956), had an export unit value of US$10.73 per kilogram, and that of the United States and Japan reached

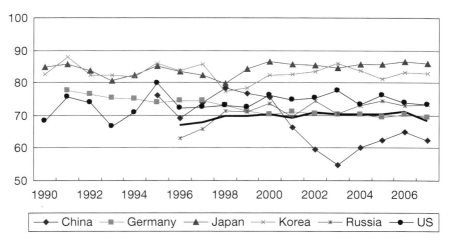

Figure 5.15 Share of flat and tube products in physical export
Source: Author's calculation, based on UNSTA (2008).

US$25.50 and US$40.72 (the highest for Japan). The highest one for the United States, stainless-steel threaded elbows, bends, and sleeves, even reached US$68.19 per kilogram in 2007. Considering the export unit value of general bar and flat products, which are mostly lower than US$1 per kilogram, the gap between different iron and steel products is quite large.

In 2007, China only had 49 products with an average export unit value higher than US$1 per kilogram among the 135 SITC 5-digit products, but

Table 5.18 Export unit value of main steel producer (US$/kg)

	1991	1996	2000	2005	2006	2007
Flat- and tube-steel products						
China		0.44	0.37	0.73	0.69	0.80
Germany	0.76	0.83	0.61	1.16	1.25	1.55
Japan	0.77	0.80	0.52	0.92	0.92	1.00
Korea	0.51	0.52	0.49	0.92	0.89	0.99
Russia		0.31	0.25	0.56	0.62	0.75
United States	0.77	1.07	0.96	1.28	1.39	1.44
Long-steel products						
China		0.36	0.31	0.49	0.46	0.54
Germany	0.63	0.62	0.44	0.87	0.92	1.14
Japan	0.71	0.68	0.57	0.86	0.89	0.99
Korea	0.59	0.57	0.45	0.73	0.79	0.99
Russia		0.26	0.19	0.46	0.52	0.70
United States	0.63	0.84	0.82	1.01	1.08	1.14

Source: Author's calculation, based on UNSTA (2008).

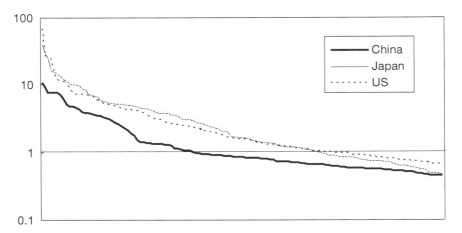

Figure 5.16 Descending export unit value of 5-digit iron and steel products, 2007
Source: Author's calculation, based on UNSTA (2008).

Japan and the United States had 90 and 92 of them, respectively. Those products contributed 25.4, 52.0, and 66.5 percent of the export values for China, Japan, and the United States, respectively, but shared just 8.4, 23.4, and 38.8 percent of the amount of physical exports. A large majority of the exports from China are still quite low-value-added products.

Efficiency and productivity

The main disadvantage of China's iron and steel industry is its labor productivity. Although China's labor input shares more than 40 percent of the world's total, its labor productivity is still lower than the world average. Compared with other leading producers, the gap is even larger, where the labor productivity of China's iron and steel industry was only one-quarter that of Germany, one-fifth that of the United States, and one-ninth those of Japan and Korea in 2005. China's catch-up only began in 1995, when it was just one-twentieth those of Germany and the United States, one-thirtieth that of Korea, and one-fortieth that of Japan.

Although China's physical labor productivity rose from 49.1 tons per employer per year in 2000 to 115.0 in 2007, 25 tons higher than Russia's, it was still only one-third those of Germany and the United States and one-sixth those of Japan and Korea. However, considering that China shares more than 40 percent of the world's total employment in the iron and steel industry and contributes one-third of the total physical output, its labor productivity is naturally just a little lower than the world's average level.

Table 5.19 Labor input and labor productivity of main steel producers

	1980	1985	1990	1995	2000	2005
Labor input (1,000 people)						
China	1,936.0	2,281.0	3,000.0	3,460.0	2,617.0	3,092.9
Germany				200.1	171.9	165.8[a]
Japan	428.0	387.0	338.0	268.3	211.7	186.2
Korea	68.9	72.9	88.3	88.2	76.0	83.4
Russia				643.6	859.3	740.5
United States	749.0	449.0	413.0	373.0	331.2	269.3[a]
Labor productivity (US$/person/year)						
China	10,758	8,077	9,051	12,667	21,846	84,744
Germany				227,000	184,521	332,836[a]
Japan	186,923	193,070	374,134	520,623	491,724	760,841
Korea	67,691	90,859	196,560	349,209	399,671	764,268
Russia				27,261	21,767	98,613
United States	103,605	135,635	183,390	245,349	267,009	421,059[a]

a Data for 2004.
Source: Author's calculation, based on UNIDO (2008).

Comparative study of three of China's industries 163

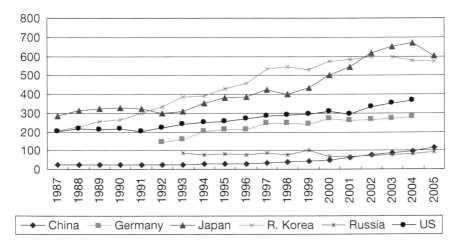

Figure 5.17 Physical labor productivity (ton/person/year)
Source: Author's calculation, based on World Steel Institution (various years) and UNIDO (2008).

Table 5.20 Physical energy and CO_2 intensity of iron and steel industry

	1980	1985	1990	1995	2000	2006
Energy intensity (kgoe/kg steel production)						
World	0.38	0.34	0.33	0.36	0.32	0.30
China	1.23	0.67	0.63	0.70	0.52	0.36
Germany	0.30	0.27	0.25	0.20	0.18	0.20
Japan	0.25	0.21	0.20	0.20	0.19	0.19
Korea	0.09	0.12	0.10	0.11	0.15	0.19
Russia			0.45	0.75	0.54	0.52
United States	0.30	0.24	0.20	0.26	0.27	0.21
CO_2 intensity (kg emission/kg steel production)						
World	1.37	1.20	1.23	1.33	1.12	1.10
China	5.07	2.95	2.55	2.92	2.20	1.70
Germany	1.12	1.06	0.93	0.83	0.70	0.71
Japan	0.92	0.78	0.73	0.71	0.68	0.68
Korea	0.33	0.31	0.31	0.46	0.58	0.48
Russia			1.54	2.60	1.53	1.28
United States	1.29	1.04	0.82	0.88	0.82	0.38

Source: Author's calculation, based on World Steel Institution (various years) and IEA (2008).

Table 5.21 R&D intensity of iron and steel industry (2710)

	Expenditure in value added (%)		Researcher (FTE) per 1,000 employees	
	2000	*2004*	*2000*	*2004*
China	1.80	2.11	5.04	7.07
Germany	2.37[a]	2.03[b]	4.57[a]	5.02[b]
Japan	4.33	3.28	26.12	34.38
Korea	0.94	1.47	6.99	9.56
Russia	0.09	0.12[b]		
United States			18.32[a]	

a Data for 1999.
b Data for 2003.
Source: Author's calculation, based on OECD (2008b).

Table 5.22 Scale distribution of China's iron and steel enterprises

Annual output (million tons)	1952	1978	1989	2000	2005	2007
0.5–0.99	1	4	9	12	–	–
1.0–2.99	0	4	8	31	29	30
3.0–4.99	0	0	3	7	13	11
5.0–7.99	0	1	1	1	8	11
8.0–9.99	0	0		2	2	2
> 10	0	0		1	8	9

Source: Data for 1952–2000 come from Chen and Zhao (2005); data for 2005 come from the China Iron and Steel Industrial Association (2006).

The proportion of energy consumption (43 percent in 2007) and CO_2 emissions (52 percent in 2007) of China's iron and steel industry is also higher than its proportion of the physical output of the world. This makes China's intensity of energy consumption and CO_2 emissions still higher than the world's average and double those of other leading steel producers, but the gap has greatly reduced from when it was three times the world's average, in 1980.

However, the R&D intensity of China's iron and steel industry is not as low relative to all main steel producers. Its R&D expenditure shares 2.11 percent of its value added, and this share is even higher than that of Germany and Korea. The number of researchers per 1000 employees reached 7.07 in 2004, which, although lower than the figure of 9.56 for Korea, was still higher than 5.02 for Germany, which was China's level in 2000. Japan and the United States have quite high R&D intensity, but China's R&D input for the iron and steel industry at least provided the possibility for technology upgrades during its recent boom years.

China's rapid development has brought a boom in iron and steel enterprises. In 1978, there was only the Bao Steel Company, with an output that reached

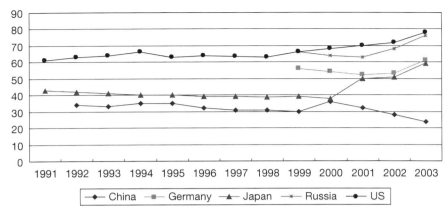

Figure 5.18 Concentration ratio (CR5) of main steel producers
Source: Author's calculation, based on Liu and Jiao (2006).

3 million tons. By 2000, there were eleven companies that had reached that scale. Seven years later, the number of such enterprises had tripled to thirty-three (see Table 5.22). Among the world's top thirty steel producers in 2007, nine were from China. Among them, Bao Steel Company ranked number five, with an annual output of 28.6 million tons.

The stagnation in the upgrading of the production structure comes from the distribution of the firms in the industry. The drop in the concentration ratio (CR; CR5 means the share of the top five firms of the total output of the industry), especially after 2000, tells us that the small firms with outputs that are mainly low-tech products (commonly the result of the scale effort) have a higher growth rate than the larger ones. Considering China's import and export structure, the deviation of the supply structure from the demand structure is the internal determinant of the development mode of China's iron and steel industry.

Main case: Baoshan Iron & Steel Co., Ltd.

Baosteel Group is the largest and most competitive steel company in China. Its predecessor, Shanghai Baoshan General Steel Factory, was built up from 1978 and began producing steel in 1985. This factory was based on a completely new mode of steel production among all the Chinese iron and steel enterprises at that time, being built far from any iron ore mine but close to the transport center of Shanghai port. This was a challenging experiment by the iron and steel industry, learning from Japan's mode, and was called "two sides (of the supply chain) abroad" (*liangtou zaiwai*) by Chinese leaders.

As a result of SOE reform from 1998 onwards, Baoshan Steel Group merged with Shanhai Steel Co. and Nanjing Meishan Steel Co. and today is the Baosteel Group. These M&As made Baosteel Group the first company with a physical output of over 10 million tons in China, and its physical output, 16.7 million tons of crude steel, made it the seventh-largest steel producer around the world in 1999. The following acquisitions happened between 2006 and 2008. Baosteel first took over the Xinjiang Bayi Steel Co., and then Guangzhou Steel Enterprises Group Co. Ltd. and Shaoguan Steel Group Co. Ltd.[7] This increased Baosteel's physical output from 22.5 million tons in 2006 to 35.4 million in 2008, and it became the third-largest steel company in the world, just after ArcelorMittal and Nippon Steel.

The Baosteel Group's revenue more than doubled, from US$14.5 billion in 2003 to US$35.5 billion in 2008, which made its ranking in the Fortune Global 500 move up from number 372 to 220 during the same period (it was also the sixth-largest company within the metal industry). Its profits reached a peak of US$2.86 billion (14.7 percent of revenue) in 2007, but dropped to US$2.31 billion (9.7 percent of revenue) in 2008, because of the current financial crisis.

The main body of Baosteel Group is the publicly listed company, Baoshan Iron & Steel Co. Ltd. It was listed on China's A-share market in November 2000, and Baosteel Group holds 85 percent of its shares. Over the following years, another one-third of the assets of Baosteel Group were merged with Baoshan Iron & Steel. By 2006, it owned 64 percent of the group's assets and contributed 89.2 percent of the group's revenue and 96.5 percent of the group's physical steel production. These proportions dropped when Baosteel acquired more companies after 2006, but Baoshan Iron & Steel still contributes 82.7 percent of the revenue, although only two-thirds of the physical steel production. This is related to the production structure of Baosteel Group and the Baoshan Iron & Steel Co. Ltd.

Baosteel Group's employment grew a little, but that of Baoshan Iron & Steel doubled because of the M&A activity in 2005. The labor productivity of each experienced a sharp rise and reached US$326,000 and US$670,000 per employee per year, respectively, in 2008, close to the levels of Germany and Japan in 2004 and more than double/four times China's average. Furthermore,

Table 5.23 Main indicators for Baosteel Group

	2003	2004	2005	2006	2007	2008
Revenue (US$ million)	14,548	19,543.3	21,501.4	22,663.4	29,939	35,517
Profit (US$ million)	946	1,537	1,395	1,622.2	2,858	2,314
Assets (US$ million)	20,792	23,421	26,523	30,259	48,795	50,755
Equity (US$ million)	11,196	12,960		17,097	26,458	
Employment (people)	102,039	94,231	92,682	91,308	110,804	108,914
Fortune Global 500 ranking	372	309	296	307	259	220
Metal companies		9	8	9	7	6

Source: Fortune (2009).

Table 5.24 Main indicators for Baoshan Iron & Steel Co. Ltd.

	2002	2003	2004	2005	2006	2007	2008
Revenue	4,093	5,372	7,085	15,688	20,216	26,224	29,356
		(36.93)	(36.25)	(72.96)	(89.20)	(87.59)	(82.65)
Net profit	516	843	1,135	1,569	1,667	1,838	966
		(89.09)	(73.85)	(112.47)	(102.76)	(64.31)	(41.75)
Total assets	7,429	7,429	7,360	17,599	19,354	25,783	29,266
		(35.73)	(31.43)	(66.35)	(63.96)	(52.84)	(57.66)
Equity	3,708	4,285	5,058	9,228	10,501	12,951	14,315
		(38.27)	(39.03)		(61.42)	(48.95)	
Crude steel production	11,582	11,547	11,867	18,361	21,741	23,776	23,124
	(58.38)	(58.11)	(55.43)	(80.81)	(96.50)	(83.34)	(65.32)
Employment	15,693	15,325	15,391	38,875	38,720	40,059	43,789
		(15.02)	(16.33)	(41.94)	(42.41)	(36.15)	(40.21)

Note: Numbers in brackets are the shares in Baosteel Group.
Source: Author's calculation, based on Baoshan Iron & Steel Co. Ltd. (various years).

168 *Comparative study of three of China's industries*

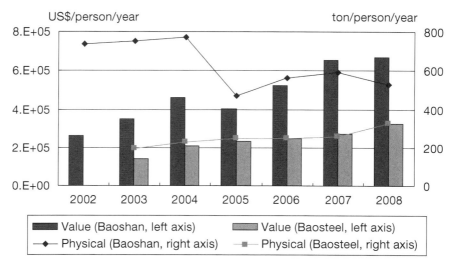

Figure 5.19 Labor productivity of Baosteel Group and Baoshan Iron & Steel Co. Ltd.
Source: Author's calculation, based on Baoshan Iron & Steel Co. Ltd. (various years).

Table 5.25 Physical output of Baosteel Group and Baoshan Iron & Steel Co. Ltd., 2006

	Baosteel Group		Baoshan Iron & Steel	
Units: 1,000 tons	*Output*	*Structure*	*Output*	*Structure*
Flat products	19,413.4	(82.84)	14,101.9	(85.48)
Plate	3,981.6	(16.99)	1,914.7	(11.61)
Wide strip, sheet in coil and length	7,591.4	(32.40)	4,837.1	(29.32)
Narrow strip and universal plate	3,930.3	(16.77)	4,292.8	(26.02)
Metallic-coated sheet and strip	2,358.5	(10.06)	1,580.8	(9.58)
Non-metallic-coated sheet and strip	679.3	(2.90)	604.2	(3.66)
Electrical sheet and strip	872.3	(3.72)	872.3	(5.29)
Long products	2,641.6	(11.27)	1,455.7	(8.82)
Concrete reinforcing bars		930.0		(3.97)
Hot-rolled bars (other than rebars)	640.7	(2.73)	631.5	(3.83)
Heavy sections				
Light sections	14.9	(0.06)		
Railway-track material	27.0	(0.12)	27.0	(0.16)
Wire rod (drawn wire)	1,029.0	(4.39)	797.1	(4.83)
Tubes and tube fittings	1,296.6	(5.53)	935.1	(5.67)
Seamless tubes	1,173.5	(5.01)	818.1	(4.96)
Welded tubes	123.2	(0.53)	117.1	(0.71)
Other	81.9	(0.35)	3.9	(0.02)

Source: Author's calculation, based on China Iron and Steel Association (2008).

their physical labor productivity also reached 325 tons and 528 tons per person per year, respectively, in 2008, similar to the levels of the United States and Korea in 2004 and also twice/four times as much as the level of China's average.

Baosteel Group's high-value-added products, such as coated sheet and strip, electrical sheet and strip, and seamless tubes etc., are produced by Baoshan Iron & Steel Co. Ltd., and the newly merged companies, such as Bayi Steel, only contribute production of low-value-added products, such as concrete reinforcing bars and wire rods (with a three-quarter share of its total output in 2006). In total, the share of flat and tube products, which are mostly high-value-added ones, in the physical output of Baoshan Iron and Steel reached more than 90 percent, which was 30 percent higher than China's average.

Among all Baoshan Iron & Steel's flat products, although galvanized sheets, color-coated sheets (which use galvanized sheets as base), and electrical sheets only contribute less than one-fifth of its total output, they are the most competitive products. Hot-dip galvanized sheets are the most advanced steel products used in automotive bodies and also the main product of the joint venture, Baosteel–NSC/Arcelor Automotive Steel Sheets Co., Ltd. After it came into operation, the proportion of hot-dip galvanized sheets in the physical output of Baosteel doubled from 3.3 percent in 2005 to 6.5 percent in 2006.

The proportion of sales of cold-rolled auto sheets (mainly galvanized sheets) by Baoshan Iron & Steel reached half the sales of all China's steel firms, and sales of home-appliance sheets (mainly color-coated sheets) also reached nearly 40 percent. The non-oriented electric sheet also shared nearly one-fifth

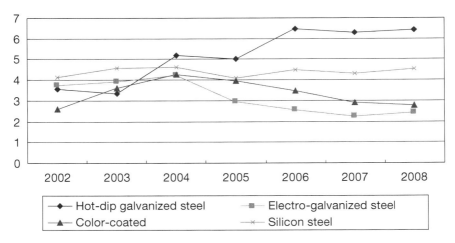

Figure 5.20 Output share of high-value-added products of Baoshan Iron & Steel Co. Ltd.

Source: Author's calculation, based on Baoshan Iron & Steel Co. Ltd. (various years).

Table 5.26 Domestic sales share of major flat and tube products (%)

	2003	2004	2005	2006	2007	2008
Cold-rolled auto sheet	45	47	52	52	50	50
Home-appliance sheet	44	35	35	37	37	37
Non-oriented electric steel	16	14	15	18	17	18
Pipeline steel	56	27	30	29	35	31
High-pressure-alloy boiler tube	19	22	34	19	23	22
Industrial-use stainless plates			10	41	27	18
Special metallurgic products				14	16	16

Source: Author's calculation, based on Baoshan Iron & Steel Co. Ltd. (various years).

Table 5.27 Share of export in total sales (%)

	2002	2003	2004	2005	2006	2007	2008
Total exports	13.90	11.84	13.53	11.08	14.07	16.12	11.24
Breakdown by products							
Hot-rolled coil & plate	6.55	5.42	6.12	4.75	6.60	9.36	5.34
Cold-rolled coil	5.70	4.48	5.08	4.02	4.87	4.01	3.68
Steel tube	0.86	1.14	1.24	0.67	1.01	1.28	1.25
Other carbon steel	0.80	0.79	1.10	1.39	0.71	0.60	0.24
Stainless & special steel				0.25	0.87	0.86	0.73
Breakdown by region							
East Asia		4.62	5.42	5.32	5.77	6.93	5.08
Southeast Asia		2.49	2.98	1.99	2.39	3.06	2.37
America		1.06	1.76	1.22	2.25	2.42	1.80
Europe & Africa		3.67	3.38	2.55	3.66	3.54	1.99

Source: Author's calculation, based on Baoshan Iron & Steel Co. Ltd. (various years).

of the total. Furthermore, other high-tech products from Baoshan Iron & Steel, such as pipeline steel (especially oil pipes, ship pipes), also amounted to one-third of China's total. After 2005, when it merged with the stainless-steel department and special metallurgic-steel department of Baosteel Group, its sales share also reached one-fifth.

At its peak in 2007, 16 percent of Baoshan Iron & Steel's steel products were exported to the international market. Most of the exports were flat and tube products, which is similar to the structure of Japanese and Korean steel companies but not of others in China. The decline in 2008 mainly came from

Box 5.1 Baosteel–NSC/Arcelor Automotive Steel Sheets Co., Ltd.

To retain the advantage of auto sheets in the domestic market and to cross the barrier of entering the supply chain of the Japanese and American automotive industry, Baoshan Iron & Steel established a joint venture with Nippon Steel Corporation and Arcelor Steel in 2004. Their shares in this new company are 50 percent, 38 percent, and 12 percent, respectively, and the contractual duration is 20 years.

The main product of this new company is auto sheets (1,800 mm in width), with a production capacity designed to be 1.7 million tons per year: 0.9 million tons of cold-rolled sheet and 0.8 million tons of hot-dip galvanized sheet. Nippon Steel also helped with the workshop building, product development, quality control, and technology transfer (the level of the factory of Nippon Steel in Nagoya). By September 2005, the four machine sets from Nippon Steel—rolling–pickling united set, continuous annealing set, continuous hot-dip galvanizing set, and dressing and finishing set, all reached the designed production capacity.

The key technologies of this joint venture are the alloying hot-dip galvanization technology from Nippon Steel and pure zinc hot-dip galvanization technoogy from Arcelor Steel. The original galvanized sheets of Baoshan Iron & Steel could not meet the technology standard of international auto producers, and these technologies provide a new opportunity to enter their supply chain. They also helped Baoshan Iron & Steel first to obtain the QS 9000 certificate from the main American auto producers, and then the auto-industry quality-management system, ISO/TS 16949.

The main clients for these products now include Volkswagen, General Motors, and Toyota. These high-value-added products have also become the most competitive ones for the trade branches, such as Baoou (in Europe), Baomei (in the United States), and Baohe (in Japan). The "learning by doing" with regard to technology upgrading in Baosteel–NSC/Arcelor is a styled mode for the companies in developing countries to climb on to the global value chain and also greatly helps the development of Baoshan Iron & Steel.

From a global perspective, the automotive-steel market is dominated by the leading producers. ArcelorMittal alone shares a quarter of the world's market, and the top five producers contribute 52 percent of the global output. Their proportion had already caught up with the market share of the top five automotive producers in 2006. Considering Baoshan Iron & Steel controlled half the market of cold-rolled automotive steel in China, its global market share may be close to that of POSCO, and this joint venture played quite an important role in that.

172 Comparative study of three of China's industries

Table 5.28 Global market share of top five automotive and automotive-steel producers in 2006

Automotive producer			Automotive-steel producers
General Motor	14	26	ArcelorMittal
Toyota	12	9	Nippon Steel
Ford	11	7	US Steel
Renault–Nissan	9	6	ThyssenKrupp
Volkswagen	8	4	POSCO
Other	46	48	Other

Source: Nolan and Rui (2007).

Table 5.29 R&D expenditure and personnel

	2003	2004	2005	2006	2007	2008
R&D investment (US$ million)	53.5	70.0	109.6	172.5	274.8	338.2
Share in revenue	1.00	0.99	0.81	0.90	1.05	1.15
R&D personnel	400	417	554	1,264	1,311	1,360
Per 1,000 employees	26.10	27.09	14.25	32.64	32.73	31.06
R&D researcher	239	285	306	819	820	753
Per 1,000 employees	15.60	18.52	7.87	21.15	20.47	17.20
Patents applied for	225	354	491	654	800	859
Patents granted	165	172	259	335	424	625

Source: Author's calculation, based on Baoshan Iron & Steel Co. Ltd. (various years).

the hot-rolled flat products, which were the comparatively low-tech products. However, the decline happened in all the main market regions, and East Asia and Europe both dropped nearly 2 percent in the total sales of Baoshan Iron & Steel.

The technology advantage of Baoshan Iron & Steel comes from its high R&D intensity, which represents about 1 percent of its revenue, the level of the Japanese iron and steel industry and twice China's average. The number of R&D researchers per 1,000 employees also reached 17.2 in 2008, which was the level of the United States in 2000—still only half Japan's level, but more than double China's average. Furthermore, the number of patents granted also nearly quadrupled, from 165 in 2003 to 625 in 2008 (113 invention patents). These indicators are all top among all Chinese steel companies and provide Baoshan Iron & Steel with great potential to develop its own technological advantage.

Baoshan Iron & Steel has been issued with registration certificates for integrated management systems of BS EN ISO 9001:2000, BS EN ISO 14001:1996, and OHSAS 18001:1999 by the British Standards Institution (BSI) and ISO 9001 by the Japanese Standards Association (JSA). Furthermore, it was also the first metal company in China to get the certificate for ISO14001 Environmental Management System from the China Certification Center, Inc. (CCCI).

Contrast case: Heibei Iron and Steel Group

In the top steel-producing companies list of the IISI, a newcomer from China, the Heibei Iron and Steel Group, became the fourth-largest producer, just after Baosteel Group, with a physical output of 33.3 million tons in 2009. It was the result of the M&A between Tangshan Steel Group (number 9 in the 2007 list) and Handan Steel Group (number 36 in the 2007 list) in July 2008. Furthermore, Heibei Iron and Steel Group also entered the Fortune Global 500 with the ranking of number 375 that year, with a revenue of US$24 billion (Fortune, 2009).

The Tangshan Steel Group is also a new company—a combination of Tangshan Steel (number 30 in the 2005 list), Xuanhua Steel (number 68 in the 2005 list), and Chengde Steel two years ago. These M&As were a series of government-dominated activities designed to advance the competitiveness of the regional iron and industry by increasing the concentration ratio. Although the physical output of Hebei Province represented one-quarter of China's total in 2006, which was about 100 mllion tons, there were more than 200 steel companies in Hehei, and only five of them had a physical output of more than 5 million tons. Only the physical output of the newly merged Tangshan Steel Group reached more than 10 million tons.

Although the Heibei Iron & Steel Group has a similar physical output to the Baosteel Group, its revenue is only two-thirds. This is related to its product structure, where the overall share of flat and tube products was only 49.5 percent of its total physical output in 2006. This ratio was even lower than China's average—53.8 percent that year—not to mention Baosteel Group's high ratio of nearly 90 percent. The Tangshan Steel Group's part had an even lower ratio of 41.7 percent. Hebei Iron & Steel Group still cannot produce electrical sheet, strip, and seamless tubes, which are all high-value-added products.

Overall, the key difference between Heibei Iron & Steel Group and Baosteel Group is that it is a loose group of several companies of similar scale, and none of them has either a production capacity or a technology advantage like those of Baoshan Iron & Steel Co. Ltd. The M&A was more a result of development policy than motivated by the enterprise itself, and so collaboration within the new group is more difficult. New regional steel groups formed by local government have become more popular in China in recent years, and it seems the form of the Baosteel Group, like the Wuhan Steel Group,[8] is more successful than the form of the Heibei Iron & Steel Group, like the Anben Steel Group[9] and Shandong Steel Group.[10]

International comparison

There have been about ten steel makers around the world to be listed in the Fortune Global 500, and they contribute a quarter of the world's physical steel output. Among them, ArcelorMittal was certainly the leading producer, even before the M&A, when the total output of Arcelor and Mittal represented

Table 5.30 Physical output and structure of Heibei Iron and Steel Group

	Heibei Iron and Steel Group	Tangshan	Handan
Flat products	12,592.9 (48.74)	6,938.9 (40.91)	5,654.1 (73.56)
Plate	2,854.1 (11.05)	273.9 (1.61)	2,580.3 (33.57)
Wide strip, sheet in coil and length	2,519.3 (9.75)	1,081.1 (6.37)	1,438.2 (18.71)
Narrow strip and universal plate	6,737.2 (26.07)	5,580.7 (32.91)	1,156.5 (15.04)
Metallic coated sheet and strip	467.7 (1.81)	3.2 (0.02)	464.5 (6.04)
Non-metallic coated sheet and strip	14.6 (0.06)		14.6 (0.19)
Electrical sheet and strip			
Long products	11,872.3 (45.95)	9,885.6 (58.29)	1,986.6 (25.84)
Concrete reinforcing bars	6,753.6 (26.14)	5,671.8 (33.44)	1,081.7 (14.07)
Hot rolled bars (other than rebars)	310.7 (1.20)	310.7 (1.83)	
Heavy sections	455.0 (1.76)	438.9 (2.59)	16.1 (0.21)
Light sections	2.3 (0.01)		2.3 (0.03)
Railway track material	28.3 (0.11)	28.3 (0.17)	
Wire rod (drawn wire)	4,322.3 (16.73)	3,435.9 (20.26)	886.5 (11.53)
Tubes and tube fittings	181.4 (0.70)	135.4 (0.80)	46.0 (0.60)
Seamless tubes			
Welded tubes	181.4 (0.70)	135.4 (0.80)	46.0 (0.60)

Note: Numbers in brackets are the shares in total physical output.
Source: Author's calculation, based on China Iron and Steel Association (2008).

nearly 10 percent of the world's physical steel output. The following team was composed of East Asia producers, who all had a share larger than 2 percent of the world's output. The share of Baosteel alone rose from 2.16 percent in 2002 to 2.67 percent in 2008 through its M&A in 2007. The revenue of these leading steel producers has an even higher share of the world market than their physical output. Their share reached about one-third of the world's market (excluding Kobe Steel), which was over US$1 trillion in 2007, because of their higher unit sales. Among them, the share of Baosteel Group rose 0.85 percent, from 2.14 percent in 2003 to 2.99 percent in 2007, which came just behind POSCO's increase of 1.21 percent over the same period of time.

However, its physical labor productivity is still lower than that of other producers. The level for Baosteel Group in 2007, 258.11 tons per person per year, is close to that of Tata steel and could only equal the productivity of Mittal in 2004. The physical labor productivity of JFE and US Steel is double that of Baosteel Group, and that of POSCO is four times as much again. Even if we consider the low labor cost, Baosteel still has a long way to go to catch

Table 5.31 Physical output of Fortune 500 steel companies

	2002	2003	2004	2005	2006	2007	2008
Share in world physical output (%)							
Total	26.50	25.68	26.13	25.16	23.86	23.60	23.78
Arcelor	4.87	4.42	4.53	4.10	9.37	8.61	7.79
Mittal	3.85	3.64	4.14	5.53			
Nippon Steel	3.30	3.23	3.13	2.81	2.61	2.64	2.83
POSCO	3.11	2.98	2.92	2.68	2.41	2.30	2.62
JFE Holdings	3.20	3.12	3.05	2.63	2.56	2.52	2.49
Baosteel Group	2.16	2.05	2.07	1.99	1.80	2.12	2.67
Tata/Corus [a]	1.86	1.97	1.84	1.60	1.46	1.96	1.84
Kobe Steel	0.73	0.75	0.74	0.68	0.62	0.60	0.61
US Steel	1.59	1.85	2.01	1.69	1.69	1.59	1.75
Share in world sales (%)							
Total			33.76	33.31	31.30	35.38	
Arcelor	3.73	4.31	5.33	5.08	6.93	10.52	
Mittal	1.14	1.40	3.15	3.53			
Nippon Steel	3.63	3.80	4.48	4.33	4.33	4.23	
POSCO	1.84	2.19	2.97	3.22	3.18	3.40	
JFE Holdings	3.20	3.22	3.70	3.43	3.28	3.10	
Baosteel Group		2.14	2.77	2.70	2.67	2.99	
Tata/Corus [a]	1.74	1.91	2.43	2.31	2.26	2.57	
Kobe Steel							
US Steel			2.00	1.76	1.85	1.69	

a Data before 2007 are for Corus Group.
Source: Author's calculation, based on IISI (various years), UNIDO (2008), and ArcelorMittal (various years).

Table 5.32 Labor productivity of Fortune 500 steel companies

	2002	2003	2004	2005	2006	2007	2008
Physical labor productivity (ton/person/year)							
Arcelor	422.10	435.56	495.77	485.16	366.25	373.72	
Mittal			260.35	280.89			
Nippon Steel	631.36	677.01	697.51	693.50	691.96	732.20	
POSCO	1,036.90	1,051.87	1,006.67	1,375.73	1,717.74	1,089.58	
JFE Holdings	534.20	574.61	601.87	562.97	596.90	599.77	
Baosteel Group		195.02	227.10	244.92	246.42	258.11	
Tata/Corus [a]	330.06	386.64	393.37	377.59	444.17	315.48	
Kobe Steel							
US Steel			433.33	419.57	481.82	438.78	
Labor productivity (US$1,000 revenue/person/year)							
Arcelor	222.51	298.57	396.74	420.97	183.97	337.81	
Mittal			135.02	125.43			
Nippon Steel	478.03	560.27	678.93	747.71	778.33	866.90	
POSCO	423.32	543.41	697.64	1,158.22	1,544.70	1,191.67	
JFE Holdings	368.15	416.69	496.88	515.26	519.97	546.79	
Baosteel Group		142.57	207.40	231.99	248.21	270.20	
Tata/Corus [a]	212.20	263.18	354.02	382.34	465.32	306.03	
Kobe Steel							
US Steel			293.92	305.20	357.16	344.35	

a Data before 2007 are for Corus Group.
Source: Author's calculation, based on Fortune (2009) and IISI (various years).

Table 5.33 Main indicators for Fortune 500 steel companies

	2002	2003	2004	2005	2006	2007	2008
Unit value of steel sales (US$/ton)							
Arcelor	527.15	685.48	800.25	867.69	502.30	903.92	1,209.45
Mittal	203.45	271.02	518.62	446.54			
Nippon Steel	757.15	827.57	973.36	1,078.18	1,124.82	1,183.96	1,266.11
POSCO	408.26	516.62	693.02	841.90	899.26	1,093.69	1,094.41
JFE Holdings	689.17	725.17	825.56	915.25	871.11	911.65	1,178.88
Baosteel Group		731.06	913.24	947.20	1,007.26	1,046.81	1,003.29
Tata/Corus[a]	642.92	680.69	899.96	1,012.58	1,047.61	970.07	1,312.21
Kobe Steel							
US Steel			678.27	727.41	741.27	784.79	1,023.88
Profit revenue ratio (%)							
Arcelor	8.40	12.34	21.18	11.96	8.88	9.85	7.52
Mittal	−0.76	2.70	7.67	11.79			
Nippon Steel	−1.88	1.42	6.51	8.80	8.16	7.35	3.25
POSCO	7.59	11.22	15.91	15.25	12.82	11.26	10.49
JFE Holdings	0.66	4.32	5.71	10.52	9.19	7.40	4.97
Baosteel Group		6.50	7.87	6.49	7.16	9.55	6.51
Tata/Corus[a]	−6.37	−3.84	4.78	4.46	2.14	11.67	3.36
Kobe Steel			3.55	5.07	5.74	4.17	−1.44
US Steel			7.73	6.48	8.74	5.21	8.89

a Data before 2007 are for Corus Group.
Source: Author's calculation, based on Fortune (2009) and IISI (various years).

up with these leading producers. Labor productivity measured by revenue per employee shows a similar pattern. That of ArcelorMittal alone almost doubled, from 183,970 in 2006 to 337,810 in 2007, which overtook the level of Baosteel and caught up with US Steel.

Compared with other main steel producers, the unit value of Baosteel's steel sales maintained a comparatively high level, which was higher than those of Arcelor Mittal, JFE Holdings, Tata Steel, and US Steel even before 2008 (even POSCO before 2007), when it merged with Guangdong Steel Group. This unit value related to the product structure of Baosteel, where the high value added products, the flat and tubes, share nearly 90 percent of its total physical output. The unit value of steel sales also related to the profit ratio of the enterprises. Except the two digit profit ratio of POSCO and Arcelor, Baosteel has a similar level with the US Steel.

Considering the productivity side, however, Baosteel seems to have no advantage at all. When we put the data into the two-dimensional graph of labor and capital productivity (the labor/revenue ratio is the inverse of labor productivity, and the asset/revenue ratio is the inverse of capital productivity), Baosteel is one of the two enterprises furthest from the leaders. From 2003 to

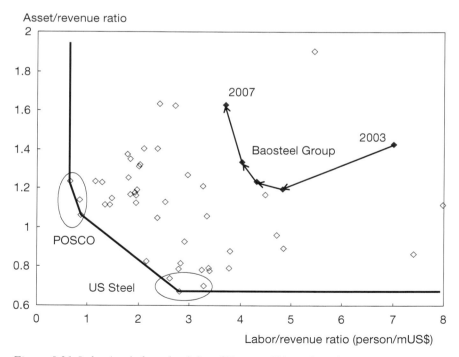

Figure 5.21 Labor/capital productivity of Fortune 500 steel producers
Source: Author's calculation, based on Fortune (2009).

2004, Baosteel's labor productivity increased a lot and it moved towards the front, but its capital productivity dropped one-third from 2004 to 2007, which made it drop behind again.

Actually, the forefront is formed by POSCO and US Steel, where POSCO has the highest labor productivity and US Steel has the highest capital productivity of all main steel producers. Even at its peak, Baosteel only had one-third the labor productivity of POSCO and nearly 70 percent of the capital productivity of US Steel.

Pattern of value added in the value chain

The patterns of value added in the generalized value chain for the two iron and steel companies are quite different. China's iron and steel industry on the one hand has comparatively higher value added on the chain, but on the other hand shows great divergence among the companies within it. The value added of the Heibei Iron and Steel Group is lower than that of the Baosteel Group in all parts of the chain.

Baosteel has a stronger R&D capacity, at double the intensity of China's average, and this provides it with higher value added on this part of the value chain than the Heibei Iron and Steel Group. Furthermore, the Baosteel Group has also been involved in the establishment of most domestic technology standards and even several international ones. These all contributed to the

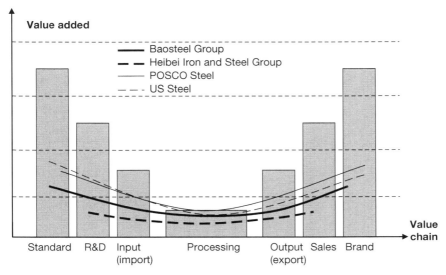

Figure 5.22 Pattern of value added of Baosteel Group and Heibei Iron and Steel Group

Source: Author's design.

technical advantage the Baosteel Group held in the value added of the high-value-added products, compared with the absence of Heibei Iron and Steel Group in this section.

On the sales side, the Baosteel Group holds a high proportion of the high-value-added products on the domestic market and also has a complete network in the main markets of the United States, the EU, and Japan. The sales of the Heibei Iron and Steel Group, however, are mostly concentrated in the domestic market and low-value-added products. Another advantage based on the product quality and international sales of the Baosteel Group is that its brand already had a recognized reputation through its buyers, which was also a source of its competitiveness.

POSCO's advantage comes from its sales capacity and successful branding, and not just the high quality of products, but also a whole set of labor-intensive and environment-friendly production modes, which are quite famous among its clients and even around the world. Similarly, the value added of US Steel comes from its R&D capacity, which brought about a capital-intensive production mode. Furthermore, its great strength in the establishment of technology standards brought even higher value added, which is key to competitiveness and which China's enterprises still seriously lacked.

Solar photovoltaic industry

In the history of industrial revolution, breakthroughs in energy systems have always been one of the key technical changes. The consumption of coal helped the United Kingdom to become the "world workshop," and, in about 1900, it edged out traditional biomass fuel as the main energy source. This kind

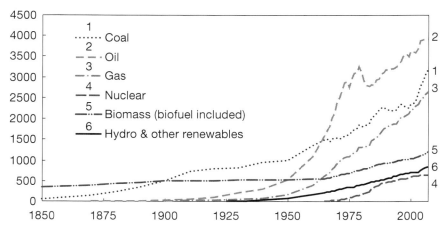

Figure 5.23 World energy production by fuel type, 1850–2007 (mtoe)

Source: Data before 1965 come from the Netherlands Environmental Assessment Agency (2006); data after 1965 come from BP (2008).

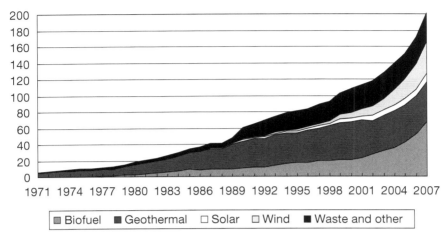

Figure 5.24 World new renewable-energy production, 1970–2007 (mtoe)
Source: Author's calculation, based on IEA (2008).

of change happened again 65 years later, when oil overtook coal to become the largest energy source, and, at the same time, natural gas also overtook traditional biomass to become the third largest. The United States is also a "world workshop" based on oil.

After the oil crisis in the 1970s, nuclear electricity and renewable energy began to be developed. By 2007, the total production of hydroelectricity and other renewable-energy sources had reached 843.6 million ton oil equivalent (mtoe), which is one-third the production of natural gas, one-quarter of coal, and one-fifth of oil. Although 709 mtoe in 2007 were produced by hydropower, which means other renewable energy only shared 1 percent of the global energy production, renewable energy is emerging quite fast under the pressures of the exhaustion of fossil fuel and climate change. The reference scenario from the IEA (2007) predicts that its proportion will rise to nearly 2 percent of the world's total by 2030.

Background of renewable energy

Among all new renewable-energy sources (traditional biomass and hydropower excluded), geothermal was always the main source before 2006. However, biofuel tripled from 22.5 mtoe in 2001 to 67.1 mtoe in 2007 and became the number one in 2007. During this period of time, wind power was the fastest-developed energy source and more than quadrupled to 39.2 mtoe. Solar energy still only represented a low proportion, even though it also doubled, from 5.3 mtoe in 2001 to 10.2 mtoe in 2007. This will not change a great deal, even if the total contribution of new renewable energy to global electricity generation were to rise from 2 percent in 2005 to 7 percent in 2030 (IEA, 2007).

Table 5.34 Existing capacity of renewable energy generation (GW)

	2004	2005	2006	2007	2008
Hydro	796	814	843	888	945
Biomass	259	264	280	291	302
Biofuel [a]	49.6	52.3	55.3	59.3	63.4
Geothermal	34.3	37.3	42.5	50.1	60
Solar	81.4	93.8	113.2	137.2	162.2
Heating	77	88	105	126	145
PV on-grid	1.8	3.1	5.1	7.5	13
PV off-grid	2.2	2.3	2.7	3.2	3.7
CSP	0.4	0.4	0.4	0.45	0.5
Wind power	48	59	74	94	121

a Biofuel here only includes the production of biodiesel (the standard thermal value is estimated as 34.4 MJ/l) and ethanol (the standard thermal value is estimated as 23.7 MJ/l).
Source: Author's calculation, based on Renewable Energy Policy Network for the 21st Century (various years).

Table 5.35 Existing capacity of solar energy generation (GW)

	2004	2005	2006	2007	2008
Solar heating					
China	45.0	55.5	67.9		84
EU	9.8	11.2	13.5		15.5
Japan	5.4	5.0	4.7		4.9
US	1.4	1.6	1.8		1.7
Solar PV on-grid					
China	0.06	0.07	0.08	0.10	0.15
EU	1.06	2.08	3.13	4.95	9.45
Japan	0.89	1.20	1.49	1.73	1.97
US	0.16	0.22	0.32	0.48	0.73

Source: Renewable Energy Policy Network for the 21st Century (various years).

Because of the low energy intensity of solar energy, its existing generation capacity was even larger than that of wind power and double that of geothermal or biofuel in 2008, but solar heating shared nearly 90 percent of the total, and photovoltaic (PV) systems only contributed 16.7 gigawatts (GW) then. Unlike off-grid PV systems, on-grid PV systems grew sevenfold, from 1.8 GW in 2004 to 13 GW in 2008, which was much faster than other systems.

The use of solar energy in China is quite unbalanced. Its existing solar-heating capacity almost doubled, from 45 GW in 2004 to 84 GW in 2008, and its share in the world's total also rose, from 58.4 percent to 66.7 percent at the same time. More than 30 million homes have the system, and 20 million tons of CO_2 emissions are saved each year (Pierson, 2009). In contrast, the share of its on-grid solar PV system dropped from 3.3 percent to 1.3 percent in 2008.

Even in China's Mid- and Long-Term Development Program of Renewable Energy, the overall target capacity of the on-grid PV system was only 0.3 GW for 2010 and 1.8 GW for 2020, which only equals the level of Japan in 2008.

Production pattern

Compared with China's small domestic market, its solar-cell output shares a much larger proportion. Although it was only 50 MW in 2003, the founding of several large solar-cell producers, such as Suntech, made it triple again and again until it reached 2,237 MW in 2008. This makes China the largest solar-cell producer and gives it a one-third share of the world's physical output, 1,000 MW higher than all EU countries. The added capacity of China's solar PV system was just under 50 MW in 2008, which means 98 percent of China's solar cells are for export.

PV technology has undergone three generations of development: the crystalline-silicon cell, the thin-film cell, and the new emerging cell. The first generation still dominates the solar-cell market, with a share of 87 percent in 2008. The thickness of the silicon material in crystalline-silicon cells is about 200 m, but just less than 10 m in thin-film silicon cells. This makes it much cheaper, even with lower conversion efficiency. Other thin-films cells, such as cadmium telluride or copper indium gallium selenide, are even cheaper but have a conversion efficiency similar to that of crystalline-silicon, and their market share has risen from 2 percent in 2005 to 8.2 percent in 2008.

The main production procedure of crystalline-silicon solar modules has four stages: polysilicon purification, wafer slicing (including monosilicon-bar or polysilicon-ingot forming), cell printing, and module assembly. Although the silicon stage only represents 7 percent of the market, its proportion of the total cost reaches 56.2 percent. This is partly because the production of silicon materials is controlled by seven global giants that can obtain an operating margin of about 35 percent. Among them, Hemlock in the United States shared 25.7 percent of global silicon-material production in 2005, Tokuyama in Japan shared 18.1 percent, and Wacker in Germany shared 17.4 percent. Their leading position comes from the technological advantage in this key stage of solar-module production. The first three steps of solar-module production are comparatively concentrated and have higher operating margins, but, at the low end of this value chain, more than 400 module firms share 45 percent of the market, with an average operating margin of 8 percent.

There has been a big gap between the demand for solar silicon materials and the actual supply, over recent years. The price on spot markets of silicon rose sevenfold, from about US$55 per kilogram in 2004 to US$350 per kilogram in 2007, because of strong speculative demand. However, the financial crisis meant that the price dropped to a more normal level of about US$100 in the first half of 2009. The problem with China's solar PV industry is that its output reached one-third of the world's total, but it can only supply one-tenth of the silicon materials. This wide gap has greatly stimulated

Table 5.36 Physical output of global solar cells (MW)

	2001	2002	2003	2004	2005	2006	2007	2008
Module production	386.0	547.1	820.4	1,193.5	1,782.3	2,500.3	4,000.5	6,850.0
China	4.6	6.0	12.0	50.0	145.7	438.0	1,088.0	2,253.7
EU	73.9	122.1	200.2	311.8	472.8	657.3	1,062.0	1,301.5
Japan	171.2	251.1	363.9	601.5	833.0	927.5	920.0	1,130.2
United States	100.3	120.6	103.0	138.7	154.0	201.6	266.0	376.8

Source: Author's calculation, based on Yin (2008) and Kuang (2009).

Table 5.37 Conversion efficiency and market breakdown of different cell types (%)

	Conversion efficiency	Market share 2005	2006	2007	2008
1st generation: crystalline-silicon cell					
Monocrystalline	16–19	38	46.5	42.2	87.0
Polycrystalline	14–15	52	43.4	45.2	
2nd generation: thin-film cell					
Amorphous silicon	5–7	5	4.7	5.2	4.8
Micromorphous silicon	6–8	3	2.6	2.2	
Cadmium telluride	8–11		2.7	4.7	7.4
Copper indium gallium selenide	~11	2	0.2	0.5	0.8
Gallium arsenide	18–22				<0.1
3rd generation: emerging cell					
Dye-sensitized cell	~12				
Multijunction cell	<40				

Source: Author's calculation, based on European Photovoltaic Industry Association (various years) and Kuang (2009).

investment in silicon production in China: more than twenty new projects had been established or were under construction in 2008, and China's production capacity was due to rise to 30,000 tons in 2009, with overall capacity reaching 65,000 tons in the future (Yang et al., 2009). This has certainly led to a great surplus in silicon supply, and that is also why the Chinese government deleted polysilicon from the 2009 version of the Catalogue of Encouraging Import of Technology and Products (NDRC, MOC and MOF, 2009) and will not have interest subsidy anymore and also treated it as one of the surplus industry as its production capacity under construction has exceeded 80,000 tons.

Another problem with China's solar PV industry is that the market is too crowded with module-assembly firms. The employment in module firms rose nearly tenfold within two years, to about one-third of the total industry, when China's output of solar modules became the largest in the world. Because more than 98 percent of China's solar cells are produced for export, the financial crisis greatly damaged Chinese module firms. They boomed from 200 in 2007 to 400 in 2008, but only 50 of them were still in operation in early 2009.

Furthermore, according to statistics produced by Global Trends in Sustainable Energy Investment (UNEP, 2009), the total employment in solar energy

Table 5.38 Global pattern of crystalline-silicon solar-module production, 2006

	Silicon	*Wafers*	*Cells*	*Modules*
Cost share[a]	56.2%	12.3%	15.1%	16.4%
Operating margin	35%	25%	20%	8%
Market breakdown	7%	11%	37%	45%
Firm number	>7	>20	>40	>400
CR5	85%	80%	60%	<50%

Source: Xiong (2008), Laurens et al. (2007), and China Optics and Optoelectronics Manufacturers Association (2007).

Table 5.39 Demand and supply of silicon materials and their price (tons)

	2001	*2002*	*2003*	*2004*	*2005*	*2006*	*2007*	*2008*
Silicon demand								
Electronic silicon	12,000	13,000	14,000	17,000	20,672	22,483	24,732	26,463
Solar silicon	5,500	7,000	7,000	8,000	13,700	16,200	31,900	
Solar silicon production					8,500	12,800	22,200	~40,000
China					60	287	1,156	>4,000
Silicon price (US$/kg)	10	23	~35	~45	55	200	350	350

Source: Author's calculation, based on European Photovoltaic Industry Association (various years), Laurens et al. (2007), and Kuang (2009).

Table 5.40 Employment in China's solar PV industry (people)

	2005	2006	2007
Silicon	1,000	3,600	7,000
Wafer	2,360	7,700	13,000
Cell	1,500	4,800	11,000
Module	2,650	9,000	25,000
Distribution	2,000	2,600	3,000
Accessory (balance of system)	1,000	2,800	4,000
Related consumption goods	3,000	8,500	15,000
R&D personnel	300	500	800
Total	13,810	39,500	82,800

Source: Zhao et al. (2008).

around the world was about 170,000 in 2008. This means that nearly half this employment is located in China. However, R&D personnel are lacking, and the share per 1,000 total employees dropped from 22 in 2005 to 9.7 in 2008, the average for China's manufacturing.

The solar PV industry today has become one of the most technology-intensive ones in the renewable-energy industry. The statistics from OECD (2008a) show that solar energy-related patents filed under the PCT overtook wind power to become number one in 2005. China has also been catching up with other leading countries in recent years. Its solar-energy-technology patents filed from 2001 to 2005 numbered 1,357, less than the 9,326 filed by Japan, 2,071 by Korea, and 2,008 by the United States, but higher than the 1,221 filed by Germany (WIPO, 2008). Most recent statistics show that, between 2006 and 2008, China had the largest number of original patent filings in the fields of wind, solar, and marine energy, followed by Japan, the United States, and Germany, in that order (Gupta and Wang, 2009).

Because the great majority of China's solar cells are produced for export, technology standards are quite important for its development. Until now, China has already had thirty-one national standards and ten industrial standards for the solar PV industry, of which eighteen came directly from IEC standards. An independent institution, the China General Certification Center, has been established to issue the Chinese "Golden Sun" certificate for solar-cell products.

Main case 1: Chinese solar-cell producer—Suntech

The Suntech Power Holding Co. Ltd. was one of the earliest private solar-cell companies in China. Its predecessor, Wuxi Suntech Power Co., Ltd., was founded in 2002. On January 11, 2005, Power Solar System Co., Ltd was established in the British Virgin Islands to acquire all the equity interests, including those from state shareholders, in Wuxi Suntech Power. The Suntech Power Holding was registered in the Cayman Islands as a listing vehicle on

188 *Comparative study of three of China's industries*

Table 5.41 Main indicators of Suntech (US$ million)

	2002	2003	2004	2005	2006	2007	2008
Net revenues	3.0	13.9	85.3	226.0	598.9	1,348.3	1,923.5
Solar modules	2.9	4.1	78.0	170.1	471.9	1,331.7	1,785.8
Solar cells	0.2	9.7	7.3	54.7	124.6	13.7	99.3
PV system		0.0	0.1	1.2	2.4	2.9	27.2
Gross profit	0.2	2.7	25.1	68.6	148.9	274.1	342.9
Total assets	10.2	17.0	68.5	481.7	1,098.0	1,957.0	3,223.8

Source: Author's calculation, based on Suntech Power Holdings Co., Ltd. (various years).

Table 5.42 Regional market breakdown for Suntech (US$ million)

	2004	2005	2006	2007	2008
China	6.7	56.4	129.7	25.7	134.9
Europe total		161.3	421.7	1,195.7	1,493.2
Germany	61.5	101.6	254.4	685.8	570.9
Spain	1.7	18.2	123.5	466.2	718.7
Others	13.0	41.5	43.8	43.7	203.6
United States			20.4	86.7	142.7
Others	2.3	8.3	27.1	40.2	152.7
Total net revenues	85.3	226.0	598.9	1,348.3	1,923.5

Source: Author's calculation, based on Suntech Power Holdings Co., Ltd. (various years).

August 8, 2005, which makes Suntech China's first overseas-listed solar-cell company (on the New York Stock Exchange, NYSE).

The initial public offering (IPO) resulted in the total assets of Suntech increasing sevenfold between 2004 and 2005, and its revenue and profit also tripled. Over the following 3 years, its total assets rose again about sevenfold to US$3.2 billion and its revenue increased 8.5 times to US$1.9 billion, but its profit only increased fivefold. Among its products, solar modules dominated its revenue with a 90 percent share, except in 2005–2006, when their proportion was less than 80 percent.

Suntech's market is concentrated in European countries, which account for more than 70 percent of its total revenue. Germany and Spain contributed about two-thirds of the world's newly added solar PV generation capacity and also became Suntech's main export destination. However, the share of the domestic market dropped from a quarter in 2005 to 7 percent in 2008, because there has been no strong demand for solar-cell products in China during recent years.

The main problem for Suntech is also the problem for most Chinese solar-cell producers—the supply of polysilicon materials. Even though Suntech signed a 10-year materials contract with MEMC, worth US$6 billion, in July

2006, the sharp increase in physical output still meant Suntech had to turn to the spot market for silicon materials. The selling price of Suntech's solar modules was just the same in 2008 as in 2006, but the rising price of polysilicon made its operating margin drop from 17.5 percent to 9.5 percent over the same period of time.

Another problem also came from the financial crisis. Suntech's stock price dropped to its lowest point of US$5.09 in early 2009, US$85 lower than its peak in late 2007 (Suntech Power Holdings Co., Ltd., 2009).

It is reported that, from late 2008, 3,000 employees had been laid off, and some employees only received 80 percent of their salaries (Ye, 2009). Its recovery has also been quite slow because its main markets—the EU and the United States—are still in recession.

The challenge of the financial crisis affected all firms throughout China's solar PV industry, but Suntech at least kept its competitive advantage, benefitting from its strong R&D capacity. Even if the ratio of R&D expenditure in revenue dropped from 1.5 percent in 2005 to 0.8 in 2008, the overall expenditure still rose fivefold, from US$3.4 million to US$15.3 million. In addition, its number of R&D personnel per 1,000 employees still maintained quite a high level of 42.1 in 2008, which is four times the industry average in China.

Furthermore, a key technology developed by Suntech, called Pluto Technology, resulted in the conversion efficiency of its polycrystalline-silicon solar cells reaching 17 percent (more than 18 percent for monocrystalline products) in mass production, much higher than the 14–15 percent of traditional products. It is reported that the efficiency might even reach the level of 18 percent (20 percent for monocrystalline products) with the next two years. This provides great technological competitiveness, enabling Suntech to lead the solar PV industry in China and even to compete with global leaders.

Table 5.43 Product price and margins for Suntech

	2002	2003	2004	2005	2006	2007	2008
Average price (US$/W)							
Solar modules	1.78	1.99	3.01	3.42	3.89	3.72	3.89
Solar cells	3.48	2.77	2.02	3.05	3.23	3.06	2.84
Margin (%)							
Gross margin	5.2	19.4	29.5	30.3	24.9	20.3	17.8
Operating margin	(34.4)	5.4	23.6	19.5	17.5	13.6	9.5
Net margin	(29.7)	6.7	23.2	13.5	17.7	12.7	4.6

Source: Author's calculation, based on Suntech Power Holdings Co., Ltd. (various years).

Table 5.44 R&D intensity for Suntech

	2005	2006	2007	2008
R&D expenditure (US$ million)				
Expenditure	3.4	8.4	15.0	15.3
Net revenue	226.0	598.9	1,348.3	1,923.5
Ratio (%)	1.5	1.4	1.1	0.8
R&D personnel (people)				
Personnel		202	247	382
Employment		3,284	6,784	9,070
Ratio (per 1,000)		61.5	36.4	42.1

Source: Author's calculation, based on Suntech Power Holdings Co., Ltd. (various years).

Table 5.45 Main technology standards issued

Technology standard	Year issued
International standard	
ISO 9001:2000 quality system certification	2002 & 2005
IEC61215:1993 test standard	2003
CE Health and Safety (European Union) certification	2004 & 2006
National standard	
TÜV SÜD certification EN/IEC61215+EN/IEC61730	2005 & 2006
UL (Underwriters Laboratories) certification	2006
VDE (Association of German Electrical Engineers) certification	2007
CCC (China Quality Certification Center) certification	2008
KIER (Korea New and Renewable Energy Center) certification	2008

Source: Author's calculation, based on Suntech Power Holdings Co., Ltd. (various years).

Finally, Suntech has been awarded almost all technology standards related to solar cells from its founding, especially in its main market countries such as Germany and the United States. This greatly helps Suntech's exports. However, Suntech only took part in the establishment of China's own standards, such as the "Golden Sun" certificate, but held no position in the IEC.

Contrast case: LDK Solar Co. Ltd.—the largest wafer producer in China

LDK Solar Co. Ltd. is one of the most successful emerging PV companies in China. Its predecessor, Jiangxi LDK Solar, was founded in 2005. On May 1, 2006, LDK New Energy, a British Virgin Islands company, was incorporated as a listing vehicle (IPO on June 1, 2007, on NYSE) and acquired all the equity interests of Jiangxi LDK Solar. In addition, the establishment of

LDK Solar International Co. Ltd. in Hong Kong, LDK Solar USA, Inc. in California, and LDK Solar Europe S.A. in Luxemburg over the following years all formed the global business of LDK Solar. In 2009, it established a joint venture, LQ Energy GmbH, with Q-Cells in Germany and bought 70 percent of the share of SGT, an Italian solar-system company, all of which strengthened its position on the international market.

The rise of LDK Solar was quite impressive, in that its revenue grew from US$0.1 billion in 2006 to US$1.6 billion in 2008, and wafer sales were its main activity throughout. By 2008, its wafer output had provided nearly one-eighth of the world's total, and it had become one of the largest global wafer producers, like Hemlock and Wacker. Unlike Suntech, one-third of its wafer products were sold to Chinese firms, and other Asian and Pacific markets also shared another third of its sales. LDK Solar's target was to dominate the wafer market in these regions. Although its gross profit dropped by half, from US$170 million in 2007 to US$88 million in 2008, its expenditure on R&D still doubled, from US$3.2 million to US$7.5 million, and it maintained its ratio to revenue of about 0.6 percent. Furthermore, of LDK Solar's 14,130 employees, there were 649 R&D personnel, a slightly higher proportion than Suntech.

The financial crisis also greatly damaged the profit levels of LDK Solar. Its operating margin dropped from 28 percent of its revenue in 2007 to 0.5 percent in 2008, and its gross margin also only had quite a low level of 5.4 percent at that time. Among its main products, the gross margin for 156 mm wafers (which accounted for 82 percent of its revenue) dropped from 34.3 percent to 3.5 percent in 2008, and this determined the overall level of LDK Solar that year. However, its processing activities and silicon materials (they both account for 9 percent of the total revenue) still maintained quite a high margin of 28.7 percent and 20.6 percent, respectively. This demonstrates that their positions on the value chain are much higher.

Noticing the big difference in the gross margins between wafer products and silicon materials, LDK Solar decided to invest in its own production basis of polysilicon materials. According to the published investment plans of PV companies in China, that of LDK Solar (about 12 billion yuan) was the largest

Table 5.46 Main indicators of LDK Solar

	2006	2007	2008
Net revenue (US$1,000)	105,454	523,946	1,643,495
Sales of wafers (US$1,000)	102,452	501,733	1,495,034
Sales of wafers (MW)	45.2	223.8	817.8
Average (US$/W)	2.27	2.24	2.35
Gross profit (1,000 US$)	41,492	170,237	88,356
Total assets (1,000 US$)	292,719	1,309,986	3,373,728
R&D (1,000 US$)	290	3,202	7,505

Source: Author's calculation based on LDK Solar Co. Ltd. (2008).

Table 5.47 Margins for LDK Solar and its products

	2006	2007	2008
Gross margin	39.3	32.5	5.4
156 × 156 mm wafers	41.0	34.3	3.5
125 × 125 mm wafers	39.1	25.8	1.5
150 × 150 mm wafers		15.4	−0.7
Processing for others	40.0	29.9	28.7
Silicon materials	20.0	22.9	20.6
Operating margin	35.2	28.0	0.5
Net margin	28.6	27.5	4.3

Source: Author's calculation, based on LDK Solar Co. Ltd. (2008).

among them, and it planned to set up a production capacity of 15,000 tons of polysilicon per year at its headquarters, about double the capacity of Yingli Power, the second-largest solar-module producer in China. Its production capacity was planned to reach 6,000 tons in 2009 and then 15,000 tons in 2010.

Another of LDK Solar's major plans involved its contract with Applied Materials for its new branch producing thin-film-silicon solar cells, Best Solar Co. Ltd. This single contract reached US$1.9 billion, which was also the largest in the history of Applied Materials. It involved a complete production line for amorphous silicon solar cells on 5.7 m^2 glass baseboards, which was the most advanced around the world. The conversion efficiency began at 8.5 percent and was hoped to reach 10–12 percent in the future. The designed production capacity of this project was 1,000 MW, and began shipping in early 2009. When it reaches full production capacity in the near future, LDK Solar will become one of the largest thin-film solar-cell producers in the world.

There are risks to these investments by LDK Solar, but if they succeeded, a new giant of the solar PV industry will have appeared, from the upstream of polysilicon-material production, to silicon-ingot and -wafer processing, and to the downstream solar cell (the Best Solar project also includes a designed capacity of 3,000 MW crystalline-silicon solar cells).

International comparison

Measured by physical output, Suntech became the third-largest solar-cell producer in the world in 2008, rising from ninth in 2004. Its physical output rose 14 times, and its gap with the leading producers also narrowed, from one-ninth of Sharp's in 2004 to nearly 90 percent of Q-Cell's in 2008. In addition, two other Chinese solar-cell companies ranked in the top ten of 2008, Jing Ao at number five and Yingli at number seven, both of which were listed on overseas stock markets in 2007. As the pioneer in China, Suntech is now facing a strong challenge from them, together with competition from other leading producers.

The global giants moved into China during the boom in this industry. For example, Canadian Solar, an integrated solar-cell producer, has already set up seven subsidiaries in China, with an overall capacity of 600 MW. ReneSola, a leading solar-cell producer in the United Kingdom, also outsourced segments of solar cells, modules, and system applications to China in a complete, foreign-owned enterprises, JC Solar, which contributed 54 percent to ReneSola's total revenue. Some leading producers, such as First Solar, also began to enter China's solar-cell market.[11]

Compared with the other two top producers, the labor productivity of Suntech and LDK still lags quite a way behind. As the main crystalline-silicon battery producer, Suntech's labor productivity is just one-third that of Q-Cell, which is the same ratio as between the leading thin-film solar-cell producer LDK and First Solar. Furthermore, they both only have physical productivity equal to one-third that of First Solar and one-fifth that of Q-Cell. Even with much lower labor costs, the gross margin or the operating margin of Suntech and LDK is still 10–15 percent lower compared with them, not to mention that LDK has been seriously damaged by the financial crisis in 2008.

The comparatively low margin comes from the higher cost of modules. The average cost of Suntech's solar modules is US$1 higher than Q-Cell's, which is the same as in 2005. This is because the price of silicon materials has more than doubled during that period of time, but Suntech does not have its own supply capacity. Even the wafer producer, LDK, has been influenced by the price of silicon material, and its average cost rose from a similar level to First Solar in 2006 to nearly double in 2008. In fact, First Solar's thin-film solar-cell technology made the average cost drop to about US$1 per watt, the lowest in the world.

Table 5.48 Top ten solar-cell producers (MW)

	2004	2005	2006	2007	2008
Q-Cell (Germany)	75.9 (4)	165.7 (2)	253.1 (2)	389.2 (1)	581.6 (1)
First Solar (United States)				207.0 (4)	504.0 (2)
Suntech (China)	35.0 (9)	82.0 (8)	157.5 (4)	327.0 (3)	497.5 (3)
Sharp (Japan)	324.0 (1)	427.5 (1)	434.4 (1)	363.0 (2)	473.0 (4)
Jing Ao (China)					300.0 (5)
Kyocera (Japan)	105.0 (2)	142.0 (3)	180.0 (3)	207.0 (4)	290.0 (6)
Yingli (China)				142.5 (9)	281.5 (7)
Motech (China)	35.0 (9)	60.0 (9)	102.0 (7)	196.0 (6)	272.0 (8)
SunPower (US)				150.0 (8)	237.0 (9)
Sanyo (Japan)	68.0 (7)	125.0 (4)	155.0 (5)	165.0 (7)	215.0 (10)
BP Solar (whole)	84.9 (3)	85.8 (7)	85.7 (10)		
Mitsubishi Elec. (Japan)	75.0 (4)	100.0 (5)	111.0 (6)		
Schott Solar (Germany)	63.0 (8)	95.0 (6)	93.0 (8)		
Shell Solar (whole)	72.0 (6)	59.0 (10)			
Solar World (Germany)			86.0 (9)	130.0 (10)	

Source: Zhao et al. (2008).

Table 5.49 Indicators of main solar-cell producers

	2004	2005	2006	2007	2008
Labor productivity (US$1,000/person/year)					
Q-Cell	360.2	461.9	737.1	740.7	678.1
First Solar	59.5	190.9	186.7	344.7	353.6
Suntech	100.1	164.5	182.4	198.7	212.1
LDK			74.3	80.2	105.8
Physical productivity (1,000 W/person/year)					
Q-Cell	156.8	216.0	262.6	228.0	226.5
First Solar	28.6	84.9	82.8	141.6	143.0
Suntech	41.1	59.7	48.0	48.2	54.9
LDK			32.8	35.8	57.9
Gross margin (%)					
Q-Cell				36.7	31.2
First Solar		35.0	40.0	49.9	54.4
Suntech	29.5	30.3	24.9	20.3	17.8
LDK			39.3	32.5	5.4
Operating margin (%)					
Q-Cell	15.2	21.1	24.0	22.9	16.4
First Solar				27.2	35.2
Suntech	23.6	19.5	17.5	13.6	9.5
LDK			35.2	28.0	0.5
Average cost (US$/W)					
Q-Cell [a]				2.50	2.50
First Solar	2.94	1.59	1.40	1.23	1.08
Suntech [a]	1.86	2.22	3.14	3.56	3.50
LDK [a]			1.47	1.61	1.82

a Estimated from average sales price and gross margin by the author.
Source: Suntech Power Holdings Co., Ltd. (various years), LDK Solar Co. Ltd. (2008), Q-Cell SE (various years), and First Solar Inc. (various years).

Distribution of value added on the value chain

The distribution of value added on the generalized value chain of China's solar PV industry shows higher value added than in the ceramics industry and iron and steel industry, because it is much closer to the world's forefront. The difference between the two cases, Suntech and LDK Solar, comes from their different position on the downstream and upstream of the industry.

For Suntech, it is closer to the module end, and so its value added in the middle part on the chain (trade activity included) is lower than LDK Solar's, which holds silicon-material and wafer-production capacity. However, on the

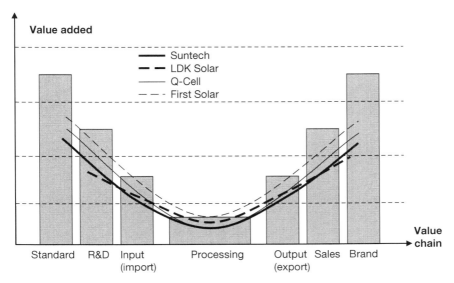

Figure 5.25 Pattern of value added of Suntech and LDK Solar
Source: Author's design.

R&D part, Suntech on one hand has higher expenditure intensity, and on the other hand has core technology that can give its products great advantages over other producers. Its value added should be higher than LDK Solar's, which mainly relies on technology imports. Besides, Suntech has already taken part in the establishment of national technology standards in China, and this brought it more value added on this part of the value chain.

They both show similar performance on the sales section, except that Suntech is much more dependent on the overseas market. However, its longer sales experience in different markets has brought Suntech a higher brand reputation, but the rise of LDK Solar with the next-generation product—thin-film solar-cell products—may also provide a great opportunity for its branding, just like First Solar in recent years.

Although still lower on most parts of the value chain, Suntech and LDK Solar are quite close to the value-added level of First Solar, which is at the forefront of this industry. In fact, the value added of the processing and trading segments of Q-Cell is at the level of the two Chinese firms, which are lifted up by their R&D and sales capacity in the international market.

Notes

1. A Chinese unit of weight, about 40 g at that time.
2. In fact, ceramic plumbing fixtures (8112) are also included in this group.
3. The physical energy consumption of structural ceramics (0.18 toe/ton) is only one-fifth that of non-structural ceramics (0.84 toe/ton).

4. The weight proportion of the glaze on all ceramic products is estimated at 10 percent, and the kaolin clay in it is about 5–10 percent.
5. Share-holding cooperative enterprises refer to economic units set up on a cooperative basis, with funding partly from members of the enterprise and partly from outside investment, where the operation and management are decided by the members who also participate in the production, and the distribution of income is based both on work (labor input) and on shares (capital input).
6. The difference between them comes from the thickness division of plates and strips in flat products: the IISI classification is 10 mm, but the division in China's classification is 3 mm.
7. Incorporating Guangdong Iron and Steel Group with Guangzhou Steel and Shaoguan Steel in 2008 (Baoshteel Group held 80 percent of the total share).
8. Formed by merger from Wuhan Steel, Egang Steel, Liugang Steel, and Kungang Steel by the governments of Hubei Province, Guangxi Province, and Yunnan Province in 2005.
9. Formed by merger from Angang Steel and Benxi Steel by the government of Liaoning Province in 2005.
10. Formed by merger from Jinan Steel and Laiwu Steel by the government of Shandong Province in 2008.
11. First Solar announced that it had a US$6 billion contract to build a 2 GW solar-power plant in the Inner Mongolia Province of China, which was the largest in the world until then (September 2009).

6 Conclusions

The research for this book focused on the key concept of the world workshop. During the past two centuries, the mode of the world's manufacture of goods has completely changed, from craft production to network specialization. The value chain has also expanded, from only production and trade to service, and is even related to regime and culture. The world workshop of today would be different from that in the time of early industrialization, such as the United Kingdom.

First of all, the networking production of much manufacturing today, especially of ICT products, is finished in several segments in many different places. The expanding value chain and offshore outsourcing activity mean that products can almost never be finished within one country. Under this new mode, the monopoly of manufacturing should be measured within the segments, not just simplified as a whole.

Related to that, exports should also be considered as a series of "quality ladders," and just producing a vital component is not enough for a world workshop. Sophistication today may be even more important, because, today, a large majority of trade is intra-industry or even intra-product. If so, the movement of intermediates of MNCs can create a large amount of trade flow but just a little value added within it, which is completely different from the age of "comparative advantage."

Table 6.1 Adjustment of the definition of world factory

Chambers (1961)	*Author's definition*
1. Monopoly in world manufacturing	1. Monopoly in the segment/s of world manufacturing production
2. Vital components of country's export trade	2. Vital components of export market and having high level of sophistication
3. Shipping and credit agencies	3. Producer service capacity, from sales to business R&D
4. Mutually advantageous relations and funds for the lubrication of the wheels of the world's commerce	4. Advantageous soft power, from technology standards to brands, with the support of finance

In addition, manufacturing services today have also expanded greatly, from the shipping and sales to more complex research and development and professional marketing. Furthermore, the "soft power" behind manufacturing also includes the regime of technology standards and the culture of branding, which is as important as financial power today. Therefore, the analysis of China as the world workshop should also include all these perspectives.

Whether China is the "world workshop" depends on it position in the international manufacturing division. According to the existing evidence, we can draft these view from the following points of view.

China as a manufacturer with a monopoly in the segments of production

Although the ratio of the value added to the gross output of China's manufacturing is only half that of the United States, that its total industrial value added will overtake the United States to become the world leader in the near future still makes this developing country create a new mode of "catching-up" with great significance, not to mention that the estimate under purchasing power parity shows that China has already completed the process.

Considering the physical amount of industrial output, China has dominated the production of numerous kinds of product in the world. Of the 616 main industrial products in UNIDO statistics, China was first in the production of 172 products, from traditional, low-value-added textiles and clothes to "high-tech" ICT products. The widespread "made in China" label simply shows that this country has become a "world workshop" to a large extent.

The structure of China's manufacturing seems already very close to that of other leading industrialized economies; in particular, the share of its high-tech sectors in either total manufacturing or in the world market has met the level of Japan and the EU in 2005. What we need pointed out, however, is that nearly two-thirds of the value added of high-tech sectors are completed by FIEs in China.

This means that China only dominates segments of the production of these products, usually processing, and the result of this kind of division means that CO_2 emissions are much more concentrated in China—about one-third of the world's total—rather than the industrial value added. If we measure from the input side, the energy consumption of Chinese manufacturing accounts for one-quarter of the world's total. As a result, some critics call China a "black world workshop."

In fact, China has also input a lot of capital and labor into its monopolized production. Although the net assets of China's manufacturing are only just over half those of the United States, its yearly fixed capital formation has already counted for double. A more significant input is the labor force, where China has one-third of the world's total and even has ten percent more than the total of the twenty-four OECD countries, which is a strong basis for China's manufacturing.

The relative efficiencies of these input factors of China's manufacturing are quite different. China has similar capital productivity to the United States and a quarter of its energy efficiency, but less than one-tenth of its labor productivity. Although the relative labor compensation in China's manufacturing sector rose a lot after its entry to the WTO, its relative labor productivity increased faster and even made the unit labor cost drop after 2001. This is certainly one of the key determinants that make MNCs choose China as the best outsourcing destination.

China as a vital exporter in the world market

Together with monopolized manufacturing, China will also become the largest merchandise exporter, both in terms of physical amount (it has had the most products ranking the first in the world's export market since 2005) and total value (very probably since 2009). China's export structure changed a lot after its entry to WTO; in particular, since 2004, China has become the largest exporter of ICT products.

Interestingly, high-tech products counted for 40 percent of China's manufacturing exports, which makes China the largest high-tech-product exporter in the world. The large proportion of processing exports finished by FIEs within China shows that China today is deeply embedded in the global manufacturing division and has become a processing center (a hub) of the production network.

Detailed analysis shows that, although China's export structure is more similar that of Japan, the United States, and the EU at both a sectoral level and a product level, its exports are more likely to be at the low end of the market, like those of Brazil, Russia, and India, than those of high-income countries, judged on unit values. This is also why we think China is much more like a "world workshop" but not a "World Factory," like the United States.

Measured by more detailed classification, we can establish that China is also a vital importer of intermediate goods, such as parts and components, in the world market. This means China's export of final-consumption products is mainly the output of the last segments of the international division, and a large majority of its trade is in fact intra-industry or even intra-product trade. In the main manufacturing sector of China, the proportion of this kind of trade reached more than 90 percent.

Furthermore, estimates using the vertical-specialization method show that a quarter of the value added of China's exports is from the use of imported inputs, which is much higher than other large economies, such as Japan and the United States, and the ratio in the ICT sectors of China is even higher. This means China has become more deeply integrated into the international division than them.

As a vital exporter in the world market, the sophistication of China's products is in fact decided by the outsourcing of MNCs. Previous "world workshops," such as the United Kingdom and the United States, had never met with China's problem—that FDI played such an important role.

China still at the low end of the global value chain

The research also examined the key factors of China's competitiveness, which is the high end of the global value chain. On the input side, the factors mean R&D and technology standards. Although R&D expenditure still has a low proportion of the value added, the researcher FTE input in China has already reached the level of the whole EU and half that of the United States. The pattern of the intensity of R&D expenditure in China is quite similar to that of other leading economies, but at a much lower level, especially in the high-tech sectors. In addition, the absence of technology standards, the superior part of the value chain, is a bigger problem for Chinese manufacturing.

Although FIEs contribute two-thirds of the high-tech-product output and 90 percent of their export, they only share one-sixth of the R&D expenditure. On the other hand, the outsourcing of development services has increased quite fast in China recently: more than 1,000 research centers have been founded by MNCs in China, and nearly 70 percent of the ODM of electronic systems is finished in China now. This makes China the second-largest net buyer of royalties and licenses around the world.

Unlike the lower R&D expenditure input, FIEs enjoyed a much larger proportion of the sales profits in China's markets and even more in the international market compared with their output. Their profit ratio in China's official statistics is not obvious, because the transfer pricing and the real sales profits eventually returned to the parent company of these affiliations. There is also the absence of brands for China's products, which makes the label of this world workshop "made in China," but not "made by China."

Overall, the absence of the "soft power" held by MNCs makes China a very weak "world workshop" that has little innovation capability. Without enough competitiveness of its own, China can hardly upgrade its position in the international division, as it wishes, by beginning from a "world workshop."

China: rising big businesses and their position

The rise of a world workshop is indeed the rise of its group of big businesses, which has been an established fact in the history of industrialization of the United Kingdom and the United States. Japan's national champions, such as Toyota and Sony, rose after the 1964 Tokyo Olympic Games, and those of South Korea, such as Hyundai and Samsung, also rose after its 1988 Olympic Games in Seoul. Another 20 years later, China's 2008 Beijing Olympic Games have just finished, and people believe a group of national champions should become real global giants in the future if China becomes a real world workshop.

China already has a similar number of Fortune Global 500 firms to Germany and France, and a similar number of *Financial Times* 500 firms to Japan, but only a few of them can be listed in the top firms ranked by R&D expenditure, not to mention that they still have almost no position among the world-famous brands. This is the result of China's position on the global value chain, where its big businesses are still at the low end, but the situation varies throughout different sectors and firms.

In the traditional manufacturing sectors, such as ceramics, the disadvantage of Chinese firms is quite obvious. Although China's physical output has dominated the world market, its firms can only enjoy an average export unit value of one-tenth that of the leading producers. The national champions of China, such as the Sanhuan Group, still lack design capacity and also can only be OEM without world-class brands. Today, these producers have already become strong suppliers in China's domestic market, but there is still a long way to go in the international market.

China's national champions in the "modern" sectors, such as the steel industry, performed like those in the ceramics industry. Measured by sector level, China's steel industry is still at quite a low level, even if it has dominated the world's physical output. Fortunately, the leader, Baosteel Group, has already emerged as a competitive global supplier with some technological advantage, although only partly introduced. Compared with other global giants, the productivity of Baosteel in terms of both labor and capital is still much lower, but the unit value of its products has reached a similar level.

In the emerging sectors, such as solar PV, China seems closer to the forefront than in other sectors. China has already dominated the use of traditional solar heating for a long period of time and has now also become the leading producer of solar cells. The leading firms, Suntech and LDK, are no longer behind their competitors in Germany and the United States. The existing problem now is that the supply of raw materials and the market are both outside China, and the sector is closely tied into the economic cycle of Western countries and seriously influenced by the current financial crisis.

Just as I finished this final part of my book, a 14-page special report on China and America in *The Economist* included the following words:

> Back in 1905, America was the rising power. Britain, then ruler of the waves, was worrying about losing its supremacy to the upstart. Now it is America that looks uneasily on the rise of a potential challenge . . . China may have growing financial muscle, but it still lags far behind as a technological innovator and creator of global brands.

The observation of China's being a world workshop is a story in Rashomon style, which is sometimes ambivalent from different perspectives. The rise of China in the international manufacturing division, just like the rise of the United States in the early twentieth century and that of the United Kingdom in the early nineteenth century, may be the most important event of the world economy in the early twenty-first century and will completely change its pattern.

Appendix 1
The broad economic categories

1   Food and beverages
11   Primary
111   Mainly for industry
112   Mainly for household consumption
12   Processed
121   Mainly for industry
122   Mainly for household consumption
2   Industrial supplies not elsewhere specified
21   Primary
22   Processed
3   Fuels and lubricants
31   Primary
32   Processed
321   Motor spirit
322   Other
4   Capital goods (except transport equipment), and parts and accessories thereof
41   Capital goods (except transport equipment)
42   Parts and accessories
5   Transport equipment and parts and accessories thereof
51   Passenger motor cars
52   Other
521   Industrial
522   Non-industrial
53   Parts and accessories
6   Consumer goods not elsewhere specified
61   Durable
62   Semi-durable
63   Non-durable
7   Goods not elsewhere specified

Source: UNSTA (1988).

Appendix 2
The International Standard Industrial Classification, Revision 3

A	Agriculture, hunting, and forestry
01	Agriculture, hunting, and related service activities
02	Forestry, logging, and related service activities
B	Fishing
05	Fishing, operation of fish hatcheries, and fish farms; service activities incidental to fishing
C	Mining and quarrying
10	Mining of coal and lignite; extraction of peat
11	Extraction of crude petroleum and natural gas; service activities incidental to oil and gas extraction excluding surveying
12	Mining of uranium and thorium ores
13	Mining of metal ores
14	Other mining and quarrying
D	Manufacturing
15	Manufacture of food products and beverages
16	Manufacture of tobacco products
17	Manufacture of textiles
18	Manufacture of wearing apparel; dressing and dyeing of fur
19	Tanning and dressing of leather; manufacture of luggage, handbags, saddlery, harness, and footwear
20	Manufacture of wood and of products of wood and cork, except furniture; manufacture of articles of straw and plaiting materials
21	Manufacture of paper and paper products
22	Publishing, printing, and reproduction of recorded media
23	Manufacture of coke, refined petroleum products, and nuclear fuel
24	Manufacture of chemicals and chemical products
25	Manufacture of rubber and plastics products
26	Manufacture of other non-metallic mineral products
27	Manufacture of basic metals
28	Manufacture of fabricated metal products, except machinery and equipment
29	Manufacture of machinery and equipment n.e.c.
30	Manufacture of office, accounting, and computing machinery

31	Manufacture of electrical machinery and apparatus n.e.c.
32	Manufacture of radio, television, and communication equipment and apparatus
33	Manufacture of medical, precision, and optical instruments, watches, and clocks
34	Manufacture of motor vehicles, trailers, and semi-trailers
35	Manufacture of other transport equipment
36	Manufacture of furniture; manufacturing n.e.c.
37	Recycling
E	Electricity, gas, and water supply
40	Electricity, gas, steam, and hot-water supply
41	Collection, purification, and distribution of water
F	Construction
45	Construction
G	Wholesale and retail trade; repair of motor vehicles, motorcycles, and personal and household goods
50	Sale, maintenance, and repair of motor vehicles and motorcycles; retail sale of automotive fuel
51	Wholesale trade and commission trade, except of motor vehicles and motorcycles
52	Retail trade, except of motor vehicles and motorcycles; repair of personal and household goods
H	Hotels and restaurants
55	Hotels and restaurants
I	Transport, storage, and communications
60	Land transport; transport via pipelines
61	Water transport
62	Air transport
63	Supporting and auxiliary transport activities; activities of travel agencies
64	Post and telecommunications
J	Financial intermediation
65	Financial intermediation, except insurance and pension funding
66	Insurance and pension funding, except compulsory social security
67	Activities auxiliary to financial intermediation
K	Real-estate, renting, and business activities
70	Real-estate activities
71	Renting of machinery and equipment without operator and of personal and household goods
72	Computer and related activities
73	Research and development
74	Other business activities
L	Public administration and defense; compulsory social security
75	Public administration and defense; compulsory social security
M	Education
80	Education

Appendix 2: ISIC Revision 3 205

N	Health and social work
85	Health and social work
O	Other community, social, and personal service activities
90	Sewage and refuse disposal, sanitation, and similar activities
91	Activities of membership organizations n.e.c.
92	Recreational, cultural, and sporting activities
93	Other service activities
P	Private households with employed persons
95	Private households with employed persons
Q	Extraterritorial organizations and bodies
99	Extraterritorial organizations and bodies

Source: UNSTA (various years).

Appendix 3
The Standard International Trade Classification, Revision 3

0	Food and live animals
00	Live animals other than animals of division 03
01	Meat and meat preparations
02	Dairy products and birds' eggs
03	Fish (not marine mammals), crustaceans, molluscs, and aquatic invertebrates, and preparations thereof
04	Cereals and cereal preparations
05	Vegetables and fruit
06	Sugars, sugar preparations, and honey
07	Coffee, tea, cocoa, spices, and manufactures thereof
08	Feeding stuff for animals (not including unmilled cereals)
09	Miscellaneous edible products and preparations
1	Beverages and tobacco
11	Beverages
12	Tobacco and tobacco manufactures
2	Crude materials, inedible, except fuels
21	Hides, skins, and furskins, raw
22	Oil-seeds and oleaginous fruits
23	Crude rubber (including synthetic and reclaimed)
24	Cork and wood
25	Pulp and waste paper
26	Textile fibres (other than wool tops and other combed wool) and their wastes (not manufactured into yarn or fabric)
27	Crude fertilizers, other than those of division 56, and crude minerals (excluding coal, petroleum, and precious stones)
28	Metalliferous ores and metal scrap
29	Crude animal and vegetable materials, n.e.c.
3	Mineral fuels, lubricants and related materials
32	Coal, coke, and briquettes
33	Petroleum, petroleum products, and related materials
34	Gas, natural and manufactured
35	Electric current
4	Animal and vegetable oils, fats, and waxes

41	Animal oils and fats
42	Fixed vegetable fats and oils, crude, refined, or fractionated
43	Animal or vegetable fats and oils, processed; waxes of animal or vegetable origin; inedible mixtures or preparations of animal or vegetable fats or oils, n.e.c.
5	Chemicals and related products, n.e.c.
51	Organic chemicals
52	Inorganic chemicals
53	Dyeing, tanning, and colouring materials
54	Medicinal and pharmaceutical products
55	Essential oils and resinoids and perfume materials; toilet, polishing, and cleansing preparations
56	Fertilizers (other than those of group 272)
57	Plastics in primary forms
58	Plastics in non-primary forms
59	Chemical materials and products, n.e.c.
6	Manufactured goods classified chiefly by material
61	Leather, leather manufactures, n.e.c., and dressed furskins
62	Rubber manufactures, n.e.c.
63	Cork and wood manufactures (excluding furniture)
64	Paper, paperboard, and articles of paper pulp, of paper, or of paperboard
65	Textile yarn, fabrics, made-up articles, n.e.c., and related products
66	Non-metallic mineral manufactures, n.e.c.
67	Iron and steel
68	Non-ferrous metals
69	Manufactures of metals, n.e.c.
7	Machinery and transport equipment
71	Power-generating machinery and equipment
72	Machinery specialized for particular industries
73	Metalworking machinery
74	General industrial machinery and equipment, n.e.c., and machine parts, n.e.c.
75	Office machines and automatic data-processing machines
76	Telecommunications and sound-recording and reproducing apparatus and equipment
77	Electrical machinery, apparatus, and appliances, n.e.c., and electrical parts thereof (including non-electrical counterparts, n.e.c., of electrical household-type equipment)
78	Road vehicles (including air-cushion vehicles)
79	Other transport equipment
8	Miscellaneous manufactured articles
81	Prefabricated buildings; sanitary, plumbing, heating, and lighting fixtures and fittings, n.e.c.
82	Furniture, and parts thereof; bedding, mattresses, mattress supports, cushions, and similar stuffed furnishings

83	Travel goods, handbags, and similar containers
84	Articles of apparel and clothing accessories
85	Footwear
87	Professional, scientific, and controlling instruments and apparatus, n.e.c.
88	Photographic apparatus, equipment, and supplies; optical goods, n.e.c.; watches and clocks
89	Miscellaneous manufactured articles, n.e.c.
9	Commodities and transactions not classified elsewhere in the SITC
91	Postal packages not classified according to kind
93	Special transactions and commodities not classified according to kind
96	Coin (other than gold coin), not being legal tender
97	Gold, non-monetary (excluding gold ores and concentrates)

Source: UNSTA (1986).

References

Abd-el-Rahman, K., 1991, "Firms' competitive and national comparative advantages as joint determinants of trade composition," *Review of World Economics*, Vol. 127, Issue 1, pp. 83–97.

Acworth, W. and G. Burghardt, 2010, "2009 Derivatives Exchange Volume Webinar," Futures Industry website, available at: www.futuresindustry.org/webinars/downloads/March_2010_Webinar_Materials_Part_1_-_Will_Acworth_FIA.pdf, March 18.

Akamatsu, K., 1962, "A historical pattern of economic growth in developing countries," *Journal of Developing Economies*, Vol. 1, Issue 1, pp. 3–25.

Alchian, Armen A. and William R. Allen, 1964, *University economics*, Belmont, CA: Wadsworth.

AlixPartners, 2009, "AlixParterns 2009 Manufacture-outsourcing cost index—overview & highlights," available at: www.alixpartners.com/EN/portals/0/pdf/AlixPartners%202009%20Manufacturing-Outsourcing%20Cost%20Index%20HIGHLIGHTS_2.pdf, May.

Ando, Mitsuyo, 2006, "Fragmentation and vertical intra-industry trade in East Asia," *North American Journal of Economics and Finance*, Vol. 17, pp. 257–281.

Ando, Mitsuyo and Fukunari Kimura, 2003, "The formation of international production and distribution networks in East Asia," National Bureau of Economic Research Working Paper 10167.

Antweiler, Werner and Daniel Trefler, 2002, "Increasing returns and all that: A view from trade," *American Economic Review*, Vol. 92, Issue 1, pp. 93–119.

ArcelorMittal, various years, *Annual report*, available at: www.arcelormittal.com/index.php?lang=en& page=638.

Arensberg, Ingrid, 2005, *The Swedish ship Götheborg sails again*, Sävedalen Warne.

Arndt, Sven W., 1997, "Globalization and the open economy," *North American Journal of Economics and Finance*, Vol. 8, No. 1, pp. 71–79.

Assche, Ari Van, Chang Hong, and Veerle Slootmaekers, 2008, "China's international competitiveness: Reassessing the evidence," LICOS Centre for Institutions and Economic Performance Discussion Paper 205/2008.

Athukorala, P., 2003, "Product fragmentation and trade patterns in East Asia," Trade and Development Discussion Paper 2003/21, Canberra: Division of Economics, Research School of Pacific and Asian Studies, The Australian National University.

—— 2005, "Component trade and China's regional economic integration," in R. Garnaut and L. Song (eds.), *The China boom and its discontents*, Canberra: Asia Pacific Press, pp. 215–239.

—— 2008, "China's integration into global production networks and its implications for export-led growth strategy in other countries in the region," Trade and Development Discussion Paper 2008/04, Canberra: Division of Economics, Research School of Pacific and Asian Studies, The Australian National University.

Backer, Koen De and Norihiko Yamano, 2008, "The measurement of globalization using international input–output tables," OECD Directorate For Science, Technology and Industry, STI Working Paper 2007/8, April 23.

Bai, Chongen, Changtai Hsieh, and Yingyi Qian, 2006, "The return to capital in China," *Brookings Papers on Economic Activity*, Issue 2, pp. 61–88.

Bairoch, Paul, 1982, "International industrialization levels from 1750 to 1980," *Journal of European Economic History*, Vol. 11, Issue 2, pp. 269–335.

Balassa, Béla, 1965, "Trade liberalisation and 'revealed' comparative advantage," *The Manchester School of Economic and Social Studies*, Vol. 33, pp. 99–123.

Baldwin, Carliss Y., 2000, *Design rule, volume 1: The power of modularity*, Cambridge, MA: MIT Press.

Banister, Judith, Catherine Guillemineau, and Bart van Ark, 2006, "Competitive advantage of 'low-wage' countries often exaggerated," Conference Board Report A-0212–06-EA, October.

Baoshan Iron & Steel Co. Ltd., various years, *Annual report*, available at: www.baosteel.com/plc/06culture/ShowArticle.asp?ArticleID=1334.

Barro, Robert and J.W. Lee, 1996, "International measures of schooling years and schooling quality," *American Economic Review* (Papers and Proceedings), Vol. 86, Issue 2, pp. 218–223.

Boyenge, Jean-Pierre Singa, 2007, "ILO database on export processing zones (revised)," Sectoral Activities Program Working Paper 251, Geneva: International Labor Organization.

BP, 2008, "Statistical review of world energy 2008," available at: www.bp.com/statisticalreview.

Brandt, Loren and Carsten Holz, 2004, "Spatial price differences in China: Estimates and implications," *Economic Development and Cultural Change*, Vol. 55, Issue 1, pp. 43–86.

Braudel, Fernand, 2002, *Civilization and capitalism, 15th–18th century* (Vol. 3), London: Phoenix.

Browning, Harley L. and Joachim Singlemann, 1975, *The emergence of a service society: Demographic and sociological aspects of the sectoral transformation of the labor force in the USA*, Springfield, VA: National Technical Information Service.

Brülhart, Marius, 2008, "An account of global intra-industry trade, 1962–2006," Leverhulme Center for Research of Globalization and Economic Policy research paper 2008/08, University of Nottingham.

Bureau of Service Trade, Ministry of Commerce (MOC), 2008, "China service trade development report 2007," available at: http://tradeinservices.mofcom.gov.cn/report/2007/.

Ccthere Net, 2010, "Collection of 2009 China's industrial data (2009 Zhongguo Gongye Shuju Huizong)," available at: www.ccthere.com/topic/2788851#C2788851, 19 March.

Chambers, J.D., 1961, *The workshop of the world: British economic history from 1820 to 1880*, London: Oxford University Press.

Chandler, Alfred D., Jr., 1977, *The visible hand*, Cambridge, MA: The Belknap Press of Harvard University Press.

—— 1990, *Scale and scope*, Cambridge, MA: The Belknap Press of Harvard University Press.
Chang, Ha-Joon, 2002, *Kicking away the ladder: Development strategy in historical perspective*, London: Anthem.
Chen, Shaohua and Martin Ravallion, 2008, "China is poorer than we thought, but no less successful in the fight against poverty," World Bank Policy Research Working Paper 4621.
Chen, Xiangbin and Yuan Zhao, 2005, "Tribology and sustainable development of the iron and steel industry (*Gangtie Qiye de Mocaxue Wenti yu Kechixu Fazhan*)," in Youbo Xie (ed.), *Engineering frontier* (*Gongcheng Qianyan*) (Vol. 2), Beijing: Higher Education Publishing, pp. 231–238.
China Association of Automobile Manufactures, 2010, "Press release of the production and sales of automobiles and economic operation in 2009 (2009 *Qiche Chanxiao ji Jingji Yunxing Qingkuang Xinxi Fabugao*)," available at: www.auto-stats.org.cn/ReadArticle.asp?NewsID=6234.
China Association of the National Shipbuilding Industry (various years), "Analysis report of the operation of national shipbuilding industry (*Quanguo Chuanbo Gongye Yunxing Baogao*)," available at: www.cansi.org.cn.
China Commodity Market, 2009, "2008 domestic steel consumption structure analysis (2008 *Guonei Gangcai Xiaofei Jiegou Fenxi*)," China Commodity Market website, available at: www.chinaccm.com/03/0315/031572/news/20090626/084350.asp, June 26.
China Iron and Steel Industrial Association, 2006, *China iron and steel statistics 2005*, Beijing: China Iron and Steel Industrial Association Press.
China National Knowledge Infrastructure, 2009, *National Standard full-text database*, available at: http://dbpub.cnki.net/scsf/, June 20.
China National Light Industry Council, 2008, "Research on the resource consumption and industrial structure adjustment of China's ceramic industry (*Zhongguo Taoci Hangye Ziyuan Xiaohao Yu Chanye Jiegou Tiaozheng Zhengce Yanjiu*)," Council Research Report, June.
China Optics and Optoelectronics Manufacturers Association, 2007, "Output and development of domestic and foreign solar polycrystalline silicon (2006 *Nian Guoneiwai de Taiyangneng Guojinggui Chanliang ji Fazhan Qingkuang*)," available at: www.coema.org.cn/news/dir/232/200707203324.html, July 20.
China Securities and Regulatory Commission (CSRC), 2010, *China securities and futures statistics 2009*, Beijing: Xuelin Press.
Chun, Chang, B. Fleisher, and E. Parker, 2001, "The impact of China's entry into the WTO: overview," *China Economic Review*, Vol. 11, Issue 4, pp. 319–322.
Coase, Ronald, 1937, "The nature of the firm," *Economica*, Vol. 4, Issue 16, pp. 386–405.
Cui, Ying, 2008, "'Made in China': A lot of room for the future (*Zhongguo Zhizao Dayoukewei*)," *People Daily* (*Renmin Ridao*), June 6, p. 10.
Dean, Judith M., K.C. Fung, and Zhi Wang, 2007, "Measuring the vertical specialization in Chinese trade," U.S. International Trade Commission, Office of Economics Working Paper No. 2007-01-A.
Deaton, Angus and Alan Heston, 2008, "Understanding PPPs and PPP-based national accounts," National Bureau of Economic Research Working Paper 14499.
Denison, E., 1962, *The sources of economic growth in the United States and the alternatives before us*, New York: Committee for Economic Development.

Department for Innovation, Universities, & Skills (DIUS) and the Department for Business, Enterprise, & Regulatory Reform (BERR), various years, *The R&D scoreboard*, available at: www.innovation.gov.uk/rd_scoreboard/default.asp.

Department of Industry and Transport Statistics, National Bureau of Statistics (NBS), various years, *Chinese statistics yearbook of industrial economy*, Beijing: China Statistics Press.

Dixit, Avinash K. and Gene M. Grossman, 1982, "Trade and protection with multistage production," *The Review of Economic Studies*, Vol. 49, Issue 4, pp. 583–594.

Duijn, J.J. van, 1983, *The long wave in economic life*, London: Allen & Unwin.

Dunning, John H. and Sarianna M. Lundan, 2008, *Multinational enterprises and the global economy*, 2nd edn., Cheltenham and Northampton, MA: Edward Elgar Publishing.

European Photovoltaic Industry Association, various years, *Solar generation*, available at: www.epia.org/publications/epia-publications.html.

Feenstra, Robert C., 1998, "Integration of trade and disintegration of production in the global economy," *Journal of Economic Perspective*, Vol. 12, No. 4, pp. 31–50.

Ferrantino, Michael, Robert Koopman, Zhi Wang, Falan Yinug, Ling Chen, Fengjie Qu, and Haifeng Wang, 2007, "Classification and statistical reconciliation of trade in advanced technology products—the case of China and the United States," Brookings-Tsinghua Center for Public Policy Working Paper Series WP20070906EN.

Fewsmith, J., 2001, "The political and social implications of China's accession to the WTO," *China Quarterly*, Vol. 167, pp. 573–591.

Financial Times, 2009, *FT Global 500 Database*, available at: www.ft.com/reports/ft500-2009.

Finger, J.M., 1975, "Tariff provisions for offshore assembly and the exports of developing countries," *The Economic Journal*, Vol. 85, Issue 338, pp. 365–371.

First Solar Inc., various years, *Annual report*, available at: http://phx.corporate-ir.net/phoenix.zhtml? c=201491&p=irol-reportsAnnual.

Fontagné, Lionel and M. Freudenberg, 1997, "IIT: Methodological issues reconsidered," Centre D'Etudes Prospectives et D'Informations Internationales Working Paper 1997- 01.

Fontagné, Lionel, Guillaume Gaulier, and Soledad Zignago, 2008, "Specialization across varieties and North–South competition," *Economic Policy*, January, pp. 51–91.

Fortune, 2009, *Fortune Datastore*, available at: www.timeinc.net/fortune/datastore/index.html?fds.

Freeman, Christopher and Luc Soete, 1995, *The economics of industrial innovation*, 3rd edn., Cambridge: MIT Press.

Gao, Jian and Gary H. Jefferson, 2007, "Science and technology take-off in China? Sources of rising R&D intensity," *Asia Pacific Business Review*, Vol. 13, No. 3, pp. 357–371.

General Administration of Custom of China, 2008, "Regulation Rule of the Custom of People's Republic of China to the Processing Trade Goods," available at: www.chinacourt.org/flwk/show1.php?file_id=125131, January 14.

Gilbert, J. and M. Wahl, 2002, "Applied general equilibrium assessments of trade liberalization in China," *World Economy*, Vol. 25, Issue 5, pp. 697–731.

Global Insight, 2007, "China set to take the lead in global manufacturing," available at: www.globalinsight.com/Perspective/PerspectiveDetail9537.htm, July 7, 2007.

Great Wall Enterprise Strategy Institute, 2004, *Science and technology innovation and "made in China"* (*Keji Chuangxin yu Zhongguo Zhizao*), Great Wall Enterprise Strategy Institute Report Series.

Greenaway, D., R. Hine, and C. Milner, 1995, "Vertical and horizontal intra-industry trade: A cross-industry analysis for the United Kingdom," *Economic Journal*, Vol. 105, pp. 1505–1519.

Grossman, Gene M. and E. Helpman, 1991, "Quality ladders and product cycles," *The Quality Journal of Economics*, May, pp. 557–586.

Grubel, Herbert G. and Peter J. Lloyd, 1975, *Intra industry trade: The theory and measurement of internationally trade in differentiated products*, New York: Wiley.

Grubel, Herbert G. and Michael A. Walker, 1989, S*ervice industry growth: Causes and effects*, Vancouver: Fraser Institute.

Gunder-Frank, Andre, 1998, *ReOrient: Global economy in the Asian age*, Berkeley, CA: University of California Press.

Gupta, Anil K. and Haiyan Wang, 2009, "China as an innovator, not just an imitator," *Business Week*, available at: www.businessweek.com/globalbiz/content/mar2009/gb2009039_914844.htm? campaign_id=rss_topStories, March 9.

Hatzichronoglou, Thomas, 1997, "Revision of the high-technology sector and product classification," OECD STI Working Papers 1997/2.

Helleiner, G.K., 1973, "Manufactured exports from less-developed countries and multinational firms," *The Economic Journal*, Vol. 83, Issue 329, pp. 21–47.

Hobday, Michael, 1995, *Innovation in East Asia: The challenge to Japan*, Aldershot: Edward Elgar.

Hollinger, Peggy, 2009, "West Europe's services sector gets FDI boost," *Financial Times*, available at: www.ft.com/cms/s/0/e7ae4fd8–3299–11dd-9b87-0000779fd2ac.html?nclick_check=1, June 5.

Hopkins, Terence K. and Immanuel Wallerstein, 1996, *The age of transition: Trajectory of the world-system 1945–2025*, London: Atlantic Highlands.

Hu, Albert G.Z. and Gary H. Jefferson, 2008, "Science and technology in China," in Loren Brandt and Thomas G. Rawski (eds.), *China's great economic transformation*, Cambridge University Press, pp. 313–314.

Hu, Albert G.Z. and Gary H. Jefferson, 2009, "A Great Wall of patents: What is behind China's recent patent explosion?" *Journal of Development Economics*, Vol. 90, Issue 1, pp. 57–68.

Huang, Yasheng, 2003, *Selling China: Foreign direct investment during the reform era*, Cambridge: Cambridge University Press.

Hudson, Pat, 2001, "The workshop of the world," BBC History website, available at: www.bbc.co.uk/history/british/victorians/workshop_of_the_world_01.shtml, January 1.

Hummels, David, Jun Ishii, and Kei-Mu Yi, 2001, "The nature and growth of vertical specialization in world trade," *Journal of International Economics*, Vol. 54, pp. 75–96.

Hummels, David and Peter J. Klenow, 2005, "The variety and quality of a nation's exports," *The American Economic Review*, Vol. 95, No. 3, pp. 704–723.

Interbrand, various years, "The 100 best global brands by value," available at: www.interbrand.com/best_global_brands.aspx.

International Energy Agency (IEA), 2007, *World energy outlook 2007*, Paris: IEA.

—— 2008, *World energy statistics: Energy balances of OECD (non-OECD) countries database*, ESDS International, (Mimas) University of Manchester.

International Iron and Steel Institute (IISI), various years, *World steel statistics*, available at: www.worldsteel.org/?action=publicationlist.
International Labor Organization (ILO), 2008, *Key indicators of the labor market database*, ESDS International, (Mimas) University of Manchester.
International Monetary Fund (IMF), 2005, *Asia-Pacific Regional Outlook—September 2005*, Washington DC: International Monetary Fund.
—— 2009, *Asia-Pacific regional outlook—May 2009*, Washington DC: International Monetary Fund.
International Organization of Motor Vehicle Manufacturers, various years, "Production statistics," available at: http://oica.net/category/production-statistics/.
International Standard Organization (ISO), various years, *Annual report*, Geneva: ISO Central Secretariat.
Isaksson, Anders, 2007, "World productivity database: A technical description," RST Staff Working Paper 10/2007, Vienna: UNIDO.
Japan Commission on Industrial Performance, 1997, *Made in Japan: Revitalizing Japanese manufacturing for economic growth*, Cambridge, MA: MIT Press.
Jarillo, J. Carlos, 1988, "On strategic networks," *Strategic Management Journal*, Vol. 9, Issue 1, pp. 31–41.
Jones, Ronald W. and Anne O. Krueger (eds.), 1990, *The political economy of international trade: Essays in honor of Robert E. Baldwin*, Oxford: Basil Blackwell.
Jorgenson, Dale and Zvi Griliches, 1967, "The explanation of productivity change," *Review of Economic Studies*, Vol. 34, pp. 249–283.
Kennedy, Paul, 1987, *The rise and fall of the Great Powers: Economic change and military conflict from 1500 to 2000*, Random House.
Kondratieff, N.D., 1935, "The long waves in economic life," *The Review of Economic Statistics*, Vol. 17, No. 6, pp. 105–115.
Koopman, Robert, Zhi Wang, and Shang-jin Wei, 2008, "How much of Chinese exports is really Made in China? Assessing foreign and domestic value-added in gross exports," U.S. International Trade Commission, Office of Economics Working Paper No. 2008–03-B.
Korea International Trade Association, 2007, "Among products ranking first in the global market share, 59 ones are made in Korea," available at: http://global.kita.net/news/02/1188600_1687.jsp, September 3.
Krugman, Paul, 1996, "Does Third World growth hurt First World prosperity?" *Harvard Business Review*, Vol. 72, pp. 113–121.
Kuang, Shaopin, 2009, "2009 development research report of global solar PV industry," available at: www.chuandong.com/publish/report/2009/8/report_1_3549.html, June 30.
Lall, Sanjaya, 2000, "The technological structure and performance of developing country manufactured exports, 1985–98," *Oxford Development Studies*, Vol. 28, No. 3, pp. 337–369.
Lardy, Nicholas R., 2002, *Integrating China into the global economy*, Washington DC: Brookings Institute Press.
Laurens, Didier, Gaël de Bray, Gerard Moore, and Colin Campbell, 2007, "Photovoltaic solar energy—in silicon's wake," Société Générale Group Equity Research Report, available at: www.sgcib.com, July 7.
LDK Solar Co. Ltd., 2008, *2008 Annual report*, available at: http://investor.ldksolar.com/phoenix.zhtml?c =196973&p=irol-investorKit.

Leamer, Edward E., 1996, "In search of Stolper–Samuelson effects on U.S. wages," National Bureau of Economic Research Working Paper No. 5427.

Lehmann, Alexander, 2002, "Foreign direct investment in emerging markets: Income, repatriations and financial vulnerabilities," IMF Working Paper No. 02/47.

Lemoine, Françoise and Deniz Unal-Kesenci, 2004, "Assembly trade and technology transfer: The case of China," *World Development*, Vol. 32, No. 5, pp. 829–850.

Li, Jingwen, 1993, *Shengchanlv Yu Zhongmeiri Jingji Zengzhang* (Productivity and economic growth in China, USA, and Japan), Beijing: China Social Science Press.

Linder, S., 1961, *An essay on trade and transformation*, Stockholm: Almqvist & Wiksell.

Liu, Yu and Yinglan Jiao, 2006, "About the concentration ratio of China's steel industry (*Shitan Woguo Gangtie Gongye Jizhongdu*)," available at: www.csm.org.cn/index/read.asp?title= %BF%C6%BC%BC%D0%C5%CF%A2&ID=788.

Lothian, James R. and Mark P. Taylor, 2000, "Purchasing power parity over two centuries: Strengthening the case for real exchange rate stability—A reply to Cuddington and Liang," *Journal of International Money and Finance*, Vol. 19, pp. 759–764.

Maddison, Angus, 2003, *The world economy: A millennial perspective*, Paris: OECD.

Martin, W. and E. Ianchovichina, 2001, "Implications of China's accession to the WTO for China and the WTO," *World Economy*, Vol. 24, Issue 9.

Marx, Karl, 1996 [1859], "'Introduction' to the Grundrisse," in Terrell Carver (ed.), *Marx: Later political writings*, Cambridge: Cambridge University Press.

McKibbin, W. and K. Tang, 2000, "Trade and financial reform in China: Impacts on the world economy," *World Economy*, Vol. 23, Issue 8.

McKinsey, 2007, "EDS, building a world-class IT services outsourcing industry in China," available at: www.beyondsoft.com/doc/BuildingWorldClassIT%20Services%20Outsourcing%20Industry%20in%20China.pdf.

Metals Consulting International Ltd., 2009, "World steel industry agenda," available at: www.steelonthenet.com, June.

Millward Brown Optimor, 2009, "BrandZ Top 100 most valuable global brands 2009," available at: www.millwardbrown.com/Sites/Optimor/Content/KnowledgeCenter/BrandzRanking.aspx.

Ministry of Commerce (MOC), National Bureau of Statistics (NBS), State Administration of Foreign Exchange (SAFE), various years, *Statistical bulletin of China's outward foreign direct investment*, available at: http://hzs.mofcom.gov.cn/date/date.html.

Ministry of Science and Technology (MOST), 2008, *China high-technology industry data book 2008*, available at: www.sts.org.cn/sjkl/gjscy/data2008/data08.htm.

Nan, Liangjin and Jinjun Xue, 2002, "Calculation of China's population and labor force 1949–1999 (1949–1999 *Nian Zhongguo Renkou he Laodongli Tuisuan*)," *China Population Science* (*Zhongguo Renkou Kexue*), Issue 3, pp. 1–16.

National Bureau of Statistics (NBS), various years, *China statistics yearbook*, Beijing: China Statistics Press.

—— 2006, *China economic census yearbook 2004*, Beijing: China Statistics Press.

—— 2007, *Data of gross domestic product of China (1952–2004)*, Beijing: China Statistics Press.

—— 2008a, *International statistics yearbook 2008*, Beijing: China Statistics Press.

—— 2008b, *Notes on national economic industrial classification* (*Guomin Jingji Hangye Fenlei Zhushi*), Beijing: China Statistics Press.

—— National Development and Reform Committee (NDRC), and Ministry of Science and Technology (MOST), various years, *China statistics yearbook on high technology industry 2007*, Beijing: China Statistics Press.

—— and Ministry of Labor and Social Security (MLSS), various years, *China labor statistical yearbook*, Beijing: China Statistics Press.

—— and Ministry of Science and Technology (MOST), various years, *China statistics yearbook of science and technology*, Beijing: China Statistics Press.

National Development and Reform Commission (NDRC), Ministry of Commerce (MOC), and Ministry of Finance (MOF), 2009, "Catalogue of encouraging import of technology and products 2009," available at: www.sdpc.gov.cn/zcfb/zcfbtz/2009tz/t20090831_299015.htm, July 22.

National Development and Reform Commission (NDRC), Ministry of Commerce (MOC), and Nelson, Richard, 1993, *National innovation systems: A comparative analysis*, New York: Oxford University Press.

National Science Board, 2008, *Science and engineering indicators 2008* (Vol. 2), Arlington, VA: National Science Foundation.

Naughton, Barry, 2007, *The Chinese economy: Transitions and growth*, Cambridge and London: The MIT Press.

Netherlands Environmental Assessment Agency, 2006, "History database of the global environment," available at: www.mnp.nl/en/themasites/hyde/index.html.

Ng, Francis and Alexander Yeats, 2003, "Major trade trends in East Asia: What are their implications for regional cooperation and growth?" World Bank Policy Research Working Paper Series, No. 3084.

Nolan, Peter, 2001, *China and the global business revolution*, Houndsmill: Palgrave.

—— and Huaichuan Rui, 2007, "The global industrial consolidation and the challenge for China: The case of the steel industry," in Peter Nolan (ed.), *Integrating China: Towards the coordinated market economy*, Anthem Press, pp. 71–94.

Nye, Joseph S., 2004, *Soft power: The means to success in world politics*, New York: Public Affairs.

OECD Steel Committee, 2009, "Presentation for the Council Working Party on Shipbuilding," available at: www.oecd.org/dataoecd/21/37/43312347.pdf, July 9.

Organization for Economic Development and Cooperation (OECD), 2003, *Science, technology and industry scoreboard 2003*, OECD: Paris.

—— 2005a, "OECD finds that China is biggest exporter of Information technology goods in 2004, surpassing US and EU," available at: www.oecd.org/document/8/0,3343,en_2825_293564_35833096_1_1_1_1,00.html.

—— 2005b, *Structure analysis database for industrial analysis*, ESDS International, (Mimas) University of Manchester.

—— 2006, The OECD input–output database: 2006 Edition, available at: www.oecd.org/document/32/0,3343,en_2649_34445_42162912_1_1_1_1,00.html.

—— 2007, *Science, technology and industry scoreboard 2007*, Paris: OECD.

—— 2008a, *Science, technology and industry outlook 2008*, OECD: Paris.

—— 2008b, *Main science and technology indicators database*, ESDS International, (Mimas) University of Manchester.

—— 2008c, *OECD statistics on international trade in services*, ESDS International, (Mimas) University of Manchester.

Panitchpakdi, Supachai and M. Clifford, 2002, *China and the WTO: Changing China, changing world trade*, Singapore: John Wiley and Sons.
Penrose, Edith, 1959, *The theory of the growth of the firm*, New York: John Wiley and Sons.
Pierson, David, 2009, "China, green? In the case of solar water heating, yes," *The Los Angeles Times*, available at: www.latimes.com/news/nationworld/nation/la-fi-china-solar6–2009sep06,0,7213756. story?page=1, September 6.
Ping, Xinqiao, Zhaoyan Hao, Liang Mao, Huasong Li, Lu Zhang, and Xiangting Hu, 2005, "Vertical specialization, intra-industry trade and Sino-America relations," China Center for Economic Research of Peking University, Working Paper C2005005.
Porter, Michael E., 1985, *Competitive advantage: Creating and sustaining superior performance*, New York: Free Press.
—— 1998, *The competitive advantage of nations: with a new introduction*, Basingstoke: Macmillan Business.
Program of "Research on China's Using FDI and Foreign Invested Enterprises" of National Bureau of Statistics (NBS), "Problem existing and policy suggestion of the development of China's foreign invested enterprises," *Guide Journal for China's Economy and Trade* (*Zhongguo Jingmao Daokan*), 2006, Issue 8, pp. 11–12.
Q-Cell SE, various years, *Annual report*, available at: www.q-cells.com/en/investor_relations/reports/index.html.
Renewable Energy Policy Network for the 21st Century, various years, *Renewables global status report*, available at: www.ren21.net/publications/default.asp.
Rodrik, D., 2006, "What's so special about China's exports?" *China and the World Economy*, Vol. 14, Issue 5, pp. 1–19.
Rogoff, Kenneth, 1996, "The purchasing power parity puzzle," *Journal of Economic Literature*, Vol. 34, No. 2, pp. 647–668.
Rostow, W.W., 1960, *The stages of economic growth: A non-communist manifesto*, Cambridge: Cambridge University Press.
Ruigrok, Winfried and Rob van Tulder, 1995, *The logic of international restructuring: The management of dependencies in rival industrial complexes*, London: Routledge.
Sanhuan Group, 2005, "Prospectus for initial public offering (*Shouci Gongkai Faxing Gupiao Zhaogu Shuomingshu*)," available at: www.szse.cn.
—— 2007, "Business circumstance of 2007," Group Report.
Schmitz, Hubert, 1995, "Collective efficiency: Growth path for small-scale industry," *Journal of Development Studies*, Vol. 31, No. 4, pp. 529–566.
Schott, Peter K., 2004, "Across-product versus within-product specialization in international trade," *Quarterly Journal of Economics*, Vol. 119, Issue 2, pp. 647–678.
—— 2006, "The relative sophistication of Chinese exports," National Bureau of Economic Research working paper 12173.
Schumpeter, J.A., 1939, *Business cycles: A theoretical, historical and statistical analysis of the capitalist process*, New York and London: McGraw-Hill.
Shafaeddin, S., 2004, "Is China's accession to WTO threatening exports of developing countries?" *China Economic Review*, Vol. 15, Issue 2, pp. 109–144.
Simon, Denis F. and Cong Cao, 2009, *China's emerging technological edge: Assessing the role of high-end talent*, Cambridge University Press.
Singtao Net, 2008, "'Made in China' ranks No.1 in seven groups of manufacturing products," available at: www.stnn.cc/chinafin/200810/t20081029_888631.html, October 29.

Solow, Robert M., 1956, "A contribution to the theory of economic growth," *Quarterly Journal of Economics*, Vol. 70, No.1, pp. 65–94.

State-owned Assets Supervision and Administration Commission (SASAC), 2009, "Five year review of SASAC (*Guowuyuan Guoziwei Wunian Huigu*)," available at: www.sasac.gov.cn/2009rdzt/yjj/wzn.pdf.

Sturgeon, Timothy J., 2002, "Modular production networks: A new American model of industrial organization," *Industrial and Corporate Change*, Vol. 11, No. 3, pp. 451–496.

Suntech Power Holdings Co., Ltd., 2009, "Stock chart," EDGAR Online, available at: http://phx.corporate-ir.net/phoenix.zhtml?c=192654&p=irol-stockChart.

—— various years, *Annual report*, available at: http://phx.corporate-ir.net/phoenix.zhtml?c=192654&p=irol-reportsAnnual.

Sutherland, Dylan, 2003, *China's large enterprises and the challenge of late industrialization*, London: Routledge Curzon.

Taylor, Alan M. and Mark P. Taylor, 2004, "The purchasing power parity debate," *Journal of Economic Perspectives*, Vol. 18, No. 4, pp. 135–158.

Taylor, F. Winslow, 1911, *The principles of scientific management*, New York and London: Harper & Brothers.

Technology Forecasters, 2006, "The evolution and future of global outsourcing," Technology Forecasters White Paper, available at: www.techforecasters.com/whitepapers/wp_read_evolution_ future.pdf.

Thorbecke, Willem and Hanjiang Zhang, 2008, "The effect of exchange rate Changes on China's labor-intensive manufacturing exports," RIETI Discussion papers 08038.

Tsuneta Yano Memorial Society, 2007, *Nippon: A charted survey of Japan 2007/2008*, Tokyo: Kokuseisha.

United Nation Conference of Trade and Development (UNCTAD), 2002, *World investment report 2002: Transnational corporations and export competitiveness*, New York and Geneva: United Nations.

—— 2009, *Foreign direct investment database*, available at: http://stats.unctad.org/fdi.

—— various years, *World investment report*, New York and Geneva: United Nations.

United Nation Development Program (UNDP), 2008, *Human development report 2007/08*, New York and Geneva: United Nations.

United Nations Environment Program (UNEP), 2009, *Global trends in sustainable energy investment 2009*, Paris: United Nations Environment Program.

United Nations Industrial Development Organization (UNIDO), 2004, *Industrial development report 2002–2003*, Vienna: UNIDO.

—— 2008, *Industrial statistics databases*, ESDS International, (Mimas) University of Manchester.

—— 2010, "China overtakes Japan as world's second largest industrial manufacturer, says UNIDO report," available at: www.unido.org/index.php?id=7881&tx_ttnews%5Btt_news%5D=450&cHash =65b1bc064e, March 18.

United Nations Statistics Division (UNSTA), various years, "International Standard Industrial Classification," available at: http://unstats.un.org/unsd/cr/registry/regct.asp.

—— 1986, "Standard International Trade Classification, Revision 3, (SITC, Rev.3)," available at: http://unstats.un.org/unsd/cr/registry/regcst.asp?Cl=14.

—— 1988, "Broad economic categories (BECs)," available at: http://unstats.un.org/unsd/cr/registry/regcst.asp? C1=10&lg=1.

References 219

—— 2002, Central Product Classification Version 1.1 (CPC V1.1), available at: http://unstats.un.org/unsd/statcom/doc02/cpc.pdf, February 21, February 21.

—— 2003, *United Nations statistical yearbook data retrieval* CD-ROM, New York and Geneva: United Nations.

—— 2008, United Nations commodity trade statistics database, available at: http://comtrade.un.org/db/.

—— European Commission (EC), International Monetary Fund (IMF), Organisation for Economic Co-operation and Development (OECD), United Nations Conference on Trade and Development (UNCTAD), and World Trade Organization (WTO), 2002, *Manual on statistics of international trade in services*, New York: United Nations.

US Census Bureau, various years, *Statistical abstract of the United States*, available at: www.census.gov/compendia/statab/.

US Department of Commerce, 2006, *Statistics for industry groups and industries: 2005*, available at: www.census.gov/prod/2006pubs/am0531gs1.pdf.

Villeroy & Boch, various years, *Annual report*, available at: www.villeroy-boch.com/en/us/home/the-company/investor-relations/reports.html.

Wallerstein, Immanuel, 1974, *The modern world-system, vol. I: Capitalist agriculture and the origins of the European world-economy in the sixteenth century*, New York and London: Academic Press.

Wang, Fenghe, 2008, "China's bicycle industry has unlimited potential (*Zhongguo Zixingche Chanye Huoli Wuxian*)," China Bicycle Association website, available at: www.clii.com.cn/zt/bicycle/.

Wang, Kevin, 2004, "China's EMS and ODM market to enjoy brisk expansion, iSuppli Corporation," available at: www.isuppli.com/catalog/detail.asp?id=6483, September 14.

Waterford Wedgwood, various years, *Annual report*, available at: http://google.brand.edgar-online.com/default.aspx?companyid=114684.

Weber, Christopher L., Glen P. Peters, Dabo Guan, and Klaus Hubacek, 2008, "The contribution of Chinese exports to climate change," *Energy Policy*, Vol. 36, pp. 3572–3577.

Wikipedia, 2009, "*Longqing (Ming Muzong)*," available at: http://zh.wikipedia.org/wiki/%E9%9A%86%_E5%BA%86_(%E6%98%8E%E7%A9%86%E5%AE%97).

Wolf, Martin, 2007, "The breath of the dragon: China and the world economy," *Financial Times*, China Report No. 37, available at: www.ftchinese.com/story.php?storyid=001016082.

World Bank, 2007a, "The 2005 international comparison program preliminary results," available at: http://siteresources.worldbank.org/ICPINT/Resources/ICPreportprelim.pdf.

—— 2007b, *World development indicator 2006* (CD-ROM), Washington: World Bank.

—— 2008, *World development indicators*, ESDS International, (Mimas) University of Manchester.

World Brand Laboratory, 2010, "2010 (the 7th) the World's 500 Most Influential Brands (*2010 nian Shijie Pinpai 500 Qiang Paihangbang*)," available at: www.worldbrandlab.com/world/2010/.

World Intellectual Property Organization (WIPO), 2008, *World patent report 2008: A statistical review*, Geneva: World Intellectual Property Organization.

—— 2009, "Global economic slowdown impacts 2008 international patent filings," PR/2009/583, available at: www.wipo.int/pressroom/en/articles/2009/article_0002.html, January 27.

World Trade Organization (WTO), various years, *International trade statistics*, Lausanne: World Trade Organization.

—— 2007, "World Trade 2006, prospects for 2007: Risks lie ahead following stronger trade in 2006, WTO reports," WTO Press Releases 472, available at: www.wto.org/english/news_e/pres07_e/pr472_e.htm, April 12, 2007.

—— 2008, *WTO statistics database*, available at: http://stat.wto.org/Home/WSDBHome.aspx.

—— 2009, "World Trade 2008, Prospects for 2009: WTO sees 9 percent global trade decline in 2009 as recession strikes," WTO Press Releases 554, available at: www.wto.org/english/news_e/pres09_e/pr554_e.htm, March 23.

Xinhua Net, 2006, "Foreign invested enterprises share sixty percent of top 500 enterprises ranked by foreign trade (*Zhongguo Waimao 500 Qiang, Waishang Touzi Qiye zhan Liucheng*)," available at: http://news.xinhuanet.com/fortune/2006-07/12/content_4823442.htm, July 12.

Xinhua News Agency, 2004, "Call China workshop instead of world factory," www1.china.org.cn/english/features/93993.htm, April 26.

Xiong, Lin, 2008, "Re-examining polycrystalline silicon from the perspective of the cost to the photovoltaic industry (*Cong Guangfu Chanye Chengben Jiaodu Zaikan Duojinggui*)," China Jianyin Investment Security Report, available at: www.cjis.cn, March 21.

Yang, Xiwei, Peng Liang, Honghe Zhang, and Xingwen Li, 2009, "Exciting polysilicon (*Kangfen de Duojinggui*)," *Liaowang*, Issue 36.

Ye, Wentian, 2009, "Fitness of Zhengrong Shi—Wuxi Suntech may laid off 30 percent of employees (*Shizhenrong Shoushen—Wuxi Shangde huo Cayuan Sancheng*)," *China Business Journal*, available at: http://news.cb.com.cn/html/56/n-3456.html, January 10.

Yin, Yifeng, 2008, "PV industry report: Broad view of solar energy development (*Taiyangneng Hangye Baogao: Taiyangneng Fazhan Qianjing Guangkuo*)," CITIC China Securities Research, http://research.csc.com.cn, April 23.

Zhang, Kevin Honglin, 2006, "The role of FDI in China's export performance," in Kevin Honglin Zhang (ed.), *China as the world factory*, London: Routledge, pp. 139–155.

Zhang, Zeqi, 2008, "Data for 30 years of China's motorcycle industry," *Enterprise Culture (Qiye Wenming)*, Issue 9.

Zhao, Ying, 2008, *The research on technology standard and international competitiveness of China's manufacturing industry (Zhongguo Zhizaoye Jishu Biaozun Yu Jingzhengli Yanjiu)*, Beijing: Economic and Management Publishing.

Zhao, Yuwen, Dacheng Wu, Sicheng Wang, Wenjing Wang, Xudong Li, Zuming Liu, Diming Qiu, Shuang Song, and Chun Ge, 2008, "Development research report of China's photovoltaic industry 2006–2007 (*Zhongguo Guangfu Chanye Fazhan Yanjiu Baogao 2006–2007*)," *Solar Energy (Taiyangneng)*, 2008, Issues 6–8.

Index

ArcelorMittal 173, 175–178
Association of Southeast Asian Nations (ASEAN) 9
Advanced Technology Product (ATP) 73, 80

Baoshan Iron & Steel 165–172, 174
Baosteel 165–173, 175–179
broad economic categories (BEC) 80, 202
business enterprise research and development (BERD) 99, 125
biological oxygen demand (BOD) 58
balance of payment (BOP) 111–113
business process outsourcing (BPO) 116
BRIC 45
British Standards Institution (BSI) 172

China compulsory certification (CCC) 148
China Certification Center, Inc. (CCCI) 172
code division multiple access (CDMA) 109–110
computers and office equipments (COE) 28–30, 69–71
concentration ratio 165

expanded balance of payment service classification (EBOPS) 113
electronic contract manufacturing (ECM) 20
electronic manufacturing services (EMS) 18, 115–116
export processing zone (EPZ) 62, 79
electronic and telecommunication equipments (ETE) 28, 30–31
European Union (EU) 20, 148, 190

First Solar 193–195
foreign affiliates trade in services (FATS) 113–114, 132
foreign direct investment (FDI) 4, 20, 39, 41–42, 113–114, 116–117, 129–132, 200
foreign invested enterprises (FIE) 2–3, 20, 27–32, 35–36, 64, 71–72, 76–77, 102, 112–114, 116–119, 129, 198–200

gross fixed capital formation (GFCF) 38–41, 55
gross industrial output (GIO) 2–3, 21–22, 102, 104, 136–137, 139, 150
Grubel–Lloyd index 86–90

harmonized system (HS) 2, 60, 73, 79, 83–84
Heibei Iron and Steel Group 173, 179
high and new technology products (HNTP) 73, 75
human resources for science and technology (HRST) 49

information and communications technologies (ICT) 9, 20, 28, 31, 33, 49, 57, 67, 69, 71, 74–76, 79–80, 83, 85, 90, 95, 102, 107–110, 128–129, 134, 197–199
International Energy Agency (IEA) 36, 42, 181
International Electro-technical Commission (IEC) 110
Institute of Electrical and Electronics Engineers (IEEE) 110
International Financial Statistics (IFS) 117

222 Index

International Iron and Steel Institute (IISI) 158–159, 173, 196
intra-industry trade (IIT) 80–81, 83, 86–87, 89–92, 95
International Labor Organization (ILO) 53, 62
International Monetary Fund (IMF) 16, 24, 83, 111, 113
initial public offering (IPO) 188, 190
International Standard Industrial Classification (ISIC) 25–28, 31–33, 48, 56–57, 96–98, 107, 128, 134–135
International Standard Organization (ISO) 108–110
International Telecommunication Union (ITU) 110

Japanese Standards Association (JSA) 172
JFE Holding 175–178

Kobe Steel 175–178

large and medium enterprises (LME) 106
LDK Solar 190–195

merger and acquisition (M&A) 127, 129–130, 132, 144, 151, 166, 173, 175
medical equipments and meters manufacturing (MEM) 28, 30–31, 71–72
multinational company (MNC) 8–9, 11, 20, 63, 77, 114, 117, 119, 132, 197, 199–200
Ministry of Commerce (MOC) 9, 73, 113–114, 132, 186
Ministry of Finance (MOF) 186
Ministry of Science and Technology (MOST) 73

National Bureau of Statistics (NBS) 3, 21, 28, 55, 117, 132, 138
National Development and Reform Commission (NDRC) 9, 186
New Zhongyuan 149–153
newly industrialized economies (NIE) 9, 31
New York Stock Exchange (NYSE) 188, 190
Nippon Steel 175–178

original brand manufacturing (OBM) 18, 145, 147, 149, 153

original design manufacturing (ODM) 17–18, 115–116, 145, 147, 153, 200
original equipment manufacturing (OEM) 17–18, 145, 147, 153, 201
Organization for Economic Development and Cooperation (OECD) 20, 26, 28, 30, 36–37, 39–43, 45–46, 49–51, 58, 70, 74–76, 94, 100, 102, 107, 159–160, 187, 198

participation ratio 45
Patent Cooperation Treaty (PCT) 85, 107–108, 187
perpetual inventory method (PIM) 40, 58
photovoltaic (PV) 133, 180, 182–183, 186–192, 194, 201
POSCO 175–179
processing trade 19, 61, 63, 71, 80
purchasing power parity (PPP) 2, 5, 18, 23–25, 37–38, 50–53, 57–58, 61–62, 97, 198

Q-Cell 192–195

research and development (R&D) 3, 5, 8–15, 17, 26, 96–104, 106, 108, 111–112, 114, 116, 123–125, 127, 132–133, 143–144, 148–149, 152–153, 164, 172, 179–180, 187, 189–191, 195, 197–198, 200–201
revealed comparative advantage (RCA) 64–67

Sanhuan Group 144–149, 151–153
State Administration of Foreign Exchange (SAFE) 132
State-owned Assets Supervision and Administration Commission (SASAC) 127
Standard International Trade Classification (SITC) 67, 69, 78, 83–84, 86–92, 135, 158, 161, 206–208
state-owned enterprises (SOE) 45, 55, 63–64, 76, 102, 116, 126–127, 130–131, 146, 165
Suntech 187–190, 193–195

Tata 175–178
total factor productivity (TFP) 54–58
transnational company (TNC) 123–124

unit cost 53–54, 56–57
unit value 77–80, 90, 139, 141–143, 160–161, 199, 201

Index   223

United Nation Conference of Trade and Development (UNCTAD) 68, 113–114
United Nation Development Program (UNDP) 37
United Nations Environment Program (UNEP) 186
United Nations Industrial Development Organization (UNIDO) 22–23, 25, 31, 40, 198
United Nations Statistics Division (UNSTA) 113
US Steel 175–179

vertical specialization (VS) 7, 17, 91, 93–95, 199
Villeroy & Boch 150–153

Waterford Wedgwood 150–153
wireless local area network (WLAN) 110
World Intellectual Property Organization (WIPO) 187
World Trade Organization (WTO) 1–2, 5, 15–16, 45, 55, 59, 71, 73, 102, 111, 113–114, 116, 132, 144, 156, 199

Taylor & Francis
eBooks
FOR LIBRARIES

ORDER YOUR FREE 30 DAY INSTITUTIONAL TRIAL TODAY!

Over 23,000 eBook titles in the Humanities, Social Sciences, STM and Law from some of the world's leading imprints.

Choose from a range of subject packages or create your own!

- ▶ Free MARC records
- ▶ COUNTER-compliant usage statistics
- ▶ Flexible purchase and pricing options

- ▶ Off-site, anytime access via Athens or referring URL
- ▶ Print or copy pages or chapters
- ▶ Full content search
- ▶ Bookmark, highlight and annotate text
- ▶ Access to thousands of pages of quality research at the click of a button

For more information, pricing enquiries or to order a free trial, contact your local online sales team.

UK and Rest of World: **online.sales@tandf.co.uk**
US, Canada and Latin America:
e-reference@taylorandfrancis.com

www.ebooksubscriptions.com

A flexible and dynamic resource for teaching, learning and research.